FUTURE JAZZ

Future Jazz

Howard Mandel

OXFORD
UNIVERSITY PRESS
1999

OXFORD
UNIVERSITY PRESS

Oxford   New York
   Athens   Auckland   Bangkok   Bogotá   Buenos Aires   Calcutta
   Cape Town   Chennai   Dar es Salaam   Delhi   Florence   Hong Kong   Istanbul
   Karachi   Kuala Lumpur   Madrid   Melbourne   Mexico City   Mumbai
   Nairobi   Paris   São Paulo   Singapore   Taipei   Tokyo   Toronto   Warsaw

   and associated companies in
   Berlin   Ibadan

Published by Oxford University Press, Inc.
   198 Madison Avenue, New York, New York 10016

Oxford is a registered trademark of Oxford University Press

Library of Congress Cataloging-in-Publication Data
   Mandel, Howard.
   Future jazz / Howard Mandel.
   p. cm.
   Includes index.
   ISBN 0-19-506378-3
   1. Jazz—History and criticism. 2. Jazz musicians. I. Title.
   ML3506.M33 1999
   781.65—dc21
   98-30134

Production by Joellyn M. Ausanka
Design by Adam B. Bohannon

9 8 7 6 5 4 3 2 1
   Printed in the United States of America
   on acid-free paper.

Contents

Forethoughts: From the Diary of a Jazz Journalist
IX

1
Maps, Myths, Arguments, Assumptions
3

2
Wynton Marsalis: First *Down Beat* Interview
15

3
The Good Ol' Avant-Garde
23

4
Birds of a Feather
47

5
Guitars and Goals Beyond
75

6
Wynton Marsalis Restarts Us
105

7
Modern Maturity
109

8
M-Base and the Black Rock Coalition
145

9
Downtowners Go for Broke
165

10
Wynton Marsalis: Conclusions, Part 3
195

11
Hothouse Culture: Jazz Clubs in the '90s
201

Acknowledgments
209

Index
211

"It is pretty clear around New York that jazz has gone back to its obscure and unprofitable limbo again."
—Otis Ferguson, "Jazz at Random," *New Republic* (February 24, 1941)

"Modern jazz is a living music, but even more, has within it a new music, clamoring to be born."
—Sidney Finkelstein, *Jazz: A People's Music* (1949)

"The world fears a new experience more than it fears anything. Because a new experience displaces so many old experiences. And it is like trying to use muscles that have perhaps never been used, or that have been going stiff for ages. It hurts horribly.

"The world doesn't fear a new idea. It can pigeon-hole any idea. But it can't pigeon-hole a real new experience. It can only dodge. The world is a great dodger, and the Americans are the greatest. Because they dodge their own very selves."
—D. H. Lawrence, *Studies in Classic American Literature* (1923)

Forethoughts: From the Diary of a Jazz Journalist

The '60s were the Janus Age of jazz, a two-faced time looking backward and forward, wearing both tragic and comic masks. Many of the greatest masters of twentieth-century America's music heyday—Louis Armstrong and Duke Ellington, to name two—were still living and active, yet there were also youngbloods turning the old styles over, raising a ruckus that came to be viewed as antithetical to the heritage. "Free jazz," "antijazz," and "the new thing," that movement was called.

From a perspective of nearly four decades later, that movement was actually a jump that landed not so far from where it started, which should be only slightly surprising, since the jumpers had come up trained in the music of their elders. The trumpeter Miles Davis and saxophonist John Coltrane had worked toward their individual early breakthroughs, respectively represented by their records *Kind of Blue* and *Giant Steps* (both of 1959), by playing the music of their predecessors and peer groups; they both soon embodied the process of continuous self-invention and spent the rest of their careers not so much shunning a hallowed past as peeling off their own skins of the previous season, reemerging with music that was seriously different, if not brand-new.

Alto sax player and composer/theorist Ornette Coleman seemed to arrive in New York, then indisputably the center of the jazz universe, out of nowhere—but really, Los Angeles wasn't nowhere, and as quasi-bootleg recordings of Coleman prior to his *Something Else!!!!* (released in 1958) prove, he was an ardent admirer of Charlie Parker, the era's recently deceased major sax figure, and remained so even after he broke "free." Pianist Cecil Taylor was steeped in the music of Ellington and his alter ego Billy Strayhorn, as well as in the music of jazz's first crossover star Dave Brubeck, the reclusive cult figure Lennie Tristano, knotty Thelonious Monk, and funky Horace Silver—and in the classically derived repertoire he studied at New England Conservatory. In Taylor's earliest recordings (*Jazz Advance* of 1956, *Looking Ahead* of 1958, *The World of Cecil Taylor* and *Jumpin' Pumpkins* of 1960), however, he took off from the path other jazz pianists trod.

These men were progenitors of what Coleman foresaw as the "change of the century," but they were not alone. Something had happened in nonjazz popular music, too: rockabilly, rock 'n' roll, rhythm 'n' blues, and so-called folk music all heralded the change, which gained momentum by the rapidly multiplying number of young music consumers, products of the post-World War II baby boom. I was among these, born on the South Side of Chicago in 1950, raised on the white side of Stony Island, a commercial boulevard that served as a racial divide.

For a lot of reasons, chief among them precocious snobbery, I never considered myself a fan of pop and rock. I dug Ramsey Lewis, Herbie Mann, and Miles Davis's *The Beginning*. But there was no ignoring the names of that era, or their sounds. The music of Elvis Presley, Frank Sinatra, Liberace, Spike Jones was everywhere in the air. And when the Beatles hit the United States in 1963, with the Rolling Stones and the rest of the British invasion close behind...well, the future was cast. Promoted by the recently dominant visual entertainment medium of television, and gladly embraced by the first generation to get its sense of fresh fun and style from TV (mostly gilding black urban blues styles forged a few blocks from my childhood home), these bands and their U.S. counterparts won what today is recognized as a huge market share. Room for jazz on radio, on records, and on stages across the United States shrank. The older-timers were around, yes. But they were hard pressed to get the work and attract the crowds they needed to survive. Of course they resented the brash, often unsophisticated music that displaced them.

Besides the musicians themselves, there were diehard fans who kept their favored musics going. Through the dogged efforts of Joe Segal, a devotee of "modern jazz" (especially bebop), grizzled yet suave hard-jazz blowers like saxophonists Coleman Hawkins, Eddie "Lockjaw" Davis, Jimmy Forrest, and James Moody (with singer Eddie Jefferson, his irrepressible pal) performed with local rhythm sections on Sunday afternoons in a rented-out party room of the North Park Hotel, not far from Chicago's quasi-bohemian Old Town. Kids under drinking age were admitted to the North Park sessions, as they were at few other jazz venues, but not that many came. For all the enviable swagger of the jazzmen, to teenagers there was something musty-seeming about them: their suits, their hats, the overly familiar songs they started with, the *ching-ching-aling* beat, the initially indecipherable streams of notes they played.

But be patient, listen, think—these guys still had *something* that was powerful. They could cast a spell that held adults rapt and gratified, without benefit of sheet music, flashy moves, or silly costumes, practicing only their mysterious, self-contained art.

In the mid-'60s my folks moved to the suburbs, and we went as a family to hear jazz at a shopping mall. Duke Ellington's orchestra, Count Basie's band, Woody Herman's Thundering Herd, and a quartet led by Stan Getz that featured Gary Burton, Steve Swallow, and Roy Haynes all had gigs in the parking lot of Old Orchard (or was it Edens Plaza?), probably to draw those shoppers nostalgic for swing and the big bands, repelled by burgeoning new nightspots such as the Electric Theater (later renamed the Kinetic Playground), where greasy longhairs yowled amid highly amplified guitar fury.

There was odd jazz then, too: Sun Ra's Arkestra, Rahsaan Roland Kirk, and Yusef Lateef, for example, delved into exotic forms of expression that were less predictable than the polished chordal extrapolations of the business-suited North Park guys, but not as blunt as the rock stuff. There were commercial appearances of jazz gestures: How could any teen boy not get off on Henry Mancini's "Theme Song for *Peter Gunn*"? There was jazz that was urgent and chaotic, for all its players' reputations. I heard John Coltrane at the *Down Beat* Jazz Festival of 1965 at Soldier Field and could make nothing of the windstorm he and Archie Shepp stirred up, except that it was dead serious art. Otherwise, why would they bother?

Exiled in suburbia, I still wanted to explore the city, and in the first year of my coveted driver's license I'd take off on weekend nights for Hyde Park, the integrated neighborhood surrounding the University of Chicago, to attend events produced by a group who called themselves the AACM, Association for the Advancement of Creative Musicians. Its members were all black, but I was fascinated by the intensity and strangeness of their outpourings and never discouraged in my curiosity. Muhal Richard Abrams conducted a big band that sounded like surrealists announcing a dramatic shift of understanding; Fred Anderson, a gentle if bearish tenor saxophonist, hunkered down as he played as if to get the air in his guts closer to the bell of his horn; alto saxophonist Anthony Braxton unraveled oblique skeins of clipped notes to the scratchy backdrop of Leroy Jenkins's violin, while trumpeter Leo Smith shot out pure, long tones; reed player Henry Threadgill made piercing sounds while a dancer unfurled herself from a wrapping of silvery foil; the Art Ensemble of Chicago celebrated a victorious homecoming at the University's Mandel (no relation) Hall.

This was my head-changing music, my soul-shaping experience, and, though I understood (or thought I did) its distinctions, it was not so different in its effect from the other things I was hearing live. Within a few months I caught Linda Ronstadt and the Stone Poneys, Dr. John the Night-Tripper, Tim Buckley, Jimi Hendrix, the Soft Machine, the Jefferson Airplane, Vanilla Fudge, Pacific Gas & Electric, the Flock, and Blood Sweat & Tears. One night after an antiwar demonstration, I heard Cream and the Mothers of Invention; one week later, the Doors,

By then I'd discovered the Jazz Record Mart, where I hung out in my abundance of spare time, sweeping the floor to justify hours spent listening to records, talking to Hank the Crank (washboard player for some scraggly trad bands) and Big Joe Williams, the blues-man, who tried to sell me his old Ford. Arvella Grey, a blind preacher, strummed a tuneless steel National guitar and sang "John Henry" for hours on end outside the JRM because it was located near the entrance to a subway station, and there was a constant flow of folks who'd poke their heads in the door wanting the hit of the month (Curtis Mayfield's *Superfly* was an especially big seller), then drop some coins in his cup.

Jim, the red-haired, black-clad Zen hipster who ran the store for the owner (and Delmark Records principal), Bob Koester, felt he could seduce any shoppers into buying *Kind of Blue*, and perhaps persuade them to check out Coltrane's *Ballads* or his album with smooth baritone Johnny Hartman. Kalaparusha—he'd changed his name from Maurice McIntyre just weeks after the covers of his debut album on Delmark were printed—was a shipping clerk, a job previously held by harmonica player Charlie Musselwhite. Tough blues guitarist Jimmy Dawkins used to show up at the store, perhaps to collect a check; he always had a restless German shepherd in his station wagon parked outside.

And sometimes dapper Junior Wells called on the phone. His *Hoodoo Man Blues* with a guitarist pseudonymously listed as "Friendly Chap" turned me on as perfectly controlled, utterly con-temporary city music, infectious as Aretha Franklin's radio hits or James Brown's "Popcorn" and "Papa's Got a Brand New Bag." This wasn't the corny country blues I'd been trying to avoid, the "folk music" sung by tired old men (though my mind changed about that too after one blazing hot afternoon at the Ann Arbor Blues Festival when I heard Son House, Lightnin' Hopkins, Fred McDowell, Sleepy John Estes, John Lee Hooker, and a host of other lately redis-covered bluesmen who'd been at it all their lives).

My point is that the music was all rolled together then, like the American population itself (and like television, which mixed com-edy, drama, news, variety shows, and sports on one small screen), becoming increasingly integrated. Concert tickets weren't very expensive; almost anyone within range who wanted to could check out any kind of music, test (if not necessarily overcome) vestigal prejudices about genre, race, age, rhythm, consonance, and disso-nance. Not only white kids like me; talking to black musicians later, I learned they too had been hearing everything, trying to figure it all out and put the elements together in some subjectively satisfy-ing way.

That was the task of the times, and sometimes we were con-founded. What had Miles Davis been up to, with his two keyboard players and electric guitarist and soprano sax player wailing loud, loud, louder than the sound mix could withstand at the Civic Opera House? Something cool, something bold—though not like the music my parents or his parents had known.

So we didn't get it; how could we? No one had heard anything like it before. Still it was respected, like the old-style blues and swing and gospel, because it sought to be truthful to itself. The black com-munity, I gathered, felt that music conveyed something which was essentially honest about life, beyond a diverting beat and hummable tune. The musicians I spoke with didn't reject their heritage as I rejected the big bands for being unfathomably mechanical, the songs of musical theater as fixed forever in their narrative lyrics, and "Doggie in the Window" or "Mairzy Doats" as insipidly cute. The black musicians seemed humble about what they'd grown up with even as they tried to get beyond it, and made their ways in the world taking art as a gift, a weapon of attack and defense, a guide.

Okay: When I was a lad the Titans still lived, and giants walked the earth. I have their posters: the etching of Medusa announcing Joseph Jarman's Quartet; a red outline of a black bluesman printed on a silver background, aside a schedule promising Howlin' Wolf, Muddy Waters, T-Bone Walker, and Magic Sam; plump Cannonball Adderley, his hooded eyes slightly sardonic, coming to the University of Illinois at the Chicago Circle campus student union. The Titans died off soon, though, and the giants shrank to size.

The jazz musicians who survived that era are now mere mortals, inevitably aged and coping with changes. They've dealt with forty years of social and economic changes, new music technologies, and new international opportunities, often paving the way for more mainstream segments of society. The jazz musicians are way out front, as self-possessed, self-employed, self-invented, self-respecting artists, discovering new models of group behavior through spontaneous interactive play.

The Janus Age is over now, though the old music lives on, and we can listen to it, love it from the here and now. Those of the elders' grandchildren who reach back, trying to capture the glorious golden era, can't help but fail. They overlook and underestimate their immediate predecessors, and seem to deny that the challenging, often unpopular moves the '60s, '70s, and '80s players made were inevitable and of great consequence. But there is no going back. We can't be our grandfathers or our fathers, however much they informed us. We can only be ourselves, revering our history but living forward. Things have changed since the '30s, '40s, '50s, '60s—yes. In fact, the rate of change seems to be speeding up, gaining momentum as though in free fall.

There is no denying, evading, or sparing ourselves the necessity of change, however much we dislike it, however much we want to hold on to our forefathers and lay claim to their powers. We must let go of those who came before us—not hold them responsible for the work we have to do, but understand them in their own times and apply what we learn along with an appreciation of the unique present so that we shape life now as we need to. For the living, there is memory, but memory comes with the onrush of experience, accruing as we go. Change *is* the engine of the universe, which is *never* static.

Oh, when I was a lad...

Spare change, buddy?

New York City   Howard Mandel
May 1998

FUTURE JAZZ

1 Maps, Myths, Arguments, Assumptions

In the final two decades of the first American jazz century, a few square blocks of lower Manhattan were all too commonly taken as the center of the musical universe. Roughly from Fourteenth Street to Canal, between Seventh Avenue and the Bowery, jazz clubs including the Village Vanguard, Sweet Basil, the Village Gate, Bradley's, the Blue Note, the Bottom Line, Visiones, S.O.B.'s, the Knitting Factory, Fat Tuesday's, Zanzibar, and Zinno's were all within a healthy walk or quick cab ride of each other.

These were some of the dens where professionally accomplished, creative, occasionally even innovative instrumentalists held forth for jazz lovers and scenemakers, newcomers and long-time listeners. The musicians hoped to make up something that would be heard, felt, and appreciated while it happened—if not remembered and treasured after that moment—changing life for each person in earshot and possibly much further beyond.

People turned these cafés and bars into hangouts where they could sit together, mill about, find diversion. Some were frankly killing time; a few sought meaning or inspiration. Most everyone was satisfied by hour-long sets of idiomatic variations on familiar riffs or chord progressions and standard songs. Most small-group contemporary music comprised a degree of melodic-harmonic abstraction of chord changes based on blues and conventional pop formulas; everything rode on propulsive, most often 4/4 rhythms. Audiences liked the musicians to be visibly absorbed in the music they made.

As such, New York jazz and its evolutionary extensions became the myth music for worldly

seekers of urbanity and surprise, who might have diverse backgrounds but shared certain longed-for destinations. The music provided intellectual and sensual stimulation, a way to rush toward the
future and trade in on the past.

Tales We Tell of Jazz in the '90s

Scenario 1: In the glory days of the Reagan reign, a winning young
trumpeter comes to the New York from the remote delta village
where our best sounds are born. Having been a childhood prodigy,
he actually studies at Juilliard rather than following the Miles Davis
example of enrolling but hanging with Bird in the beat streets till
dawn. This upright, well-spoken youth wears his suits as to the
bebop manner born, yet expresses himself playing Haydn, Hummel,
and Handel concertos with a chamber orchestra as truly as he does
rip-roaring through jams in smoky clubs, at first in the band of a
drummer belonging to his father's generation.

In no time at all this young trumpeter rescues his people's music
from anarchy and commercialism. He rousts an army of protégés by
conducting instrumental clinics at ghetto schools, hosting jam sessions wherever he plays, and simply being a fine role model. He's
blessed by his elders—and by execs of the industry that disseminates
the culture he's revived. His followers, an elite corps known as the
Young Lions, are signed to long-term contracts by major record
labels and tour international festivals.

Scenario 2: In far-flung corners of the world, orphan artists of
unappreciated talent labor in obscurity to create distinct but con-
gruent musics that reflect heights of the imagination, depths of the
soul, infinite varieties of celestial melody, wond'rous harmony and
earthy rhythms always known yet ever ripe for rediscovery. These
savage innocents are graced with inherent understanding of structure
and tradition, but stubbornly believe they have "new ideas" and hold
fast to the notion of absolute freedom. A vast conspiracy, an evil
cabal, prevents them from casting their rough spells before any but
the eager few who seek them out in low-rent caves, where they are
paid a mere pittance.

Now and then one of these benighted worthies makes his (usually) or her way to the Dreadful City, and desperately strives to gain
audiences with the gatekeepers, courtiers, and high priests guarding
the Eternal Flame. If the musician is young and handsome or fasci-
natingly exotic, the way is sometimes cleared and he or she is

allowed to draw near this fire that feeds on beauty and truth, emits smoke, heat, and sometimes the light of effort—but just as often all that results is an ash of failed hopes and cutout recordings.

Only the cleverest and luckiest pilgrims withstand the Flame's lure, defend themselves from its dangers, draw upon its warmth for sustenance, and can depend on its hot currents to carry their brilliant magic, forged in its crucible, to listeners at large. And even most of *these* burn out, go mad, fall away, or die young. The rare soul who forbears seemingly must pay a price—perhaps isolation, dissolution, and/or corruption by Mammon.

(There is a variant of this tale, whispered seldom and then softly, of some players who are patently insane but snowy pure. These radicals roam the globe in ragged coats of many colors and survive as best they can. They care for neither public recognition nor material goods, make friends where'er they wander, pay no heed to the occasional flattering summons of the court, and leave no trace but in the memories of those who hear them. Since there is no evidence that this clan—or even one member of it—has existed, I can't vouch for the rumor's truth.)

The Lion King?

Wynton Marsalis pounced into the limelight in the early '80s, "age 20, insisting on playing acoustic jazz and lecturing his elders about selling out," according to Tom Piazza in a controversial *New York Times Magazine* article of May 1990. "His integrity, sharp appearance and musical wizardry caught the eyes and ears of young musicians and fans alike. Suddenly, someone their age, or just a little older, was playing a kind of music that was more interesting, and more demanding, than rock, and being cool doing it."

Definitions of "interesting," "demanding" and "cool" change, almost with the seasons—and there's something about the synopsis of jazz history by Piazza, who also writes fiction, that's not precisely either/or. "Jazz was a single language," he claims, "with a common repertory and a canon of techniques that enabled people from different musical (and social) backgrounds to build something spontaneously…Things began to change in the '60s. The common language broke down…with the advent of electronics, the sounds of instruments were distorted…."

One might argue that the "single language" didn't precede, *or* survive, the Swing Era. That bebop was the Big Bang that announced a universe of jazz possibilities. That '50s hard bop was not just a codification but also a simplification of bebop's abstractions, as well as a reaction against new studio techniques, the rise of individualistic arrangers, and the entry of non-Negro ideas in the form of Caucasian "cool" and Euro-derived "Third Stream" elements into the jazz gene pool.

Then it's conceivable that the new things Miles Davis, John Coltrane, Ornette Coleman, Charles Mingus, and Cecil Taylor—all steeped in "the jazz tradition"—were trying at the '50s end further extended the bop founders' repositioning of jazz as an art form. That the essential breakthrough of bop was its denial of *any* shackles, its insistence that blacks—and whites, and Latins, and even guys playing what Louis Armstrong called "Chinese music"—could, nay, *must,* integrate their broadest life experiences into whatever music they think of, going as far as their energy could take them. That neither electronics nor the language's changes, nor pop influences, nor dissonant or square charts can "distort" jazz. Jazz belongs to artists and audiences. The business…well, that's something else.

If these suppositions are accepted, it's natural that some of the resulting music will be unpopular. There are folks who just don't want any ol' new thing: They'll stick with what they know, thanks, preferring the tried-and-true. But jazz musicians by definition and practice resist repetition and stasis. From the '60s through the U.S. bicentennial (celebrated by President Jimmy Carter singing "Salt Peanuts" with Dizzy Gillespie during a National Public Radio broadcast from the White House after performances by Cecil Taylor and Ornette Coleman, ailing Charles Mingus also among the guests) to the millennium, innovative jazz musicians were out front experimenting with advanced technology, attempting new structures blending composition and improvisation, testing standards of beauty, taste, and logic, sometimes in wildly expressive tongues. Some of these musicians were, incidentally, recorded, promoted, and marketed by major labels.

It's been bruited about that Miles Davis's last twenty-five years were a waste of cynical self-indulgence, that John Coltrane's spiritual ascension was mostly inchoate pain, that Charles Mingus sold out to Joni Mitchell, that Ornette Coleman is a spacey charlatan, Cecil Taylor simply *too* much, thirty years of fusion has led to a dead end— pace Zawinul and Shorter, Hancock, Metheny, Corea, et al. There's the notion that young musicians lost their senses of direction when presented with too much freedom, not knowing what to do—then came Wynton Marsalis, to save the CBS jazz catalogue for Japanese-owned Sony Music; polish the names of Armstrong, Morton, and Ellington for the canon; and knight the Lions whose chief distinction, at the start, was an acceptance of conventions, despite their roaring youth.

Words from the Wise

"The Young Lions concept is something a number of people used to define Wynton and Branford Marsalis, Roy Hargrove, and some others," explains Dr. George Butler, in the '80s and early '90s head of jazz A&R at Columbia Records. "When I signed Wynton, there was talk of Young Lions by George Wein and Bruce Lundvall. It was a commercial hook.

"The point was to sign young artists who would allude to the '50s—the time of Miles, Trane, Dizzy, Bud Powell, Kenny Clarke, and Thelonious Monk—and start a period comparable to bebop. While that's happened, and continues to develop, a lot of commercial jazz still gets airplay. It's getting thin. And I think people at the major labels are now concentrating on young players who not only are proficient but also suggest longevity, who might be able to produce enduring statements."

Besides the senior Marsalis brothers (Delfayo, their younger sibling, trombonist, producer, and liner-note writer, contracted with BMG/RCA/Novus Records), Dr. Butler signed Young-Lionized trumpeters Terence Blanchard, Marlon Jordan, and Ryan Kisor, organist Joey DeFrancesco (Piazza reports eighteen-year-old Joey won the grudging respect of veteran big-band sidemen at his recording sessions), pop-jazz tenor saxist Kirk Whalum, Turkish-born keyboardist Aydin Esen, commercially oriented guitarist Dwight Sills, multicultural improvisers Tony Vacca and Tim Moran, and keyboardist Rachel Z. "We might call what she does hip-hop jazz or acid jazz," Butler says.

Gone are CBS cubs of years back such as saxists Tim Berne, Jane Ira Bloom, Arthur Blythe, and Paquito D'Rivera, keyboardist Rodney Franklin, flutist Kent Jordan (Marlon's brother), and guitarist James "Blood" Ulmer. Things change, yet stay the same: Columbia once laid off Ellington. Does CBS have a rule against over-thirty players, or those inclined to iconoclasm, experimentation, dissonance?

"A while ago there was an indifference to that kind of artistry,"

Butler concedes, "but I'm trying to resurrect interest in it. I started the Masters' Series, negotiating with Doc Cheatham, Dorothy Donegan, Frank Wess, and George Coleman—veteran jazz artists whom major labels have ignored. They're the predecessors of the young guys and need to be heard. We also struck a deal with Disk Union, the Japanese label, to release the Art Ensemble, David Murray, Harold Mabern, and others they've recorded. We don't want to ignore traditional artists or guys coming from an outside bag."

The "new balance" of artists and styles Butler sought to strike in the '80s was heavily affected by the weight of one Harry Connick Jr., a sudden crossover king. "Do you call what he does jazz?" asked a longtime Columbia publicist. "The Grammy committee didn't put him in the jazz category. Sales-wise, the selling of 350,000 to 500,000 copies of a jazz album are over, except for Harry. Sales-wise, except for good-selling albums by Wynton or Branford, the days of a 150,000-to-200,000-unit jazz album are long gone."

Sales-wise or otherwise, Columbia's own catalogue proves mainstream jazz was not forgotten before Wynton, Branford, Harry, and the Young Lions arrived on the scene. The label did handsomely by straight-ahead/progressive trumpeter Woody Shaw, for one. And mainstreamers like Shaw coexisted with "outside" explorers—for instance, Miles Davis. But to be fair: Until Wynton Marsalis's opus *Blood on the Fields*, released in 1996, Columbia Jazz (nor any other label or artist) had never produced a Pulitzer Prize-winning composition. Later in 1996, a couple of years after Dr. George Butler left Columbia Records, Branford Marsalis succeeded him as head of the jazz wing's artists-and-repertory department.

A Company's Bottom Line

Bruce Lundvall, a longtime record executive and former president of CBS Records Division who moved on to become hands-on chief of Blue Note Records, a division of Capitol/EMI, is candid about the Young Lions concept he helped initiate, and its disappointments.

"When I had the Elektra/Musician label I handpicked some of the more important young players, most of whom were also composers: Wynton, Bobby McFerrin, Anthony Davis, Paquito D'Rivera (who'd just come from Cuba), the flutist James Newton, drummer Ronnie Burrage, trombonist Craig Harris. Some made it, some didn't."

Lundvall's average was exceptional: Everyone on the out-of-print album documenting their Kool Jazz Fest concert of 1982 is still active. The rest of that litter was violinist John Blake, bari sax player Hamiet Bluiett, guitarist Kevin Eubanks, tenor man Chico Freeman, vibist Jay Hoggard, bassist Fred Hopkins (who died in January 1999), reeds doubler John Purcell, McCoy Tyner's bassist Avery Sharpe, and cellist Abdul Wadud.

"It's healthy, this serious interest in acoustic jazz by young black and white players," Lundvall goes on, "but some of them are being recorded as leaders prematurely. The emphasis is on youth as opposed to who has the magic. Our first signing to Blue Note was the guitarist Stanley Jordan when he was nineteen or twenty years old and totally unique. The first album we released was *The African Game* by George Russell, a man in his sixties.

"What I'm trying to find is someone doing something fresh and special, not just regurgitating the past. I'm proud to have young people like Geri Allen and Greg Osby, who've tried new things. Benny Green is a young traditional player with his own style, and his records are starting to sell. Joe Lovano should be the most-talked-about tenor player on the scene; he's in his forties. Kevin Eubanks returned to us [after a fusion foray] to make serious jazz."

The roster continues: "Gonzalo Rubalcaba's a miracle to me, one of these virtuosic masters who come along maybe every twenty years. Jack DeJohnette's planned an album with John Scofield and Vernon Reid and Will Calhoun from [black rock band] Living Color [which never came to fruition]. We had Bobby Watson, who was in his thirties; he has something to say in a voice of his own. Same with Bobby McFerrin. That's what I look for."

This being a music *business*, Lundvall *must* and *does* keep an eye on the bottom line. McFerrin and Dianne Reeves are his top-selling artists, but Blue Note shares them with Capitol/EMI's pop division. Andrew Hill's records were not self-supporting, though the composer-pianist-bandleader, in his fifties and comparable to Monk in terms of gnomic originality, employed members of the youth movement. *The Dreamkeeper* by Charlie Haden's Liberation Music Orchestra with the Oakland Youth Chorus was nominated for a Grammy but sold modestly; the expensive production was licensed from Japanese Disk Union. How do *they* do it?

"You have to look at the worldwide picture, do business in Japan and in Europe. If you have just the States, you're in trouble," Lundvall maintains. Blue Note invested in no-longer-a-kid but creatively rampant pianist Don Pullen, young drummer Ralph Peterson Jr., young pianists Renee Rosnes and Michel Petrucciani (who also died in January 1999). "We're making money at Blue Note, and I'm proud of that," says Lundvall. "It's hard to do with jazz records."

Views from In and Out Sides

Come on, aren't all the larger jazz labels making money? Just a little bit? Enough to retain offices, pay decent salaries, break even? Don't the Young Lions of each successive semester appeal to their record-buying classmates?

"The young bebop guys' records can be economically viable—maybe not from the very beginning, but you start something and make it grow," Richard Seidel of Polygram's jazz label Verve (which in '99 merged with rival GRP Records into the Universal Music Group) says. "They're not expensive to record—all acoustic, no big equipment rental—and some of them get press attention, depending on their personalities, not their music." Tenor sax veteran Joe Henderson's *Lush Life: The Music of Billy Strayhorn* with Wynton Marsalis and a Young Lion trio was Seidel's spring 1992 prestige release, beginning a series of Henderson concept albums that came to include a jazz version of the Gershwins' *Porgy and Bess*.

"But writers like to write about what's on the cutting edge, which is often other than what radio wants to play. Radio alone is insufficient to sell records; it's got to be combined with a strong retail profile, touring activity, and press. *Then* you've got some-thing…maybe. For straight-ahead records, there's nothing more important than attention in the nonmusic press: *Newsweek, Time*, the *Wall Street Journal, USA Today*."

"It's true—the tastemaker publications that are perceived as read by important, chic, and prosperous demographic segments and sup-posed to influence their readers' behavior—that's where the action is," agrees publicist Don Lucoff, whose Philadelphia-based DL Media approaches assignment editors at newspapers, magazines, and radio and TV shows for more jazz coverage.

"What does it take to get *Newsweek* or *Good Morning America* to cover Abbey Lincoln, who's not a kid but has a great new release [*You've Got to Pay the Band*] on a major label [Verve]? A film career; recognition at last as the heir apparent to Billie Holiday; rave reviews and coverage in other publications—which can be a catch-22.

"That's always the way," Lucoff says, "'cause the big magazines and news programs don't make or break news—they *follow* it. And once the mainstream press writes about someone, that's it. They drop 'em and move on to others.

"You'd think the mainstream would have moved on by now to cover the musicians of the Knitting Factory," he says. The Knit's a busy if grungy New York nightspot, described by the *New Yorker* as "frat house of the avant-garde."

"But politics now aren't in sync with what's happening at the Knitting Factory," he observes. "Music is ahead of politics, always has been. Even though the media and record companies covered jazz in the '60s when Charles Lloyd opened for Jimi Hendrix and the Grateful Dead."

Surely there are editors more responsible and responsive to maturity and diversity in jazz—probably at *Down Beat,* the jazz Bible for more than sixty years.

"We've paid a lot of attention to Young Lions because they've been a natural outgrowth of our work twenty to twenty-five years ago, when we helped fund the first college jazz festival at Notre Dame," Dave Helland, a former associate editor of the suburban Chicago-based monthly, explains. "Roy Hargrove, Joey DeFrancesco, Ryan Kisor were all presented in *Down Beat's* 'Audition' pages as winners of high school student awards. We've watched them develop, and they're good, and they have recording contracts. There's a progression from learning big-band jazz to playing bebop that I don't think happens with any other style. I don't know if you can teach free jazz or find schools that will pay for electric gear so the students can get into fusion.

"We've devoted less editorial space to electric jazz in the past five years, but how many of those in the forefront of fusion in the '60s stuck with it? Are there as many hot fusion bands to cover now? If not, it's logical they get less space. If there's less of an audience, it's logical they get less space. If there's less audience, the artists get lesser record contracts.

"It's notable, too, that at a time when the record companies are interested in selling CDs from their catalogues, they come up with people who play well, talk well, and say, 'Pay attention to the traditions.' As far as free jazz, I'm not the guy to talk to. My predecessor liked free jazz. But did his taste extend to the middle-aged Basie-ite who went on to have a career of his own?

"We're always looking for the new thing to sell, and *DB's* always been interested in the new thing. Maybe youth has the same old story, with a new person telling it. Certain guys make good copy. Wynton is always prepared to mouth off in print."

Tree Falls in Forest

"The Young Lions? They should put 'em in the zoo, wait till they get old enough, then farm 'em out," says Roy Nathanson, saxophonist and coleader of the Jazz Passengers, a sextet of guys a little older and odder than the Young Lions. This band received scant interest from major labels but built a following in the United States and Europe with several distinctive, independently issued albums.

"It's not about age—it's the conservatism of the whole country now, which says musical information has to be cleaned up and recycled. A lot of these guys can really play. If they had some political consciousness, they'd produce some great stuff. Or maybe they *do* come from a social movement, one I don't like."

Nathanson is a Marxist of the Groucho persuasion; his band was a critics' darling. Jon Pareles wrote of their 1990 JVC Jazz Fest appearance in the *New York Times*: "The Jazz Passengers show what's missing from the hard bop revival…with their jagged tunes and abstruse harmonies…extended solos…droll humor…and a sense of timing that takes into account the fractured continuity of a television-wise generation.…They back their innovations with genuine musicality."

Something you might want to hear? Seek out the indies labels, which have more to gain and less to lose from taking esthetic chances. Those noisy young, middle-aged, and old animals who the majors say aren't lions—sorry—aren't necessarily turkeys either. Maybe they're…*swans*?

As for the cabal, the gatekeepers and guardians of major-label resources, hear BMG/RCA/Novus producer Steve Backer: "The industry's in lockstep? That's a crock. We don't collaborate, we *compete*! I make decisions by intuition. Money can be a factor, but each company reflects the individuals overseeing it.

"I've always said that the record industry is simply people trying to do the best they can. It may seem monolithic and impersonal, but it's just people struggling with lots of variables."

As Sun Ra asked: "If you're not a myth, whose reality are you? If you're not a reality, whose myth are you?" But when we try to survey the border between hard fact and wishful fiction, we should concede that the jazz omniverse is neither so polarized nor so Manichean a construct.

Ornette Coleman maintains, "There are as many unisons as there are stars in the sky." Each star beams its own insistent light, the brilliance of which travels vast distances to reach us, sometimes after the star itself has burned out. Too often the wisdom and/or beauty of the less prominent jazz suns isn't sighted until it exists as just a faint glimmer, growing dimmer all the time. That's a sad way to receive future jazz.

2 Wynton Marsalis
First Down Beat *Interview*

Wynton Marsalis was already an enthusiastically acclaimed and much-promoted jazz wunderkind at the time of our interview for a *Down Beat* cover story, April 24, 1984. A twenty-two-year-old scion of New Orleans bearing the trumpet that, since Louis Armstrong, has been regarded as a scepter conferring high profile and inestimable power upon its master, Wynton accepted critical and audience accolades and jazz industry support with equanimity. Onstage he had a manner of serious concentration to high purpose. Offstage he was little-known, but seemed to embody the very image of articulate professionalism.

Marsalis first recorded his own compositions backed by pianist Herbie Hancock, bassist Ron Carter, and drummer Tony Williams, Miles Davis's acoustic rhythm section of the mid-'60s. In 1983 Marsalis became the first musician ever to win National Association of Recording Arts and Sciences' Grammy awards simultaneously in jazz and classical categories (testimony to a recording's retail availability and sales as much as proof of its esthetic excellence, but an honor nonetheless).

He sauntered into Black Rock, headquarters of CBS Records in midtown Manhattan, late in the morning, having spent the previous day traveling from his hometown New Orleans to New York, to Philadelphia to rehearse for a classical recital, then back to the Brooklyn brownstone he shared with his older brother, saxophonist Branford, to sleep. Wynton had a soon-upcoming concert with the Boston Pops, but was eschewing the typical jazzman's summer European festival tour in favor of a trip through the United States and to Japan with his quintet (Branford on tenor, pianist Kenny Kirkland, bassist Charles Fambrough, and drummer Jeff Watts). Getting the best gigs on his own time frame, Wynton seemed in command of his career trajectory—rare for any but the most successful artists of any medium.

It took a few minutes for the young man—opinionated yet sensitive, good humored if wary, highly articulate (he does talk in page lengths)—to warm up. He needed breakfast, and when he got it he began speaking in the style of his horn solos. His confidence was founded in a well-considered and consistent viewpoint; he stretched across bar lines to connect ideas one to the next; he took some high, steep turns but followed through to credible conclusions.

The following transcript was slightly edited for grammar and redundancies.

HM About your early playing experience in New Orleans. I've read your bio...
WM A lot of that stuff is incorrect, though.
HM What's the truth?
WM Let's see, this is difficult. Well, you know my father [pianist Ellis Marsalis] is a musician. I had a trumpet when I was six. I wasn't really serious about music, but when I was eight or nine I played in the Fairview Baptist Church marching band, led by Danny Barker for young kids like us.

I was the saddest one in the band. We played at the first New Orleans Jazz & Heritage Festival, but I remember I didn't want to carry my trumpet because it was too heavy, so after an hour somebody else was carrying it for me.

As we grew up my father was always working gigs, trying to make enough money to feed all of us, because New Orleans is rough on jazz musicians; there are not that many gigs. He worked on and off in different places, freelance, then he started teaching at the New Orleans Center for Creative Arts. At that time I was twelve; I had a trumpet but didn't really play. I knew tunes like "When the Saints Go Marchin' In" and second line, but I didn't have any technique. I just heard music.

In New Orleans you have a lot of really hip culture, and I really love the city. The drag is, I didn't really know much about its heritage until I left New Orleans. I didn't believe in studying like that. I was just figuring stuff out, getting stuff by osmosis.

HM In a previous interview, you said playing together wasn't part of your family life.

WM My father was always working at night, and we were going to school during the daytime. But once I got serious about music—The best thing about New Orleans for young musicians is that we had a generation of older musicians, maybe only seven or eight people, who loved the music so much that they would do anything for us because we were trying to actually play it. My father would stay up with anybody—not just me 'cause I'm his son, but any musician—could come to our house after 11 p.m., and if he was home, my father would show them tunes, play changes and all.

Get these names, they're important. Besides my father there was clarinetist Alvin Batiste. John Longo, my first teacher—I hardly ever even paid him, and he used to give me two- and three-hour lessons, never looking at the clock. Clyde Kerr. Alvin Thomas—he died. Kidd Jordan, who put on the concert that first brought together the World Saxophone Quartet; I was there, but I didn't know any music except pop music then. George Jenson was my teacher; he just died, too. Danny Barker, who had the band. All these guys wanted us to learn how to play.

HM Did they steer you away from playing junk?

WM No. As a matter of fact, my father told me to go play in the funk band when we were in eighth grade. He said, "Man, go play in the band, get some experience at playing music." I've told this to people in interviews, but they always write the same thing, using me to express what they want to express. I've never said popular music is not good. All I said was it's not jazz. That's just clarification for purposes of education.

Man, I played in a funk band for four years; I know all those tunes from the '70s by Earth, Wind & Fire, Parliament/Funkadelic. I played that music. That's why I know it's not jazz. People think a simple statement like that is condescending to some other kind of music. But all music is better than no music.

HM But you have a good idea of what you want to do yourself, and it's in the jazz vein...

WM What I'm saying is, I'm a student of music. I'm humbled by music, not by people. Great music is what humbles musicians, and it's the precedents set in music that keep musicians honest. When you start redefining what music is, and replacing something that's great with something that's mediocre, then the next generation of musicians doesn't know what their job is. I'm embarrassed to admit it, but when I joined Art Blakey's band, I hadn't even listened to Art Blakey's records. I was just playing scales on chords. I didn't know you were supposed to *construct* a solo.

HM You must have studied assiduously from Blakey on, because your music seems closely linked to the jazz of the time you were growing up.

WM People miss a great part of what my music has. They don't understand what we're trying to do, but they think they do, and they lash out against it.

I have to phrase this very delicately. My music is a very intellectual thing—we all know this—art music, on the level we're attempting. Sonny Rollins, Miles, Clifford Brown, Charlie Parker—we don't have to name all the people, maybe just the main ones—Monk, Duke Ellington, Louis Armstrong. These were extremely, extremely intellectual men. Whoever doesn't realize that is obviously not a student of their music, because their intellect comes out in that music. It's obvious that the average person couldn't stand up and play like that.

See, the faculty of creating comes with observation, hand in hand. The ability to translate what is observed into a very precise language, that's where the intellect comes in. People have every kind of tragedy imaginable befall them—that doesn't make them able to translate their experiences into as precise a language as music, 'cause they don't have the technique to do it. They might have the imagination, but they don't have the invention. Invention means worked out.

But in jazz, people write it backward. They think the opposite way, most jazz critics. They think that because Louis Armstrong sat back all folksy, in his mind he didn't *know*. How many times have you heard, "Louis Armstrong was an intuitive genius"? That implies he didn't know he was great, he just naturally could do that. It implies that he was just lucky. But if you're lucky, you can't be consistent. Pops was not an intuitive genius, he *knew* what he was doing, and I've read interviews he gave where he let people know that he knew what he was doing.

HM But Armstrong, Ellington, all the great artists, had spiritual and emotional resources too, not just intellect, didn't they?

WM You never find a musician with technique as great as theirs who didn't have the other two. Never. People get confused and think of velocity as technique. It's not. Emotion is an aspect of technique. If your intellect is on a certain level, like Ellington's was, you automatically experience those other things.

We think of intellect as sitting down, reading, and spewing out the words we read. Then there's somebody who has the sensitivity to observe what's going on around them, process it, and make something out of it. Someone has intellect who knows what their relationship is to what goes on around them; great artists always have that. That's the key to any music.

And that's what makes them have the technique: They want to be great, they understand that they aren't great, and so they develop the technique to be great. You have to defer to the musicians who keep you honest, like Beethoven writing in his letters, "Don't compare me to Mozart and Haydn, yet." Bird spoke of Lester Young; Pops talked about King Oliver; Duke Ellington deferred, too. Duke had everything, but that's because he experienced life on a more acute level than most of us do, because he was so aware of what was going on around him. That's what's important.

Jazz is about elevation and improvement. Jazz music always improves pop music. What Louis Armstrong did, singing songs by Gershwin and Irving Berlin, was improve them. Bird improved "I'll Remember April," just like Beethoven improved folk melodies. What we have to do now is reclaim, because the cats went astray in the '70s.

HM On reclaiming music: I take it you're reacting to music watered down by fusion, simplified by funk. You think there's nothing there.

WM Everybody knows it, too.

HM But rather than reclaiming, you're exploring things from the '60s.

WM People don't hear what we're doing on *Think of One*. I'm doing things from the '70s, too, because that's the era I grew up in. I had all the records, man. We're playing funk beats, too. We don't reclaim music from the '60s; music is a continuous thing. We're just trying to play what we hear as the logical extension. Before you understand what the *extension* of something is, you have to understand what *something* is. If you don't study and understand it, a large part of your program's missing—to me, the most important part. A tree's got to have roots.

In the '70s, the tunes were static. They aren't like Monk's tunes, man. The goal of the music was different; a different element was introduced, and if it's good and popular, well, good for that. But the musicians know that what Trane and Mingus, Monk and Miles did in the '60s was the baddest stuff. Duke Ellington's bad, man. That's the level the music must exist on.

HM What got established in the '70s, within the jazz tradition, that moved the music along?

WM Nothing. Not one thing. I don't think the music moved along in the '70s. I think it went astray. Everybody was trying to be pop stars, and imitated people who were supposed to be imitating *them.* Then there's the school of music that sounds like European music people were writing in the '30s.

HM You're very interested in European music.

WM I love European music, great European music that Europeans wrote. 'Cause it's great music. I like pop music too. But neither one is jazz.

HM Are you particularly fond of the Baroque period?

WM No, I love every period. I love Bartók. I put out one record and played classical concerti because on your first record you have to show people you know this part of the literature, because it's standard. I love Bach, too. My new album has Baroque on it, too. My recital program includes some modern music by Hindemith and Halsey Stevens which is Copland-sounding. I played a Hale Smith piece, "Exchanges," when I was in school.

HM When do we get to hear some of that?

WM I'm twenty-two years old, man! I can't record everything at once. Rome wasn't built in a day; we all have to wait to find out what we're gonna do. Right now I'm just doing this; Baroque music is cool. All music's the same, saying different things about human existence at the time. Pop music is here today, gone tomorrow. Great music is idealistic, but it's realistic.

HM Maybe pop music's trying to be great studio music?

WM Ain't nothing happening in pop music today. In the '70s you had Marvin Gaye, Stevie Wonder, creative cats, geniuses, making music that musicians would try to sit down and figure out. Now in pop music they're just trying to see who can wear the most sweaters and dresses and Jheri-Curl their hair. All they're talking

about is screwing somebody up the asshole. Which is not interesting, whether you're pro or con. It's like all the cursing the
comedians do, just to get a reaction. The arrangements behind
Michael Jackson are nice arrangements, but compared to what?
Duke Ellington did arrangements in 1930. What standard are we
using? Louis Armstrong made statements for all time about the
condition of American humans at the time he lived. To me, in
music in the past five years, I don't hear anything great.

HM What's the greatest thing you could do?

WM *(long pause)* We're going astray now. Come up with some new
music that has everything in it. You don't limit your universe. You
take from everything, then you refine it, present it, and be very
precise.

Let's start from the beginning again. I'm serious. You started
to ask me, "What did you do in New Orleans?" and then we just
went totally off that, we never finished it. Let's start again.

3 The Good Ol' Avant-Garde

I'm not ashamed of the label 'avant-garde,'" pianist Don Pullen said during an interview held in his modest New Jersey apartment during the mid-'80s. New York City's World Trade Center towers were visible from his balcony, looming at once near and far. "But I never considered myself avant-garde. For one thing, I never knew what the two words meant. And I always played so many different ways, anyhow. What they called avant-garde players, to my recollection, were people who played only one way."

Which way was that?

"Avant-garde." With that invocation of a tautology derived from ignorance and misapprehension, Pullen—usually dry, elegant, and self-contained—cracked up in giggles.

A healthy appreciation of the absurd may be the best defense to categorically circular reasoning. But Pullen, like many of his generation of jazz iconoclasts who emerged in the '60s and achieved esthetic maturity in the midlife of their careers, may have been hampered earlier on because of a reputed association with a term—avant-garde—in much the same way that those labeled liberal have been stereotyped negatively by illiberal politicians.

Pullen himself didn't immediately link any career slights to his reputation as an avant-gardist. "I'm only beginning to wonder about that now," he remarked. "I don't know what people think. Because I never cared much what they thought, I never inquired. But then you hear certain things that really surprise you.

"There are quite a few cats out there who *are* avant-garde players; that's all they know. I'm not knocking them. But if I find you in every different category, playing all different kinds of music, then how can I say you're avant-garde? And if that's what avant-garde means, that's what I am."

The Curse of the Front Runners

People with a fleeting impression of jazz, as well as some music professionals—writers, club owners, concert and record producers, teachers, radio deejays—think "avant-garde" means weird and ugly. This notion persists from the '60s, when "avant-garde," synonymous with "new thing," "free jazz," and "black music," typified the experiments—like other social and cultural movements of the era, sometimes rhetorically extreme, amateurish, and/or unformed, energized to sheer brute physicality, raucous, dissonant, and persistent—of musicians eager to challenge the habits and conventions of jazz past.

Some of the music was weird: surreal, expressionistic, purposely or defiantly raw, countermelodic, arrhythmic. But ugliness is a bump in the ear of the behearer. Webster's dictionary defines *avant-garde* as "advance guard, vanguard." As '60s rock musicians used new sounds in their excited messages of protest and to mirror their use of psychoactive drugs—affecting fresh juxtapositions of influences, exploring advanced studio techniques, and convening new audience coalitions—so vanguard jazz musicians who bespoke their personal, social, and spiritual experiences were assumed to be breaking ground. Jazz commentators persuaded by '60s politics thought jazz's leaders were heading to the fore, advancing on musical frontiers which subsequent musicians would occupy, settle, perhaps civilize and refine.

So it happened. Musicians of the '70s, '80s, and '90s—Don Pullen among them—built on foundations established by Albert Ayler, Ornette Coleman, John Coltrane, Miles Davis, Charles Mingus, Sun Ra, Cecil Taylor, and others of the '60s, absorbing, consolidating, and eventually expanding on their innovations.

The assumption of a vanguard, though, is linked to the idea that music advances in one progressive direction over time, continually evolving and improving. When the glorious future—the golden age of complex, subjective jazz, teeming with freely emotive melodies, open forms, and far-reaching harmonies upon multilayered polyrhythms—failed to arrive by attracting a mass audience, vanguard musicians were written off by many in the jazz industry as a going *wrong* rather than going *on*.

Ideas that were once thought way out front can grow old and stale, lose ability to shock or provoke, when assimilated into the cultural mainstream or unanimously discarded as unsuccessful, unappealing, irrelevant. But the avant-garde isn't rendered automatically passé by the passage of decades; individual artifacts can remain "avant-garde" for centuries—as long as they endure as something other than clichés.

What Has He Done for Us Lately?

Pianist Pullen was initially lumped among the avant-garde because of his earliest professional New York association with the shamanistic saxophonist Guiseppi Logan, who by the mid-'70s had disappeared.

"Lewis Worrell, the bassist, was the only person I knew in New York when I came here," Pullen recalled, "and through him I met both [drummer] Milford Graves and Guiseppi Logan. Right away Guiseppi said, 'Come play with me.' He was very influential to me, musically, supplying direction and concept—and a lot of other ways. He was very gifted in many areas. I haven't seen him in years, and have no idea where he is or what he's doing."

Logan's music was incantory, murky, static, as though accompanying a secret, sacred ritual. Pullen strummed his piano's wires or comped repetitiously, as in a trance. Though Logan's quartet brought heat to its music, there was less light. In '67, before a Yale University audience with the heroic Graves, Pullen recast his obsessive style as a sort of cathartic endurance test. Graves and Pullen marketed via mail order two volumes of their concert's continuous (for at least forty minutes), dense and high-energy "free" improvisations. A cover photograph by Roy DeCarava shows the duo dressed in natty business suits, belying their music's relentless firepower.

Power was a keystone of the '60s black jazz avant-garde, but its display could not in itself capture listeners. Apprenticing to the composer-improviser-bandleader Charles Mingus, but drawing also on musical idioms of his childhood and early manhood and of seemingly distant cultures, Pullen became one of a handful of pianists to develop a personal, durable, adaptable vocabulary out of the '60s imperatives.

Taking the next step in exploiting the piano's linearity (a dimension Bud Powell championed during the bebop revolution), Pullen swept the keyboard with his strong hands' palms, heels, and knuckles to create broad, flowing phases and percussive clusters of virtually orchestral density. Like most jazz pianists, he was adept at fast-fingering distinct single notes to create melodic variations, but when inspired Pullen would build to climaxes with chorus after chorus of glisses, stirring up so many tones that one was held in suspense as to their resolution. Pullen also developed a rhythmic mastery that embraced beat patterns common to Caribbean, Central and South American, flamenco, West African, American gospel, pop-rock, and, finally, American Indian idioms—rhythms he'd suggest, seemingly abandon, then reinstate with emphatic yet graceful rigor.

In Pullen's own '90s projects—which included two trio recordings (*In the Beginning* and *Random Thoughts*), four albums with his African-Brazilian Connection (*Kele Mou Bana, Ode to Life, Live...and Live Again, Sacred Common Ground*—all on Blue Note), and the touring band Roots, in which he anchored a rhythm section for four soloing saxophonists—the pianist deployed his signature sweeps, slurs, and clusters in conventional head-solo-solo-head-out song structures. His hummable original compositions—drawing on youthful memories, romantic themes, diverse folk and classical repertoire, standard progressions, vigorous vamps, minor modes, and bluesy boogies—suggested he didn't arrive at his style fully formed, and proved he hadn't meant to stake out an inaccessible or stubbornly "avant-garde" position. Pullen's interest in these forms reiterated his ties to a jazz continuum. In *Sacred Common Ground,* collaborating with Indians of the Salish-Kootenai reservation in Montana, he constructed a firm, long-sought bridge between contemporary jazz and aboriginal chant.

While in college in North Carolina, Pullen had worked in a dance band: "More or less in the rhythm 'n' blues area if we had a black audience. For a white audience, we'd play more standards." He didn't chafe at the strictures of the material: "I always considered that I was fortunate to be in *any* circumstances where I could play, and always tried to take advantage of it. That way I had a foundation in all the different kinds of music I was experiencing. Because when I first went to school, all I knew how to play was the blues."

In time-honored fashion, Pullen, born at the end of 1944, learned the blues from his cousin Clyde "Fats" Wright, "a very good professional pianist who had been on the road with Dinah Washington. I used to follow along behind him like a shadow. He being family, I took total advantage. But he was always glad to help me out." This help, his early experiences in black churches near his home in Roanoke, Virginia, and his work backing local vocalists in semiprofessional recitals stood Pullen in good stead when he arrived in New York.

"I was an avant-garde pianist only as far as the jazz world was concerned," he explained. "In the *other* world"—comprising unheralded neighborhood clubs of Harlem, the outer boroughs, and New Jersey—"I was known as an organ player.

"I stopped playing organ shortly before I joined Mingus...Well, I never stopped, really. Nobody knew, but I was always playing uptown *somewhere*."

His organ expertise brought him commercial projects as writer, arranger, and conductor with vocalist Arthur Prysock and Cincinnati-based King Records, a premier independent rhythm 'n' blues label; Pullen revitalized jazz organ playing in the early '90s, on separate projects with guitarist John Scofield, saxophonist David Murray, and auteurist-bandleader Kip Hanrahan. But during the late '60s the organ simply paid his bills. "I did an album with Irene Reid and one with a girl named Queenie Lyons. But just as I was going good, King was acquired by a country label from Nashville."

So he spent a year accompanying singer Nina Simone and a short time as one of Art Blakey's Jazz Messengers before Mingus called him to join his combo: longtime drummer Dannie Richmond; the bluesy, leather-lunged tenor sax player, flutist, and casual vocalist George Adams; trumpeter Jack Walrath; and baritone saxophonist Hamiet Bluiett. This working ensemble tore through kaleidoscopic changes of theme, time, and tempo with convincing passion. They never recorded with Bluiett (though Pullen claimed there was a bootleg album of a European date). *Mingus Moves* and *Changes One* and *Two* (all on Atlantic Records) feature the group as a quintet.

"Those were more carefree days," Pullen said wryly, "only in retrospect. Nothing to do with the reality of the situation, but when I see now what I have to consider, that seems like another lifetime. Being with Mingus and playing quality music—the music was *always* on an advanced level—was a valuable opportunity to grow. Being with high-caliber musicians all the time, the worldwide exposure—there were many benefits. Plus, it was a lot of fun.

"Oh, Mingus's music was difficult; he had an uncivilized edge, definitely, and his bass had that certain *sound*. Mingus didn't play many notes, but I heard him play some fantastically beautiful solos—short, maybe just a chorus or two—that were *deep*. His sound had a lot to do with his music. When anybody else plays it, unless Mingus's sound is there, it's going to lose something. You could say the same about Monk."

Thelonious Monk, who expressed his acute insights and partic-ularities within the parameters of conventional song form, might seem Pullen's nearest predecessor in the lineage of jazz piano inno-vation, though Pullen was throughout the '70s and into the '80s often identified with Cecil Taylor (for the supposed ferociousness of their approaches). And Pullen was seldom spare, as Monk often was; his touch and density of incident was full, in a manner resembling, perhaps, McCoy Tyner's—though, like any worthy jazz musician, Don Pullen struggled hard to sound like himself.

Pullen did record an homage: "Thank You Very Much, Mr. Monk" (also known as "Gratitude") for the Japanese label Why Not. He'd penned the piece for his post-Mingus quartet with drummer Richmond, saxist Adams (who died in autumn '92), and bassist Cameron Brown; they performed it often. However, most of Pullen's music is less like Monk's, with its craggy intervals and oblique turns, or Tyner's, characteristically modal, than like Horace Silver's hum-mable tunes buoyed by compelling Cape Verde island rhythms. The similarity seems founded on a syncretism Pullen pursued even before the aptly titled 1984 album *Well Kept Secret*, wherein he co-led the 360 Degree Experience with drummer Beaver Harris in tracking the African diaspora.

That album (very rare, the first and only release from producer Hal Willner's Shemp Records) begins with "Goree," a seventeen-minute suite named for the tiny isle off Dakar, Senegal, where sev-enteenth-century ships boarded slaves bound for the Americas. French-hornist Sharon Freeman's arrangement for sextet (including Bluiett, tenor saxist Ricky Ford, bassist Buster Williams, and steel drummer Francis Haynes), four French horns, and Cuban conga drummer Candido, may seem to echo the Coltrane-Eric Dolphy '60s classic *Africa Brass,* but the clash of Pullen's piano with Haynes's "pan" diverges from that model to represent humans at sea. The choir of brass and reeds that rises against them evokes the pride of African history and perhaps the captives' vows to overcome servility. Then there's a conga-piano duet of earthy, stomping communion.

"I think I've always had an affinity for Latin music, African music," Pullen reflected after the concert debut in autumn 1990 of his African-Brazilian Connection, a band comprising Senegalese percussionist Mor Thiam, Brazilian percussionist Guilherme Franco,

Brazilian bassist Nilson Matta, and saxophonist Yebga Likoba from Cameroon. Pullen's ABC came together during a two-week residency sponsored by the not-for-profit Yellow Springs Institute of the Arts in Chester Springs, Pennsylvania.

"The very first composition I ever wrote when I was a kid was a samba," Pullen said in a backstage dressing room following an enthusiastic reception for the ensemble, which survived into 1995 with the personnel changes of Panamanian-born reedist Carlos Ward for Yebga, and traps drummer J. T. Lewis for Franco. "I play those kinds of tunes very easily, and they feel very good. So I've been wanting to investigate the music of Brazil, the music of Africa and flamenco too, to get more familiar with the roots of the music that we play in America—blues, jazz, and so forth. All of it has its roots in Africa.

"There are differences, but I think the strain that runs through us all in this particular group is African music—it all comes through that. Mor can tell you where specific Brazilian rhythms came from in Africa. Some of the stuff we play in jazz we know came from Africa. I've felt for a long time that playing with African and Brazilian musicians would get me closer to the origins of my music. Because on a higher plane of thought, there's not that much difference, perhaps *no* difference, between African and Brazilian musics and jazz.

"I think that's why we can all play together so easily. What I've heard in Brazil touched me; I knew I could be a part of the creation of that kind of music. The same with some African music; I knew I could find a place for me in that too. Especially the rhythmic pieces. My approach to piano is percussive, and very rhythmic—like another drum at times. These ideas are just kind of circling around in my head, but I have a very intense feeling about them. I guess that intensity helped our collaboration *happen*," the '90s jazz musician's term for "succeed."

Is it only rhythmic aspects that bind this band?

"I think it's a common level of maturity, personal growth, and spiritual evolvement"—development, evolution—"that allows us to work well together," Pullen answered. "But the rhythmic aspects definitely help. I just love percussion, and there's no way I'm going to have master percussionists available and not make use of them."

In the African-Brazilian Connection Mor Thiam played indigenous African hand drums including the *djembe, tabula*, and *joum-joum*—distinguished by their size, shape, and pitch—rattles such as the *shekere* and rainsticks. Franco played a setup of his own design that he called *timba:* a hi-hat cymbal and a cylindrical, horizontal, one-headed balsa drum over which he sat on a chair, supporting it with an ankle, the better to be able to strike its every surface.

"I hear them as one drummer," Pullen said, "but also as two separate ones, depending on what I need to hear at the moment. Basically, I want to hear them as one but be able to distinguish everything. That's how I listen to music. I hear all the different parts separately, and at the same time I hear them all together. If I need to hear a particular thing, I can zero in on that, but at the same time keep sight of everything going on with the group."

Though his ABC had just taken its first bows, Pullen knew it was going to last beyond the Yellow Springs Institute residency. "The guys want to continue and I want to continue," he explained, without worrying whether a precedent or audience for an African-Brazilian jazz quintet existed. "They came to me early on and said they did not want this to be our last concert. I immediately agreed. It's very exciting. These are great musicians who are talking about staying together with me; I'm honored they feel that way. The music is great; it's *on-time* music. The people here really responded well, by being really happy about this music, as though they've been transformed. I haven't seen this kind of excitement about anything I've done in years.

"I undertook this project because I wanted to realize some ideas I had about some tunes running around in my head. How to play them, would they work, could they be played, were they possible. These questions run through my mind when I'm composing. But making music, making jazz, is not just about composing as a skill or craft. It's a way of living, a way of thinking, a way of looking at things. The music gives you a different vision. The really adept musicians have that, which I noticed early on.

"The good players always saw things differently; they even spoke differently. I remember the first time I was in Chicago and met Muhal Richard Abrams through Lenny Martins, a bass player from my hometown. Lenny and Richard talked, and I listened, but I had no idea what they were talking about. They used words just like anybody else; they weren't speaking a foreign language. But I couldn't relate to what they were saying because I hadn't grown to that point in the music. Now, through the music, I understand what they were talking about. The music brings enlightenment."

Would Pullen have had difficulty making music with players of greater—or different—enlightenment?

"The only people I couldn't work with would be those who didn't have a respect for this music," he avowed, "someone who was so afraid of his own music that he couldn't allow it to be expanded by the use or insertion of any other kind of music that's different from his. But that's the thing about jazz: its universal nature, that quality that can absorb any kind of music from anywhere. A great jazz musician can adapt to any music. And jazz can cover all kinds of influences. It has and always will."

Do diverse influences water down jazz?

"Only players water down jazz. Jazz itself is *never* watered down. Jazz is a high cultural thing on its own. What people do with it might water it down, but *jazz* can't be watered down. Players' ideas, usually about commercialism, are what make a person try to water jazz down.

"What I do used to be considered avant-garde, but it's not avant-garde anymore," Pullen insisted. "It's changed. I've changed it so that it fits about anywhere. I've adapted it and do so many things with it that it's not really strange to most people who've been exposed to jazz. I have more control; I developed what I already did. I can play things cleaner now, more exactly, if I want to. I can roll my hands exactly, but...

"I don't like exactness, or too much refinement," Pullen admitted with a shy smile. "I never want to lose that raw edge, which I think is one of the qualities of jazz—that looseness, you know. Of course, we're in a stage of refinement now, but there should still be that earthiness, that rawness. I think when they hear it, people respond to that more than anything else."

Who Said He Could Do It His Way?

Pullen, like most artists, sought stimulation and support from respected elders at important points in his career. Mingus, Logan, even baritone balladeer Arthur Prysock helped the pianist, but he identified Muhal Richard Abrams as one of the most positive mentors in his life.

"That summer my friend Lenny and I went to Chicago, I was there only two weeks," Pullen said, "but I hung around Muhal's house the whole time. It seemed like much longer because we were

the good ol' avant-garde

at his house first thing in the morning and stayed until the landlady said we had to leave, late at night. I was fascinated. I was very young, and here was this real live musician!

"I learned a lot from him. Not what to play, or to imitate him. Muhal's greatest contribution was to give me confidence that I *could* play, that my ideas were valid. My bass player would say, 'You should- n't play *that,*' but Muhal would say, 'Yes, you should, you *should.*' And I'd think, 'Yeah!' because *that's* what I was hearing. I grew tremen- dously in that short period, and have always been grateful to Muhal."

Abrams has exerted the same effect on scores of musicians, start- ing with members of his Chicago-based Experimental Band of the early '60s, later renamed the AACM Big Band in accord with the cooperative Association for the Advancement of Creative Musicians he cofounded.

"Let me tell you about the first time I heard Muhal's big band." Pullen's eyes lit up. "I thought everybody in it was crazy! Honest to God, it was the most shocking and surprising thing I'd ever heard, and I started to go home. But then I sat there thinking, 'No, these cats are *not* kidding.'

"Muhal had charts and music for them to play—even *more* amazing. When they hit the first notes I thought, 'Wait a minute, they're gonna start over.' They didn't—they kept going!"

What Pullen heard that so disturbed him is impossible to pin- point—there are not now and never have been any commercially available recordings of the Experimental or AACM Big Band. But the Band was characterized by highly specified, complexly detailed mixtures of not only trumpets, trombones, saxes, and rarer reeds, but also violin, organ as well as piano, vibes, electric guitar, multiple basses, and sometimes a poet, arranged to blend in shimmering col- ors yet retain the individuality of players' personal sounds.

Each piece was different, employing themes and forms that wandered far from basic blues-derivations, yet kept something of the blues in their core. Thunderous, splashy, provocative—anyway, *active*—drumming neither obviously underscored the orchestra nor stood totally independent of it. Space was afforded for impassioned solos, hastily conceived duets and trios, and other spontaneous, unusual combinations.

In the late '60s, when the AACM took Monday night stands at Chicago South Side clubs like Las Brisas Lounge and the Pumpkin Room, musicians relieved of jazz's genre restraints let their bristling energy erupt in exploratory self-expression. More grounded than

Sun Ra's Arkestra and not so coolly disaffected as Gil Evans' studio assemblies, members of the AACM ensemble followed Muhal's conducting and each other's charts through Afro-mythic anthems, time-suspended abstractions, dramatic tone poems, and structured collective improvisation. Some members formed smaller working units (including the Art Ensemble of Chicago and the trio Air); some (like Anthony Braxton, Leroy Jenkins, Amina Claudine Myers, and Leo Smith) were ready to tour the world, and some (such as tenor man Fred Anderson, reed player Vandy Harris, trumpeter Billy Brimfield, and drummer Ajaramu) seldom left Chicago. Theirs was a brave, hungry, underfunded music that announced: "Our revolution is *now*."

Inspired by the freedom from hard-bop formulas that Ornette Coleman, Albert Ayler, John Coltrane, Eric Dolphy, and Cecil Taylor, among others, had claimed in New York, the Chicagoans were nonetheless disinclined to simply vent. They wanted to create what hadn't previously existed—and not only by developing *music* of their own.

They discovered and/or converted unusual spaces at odd times. Trombonist Lester Lashley engaged trumpeter Leo Smith or reeds player Kalaparusha Maurice McIntyre on Sunday mornings amid his paintings at the Afam Gallery; guitarist Pete Cosey plucked Fender bass in the lead of a galloping quartet at the Child City community house. Perhaps most significantly, the AACM established its own music school at the Abraham Lincoln Center in an area decimated by Mayor Richard J. Daley's "urban renewal."

AACM performances were seldom straitlaced; this *was* the '60s, after all. Once, ticket holders at the University of Chicago's Ida Noyes Hall were given crayons with which to decorate paper bags they were to wear on their heads during the performance. Once, trumpeter Lester Bowie announced from the stage at the scheduled starting time that the concert had begun—then split, to return forty-five minutes later in higher spirits, blowing comic splats of horn while singer Rita Warford paraded with him through the crowd, tossing confetti and whooping up a festive mood. Once, at the Hyde Park Art Center, saxophonist Henry Threadgill engaged other improvisers in concentrated interplay while dancer Christine Rrata Jones uncoiled from her wrap of aluminum foil and cellophane, slowly and steadily as a hatchling.

If these frills were extramusical, the AACM music itself, created with scant reference to commercial format imperatives or the social functions of nightclubs, was from its recorded beginnings truly something else. Tiny Delmark Records, with its funky retail outlet the Jazz Record Mart and its catalogue of rediscovered rural and new urban bluesmen, was the unlikely purveyor of the first AACM efforts.

Shamanistic reeds player Joseph Jarman's *Song For* partook of imagistic street poetry and subtle "little instruments"—finger cymbals and such—gradually building to torrents of righteous passion. Saxophonist Roscoe Mitchell had compositions emerge from timbral qualities in *Sound,* leaving sarcasm and satire in the wake. Anthony Braxton released *For Alto,* a two-disc set of virtuosic solos recorded in his living room, and complex structures apparently informed by contemporary classical music on *Three Compositions of New Jazz.* Kalaparusha offered primordial pantheism in his *Humility in the Light of the Creator.* Despite their exotic elements, each AACM album demonstrated a conceptual rigor foreign to the era's self-promoting but shorter-winded blowhards.

Until 1967, Abrams was best known for his mainstream piano work with Eddie Harris and the MJT+3. He emerged reborn on *Levels and Degrees of Light,* which opened with an oceanic wash of vibes pierced by a clarinet's shriek and a woman's wail. Then came the chant: "My thoughts are my future…Now and forever," and volcanic sax solos rendered all too indistinct by dreamlike reverberation.

More than twenty years later, in 1989, the fifty-six-year-old Abrams was the first recipient of Denmark's twenty-five-thousand-dollar Jazzpar Award—"the Nobel Prize of jazz," *Village Voice* jazz critic Gary Giddins called it, though the U.S. National Endowment of the Arts annually granted fifty thousand dollars to "American Jazz Masters," a role composer, pianist, bandleader, and infrequent clarinetist Abrams exemplified. To date, he's not been NEA-certified, and his name is known mostly to jazz aficionados. A small percentage of them know his music, and those who do may be hard put to repeat a motif, identify a passage or even a title of one of his compositions. That's due in part to the abundance, diversity, and elegant intricacy of his work, and his apparent indifference toward marketing or publicizing it.

Abrams's albums of the early '90s, such as *The Hearinga Suite* (Black Saint) and *UMO Plays the Music of Muhal Richard Abrams* (featuring a Finnish new music orchestra), may not inspire quite the wonder of his first broad-sweeping documents—he followed *Levels and Degrees* with *Young at Heart/Wise in Time,* weaving varied strands from jazz piano's past and promoting a combo of protégés including saxophonist Henry Threadgill—yet they plumb very specific complexities, mysteries, depths. Muhal's well-rehearsed concerts—since relocating to New York in the '80s, he has produced himself and colleagues under AACM auspices at Merkin Concert Hall, Symphony Space, and the Society for Ethical Cultural—may de-emphasize the bracing discoveries improvisers make during play. Yet his writing always probes instrumental relationships, contrasts, and shape-shifts of the high order that issue only from a single sharp mind or a group consciousness bonded by purposeful fellowship and lengthy shared experience.

In a rare interview conducted by Leigh Silverman and Larry Birnbaum for *Ear* magazine in the mid-'80s, Abrams explained: "I don't think the intention of people who cause or allow certain ideas to manifest is change. They're responding to change.... But from my point of view I [am] dealing with music, and the essence of music is movement and change and variety. So if you deal with that in certain ways, you may find yourself in an area that is more original—not necessarily original, but definitely a departure from the mainstream. I was born into *not* being mainstream."

Seeing and Speaking Differently

Abrams described himself as "a musical historian as well as a practicing musician...I feel it's an all-in-one thing. When you grow up in the Black Belt, especially during the time when I grew up, you hear it all. But the music in vogue at the time that I started to play music was bebop.

"Reaching back did actually propel [my] move to more original approaches. I think humanity is well steeped in reaching back, even when you don't realize that's what you're doing. You could just be remembering something out of some distant past that will accommodate some current move...

"Can you name anything today that can't be connected to the past? The past as a teaching tool can certainly give impetus to future actions far beyond that which we can imagine. I've tried to take all this information that I could gather, and that I'm still gathering. The past gets further in front and further behind at the same time. So I'm looking in all directions. But with this information, I compose and perform from the impressions I get.

"I've always found myself addressing the world of music—not just styles.... Naturally, in composing you can specialize in the world of music, but certainly in performance it's quite a bit more difficult because you have to spend time in different camps. So my process has been to make a mixture of the things of the music world in performance and composition.

"I think in every area of the arts you always have these keepers of the flame, and sometimes the torch is passed to very young people, and they remain keepers of the flame even on into old age. Some of the more established or older musicians today...didn't do anything new; they inherited their style from some other person. But they perfected their ability, and they dazzle you now, and they're the ones you look to as the masters. To me, if you don't know anything about the history or the basis of what you're doing, you've got a few problems. But music has to touch you in some way...and that thing that touches you is the thing that a performer went down into him or herself to get."

Though Abrams sits on myriad arts-organization advisory boards and speaks with considerable self-assurance, he intends no pronouncement to be final or definitive. In fact, only his disclaimers are written in stone.

"If anyone is looking to perceive there's been some great achievement, something we [the AACM] did or some groups did, they're not being accurate in their view yet," he warned the fans attending a discussion during the AACM's twenty-fifth-anniversary celebration in Chicago in November 1990. Among the participants were Lester Bowie and Joseph Jarman of the Art Ensemble; Jamaican-born reedist, composer, instrument maker, and former AACM president Douglas Ewart; and longtime AACM observer John Litweiler, author of *The Freedom Principle*. Deflecting queries regarding his own or any other AACM member's achievements has been one of Abrams's consistent themes.

"The *idea* of the AACM is what we're focused on," he continued, "an idea that sustains us and other organizations that attempt to organize in this manner. Viewing the individual, you have to consider human frailties in their many manifestations. It's an idea we're celebrating here—twenty-five years of an idea lasting."

The idea is collectivity—as practiced by the AACM as a whole, by its constituent bands such as the Art Ensemble, and by other ad hoc musicians' organizations including the Black Artists Group (BAG) of St. Louis.

"We were musicians who had the desire to have more control over our own destinies," Roscoe Mitchell has recalled. "That's what the AACM was all about. We were able to sit down together, analyze the past, and figure out our plans for the future. The philosophy of the AACM and the Art Ensemble—to go out and get what we want, to do the type of work we all want to do—has spilled over into other things besides playing."

In its statement of purpose the AACM vowed to "cultivate young musicians...magnify the importance of creative music...conduct a free training program for inner-city young people...encourage sources of employment...set an example of high moral standards...increase mutual respect between creative artists and musical tradesmen...uphold the tradition of elevated, cultured musicians handed down from the past."

The Shameless and the Bold

The Art Ensemble's slogan "Great Black Music—Ancient to the Future" is a working strategy, by which the musicians stake claim to all the world's rhythms and any or every compositional technique as well as the Afro-American tradition of collective improvisation. Always self-aware, often ironic, and sometimes downright sarcastic, the Art Ensemble of Chicago draws on tics and tropes of bebop, doo-wop, swing, soul, reggae, South African song, minimalism, Dixieland, sound concrete and theatrical performance art, and anything else its members come upon to redefine "jazz"—a term they deem inadequate.

"'Jazz' applies to only one of the idioms we deal with," AEC percussionist Famoudou Don Moyé has declared. The Art Ensemble's collective decision-making process has kept it together and working with regularity for more than twenty-five years, but Moyé, Lester Bowie, and Joseph Jarman (who retired from it in '97 to concentrate on his Buddhist dojo in Brooklyn) spoke for the group more often than Mitchell or bassist Malachi Favors. "It's all great black music, and we respect all its forms; they're part of our musical heritage. We have some quasi-funk tunes in our repertoire, too, on which we use our own approach."

The Art Ensemble's approach includes taking care of its own business without relying on record-company financial support for its recordings or tours. The band has its own business office in Chicago, has often produced its own records, determined its own next steps, and even "refined all the technical aspects of touring," according to Moyé.

"We hired our own crew of four roadies, including a soundman, and got a bus" to transport them coast to coast, border to border, during a U.S. tour celebrating their twenty-fifth anniversary. "We have more stuff than most so-called jazz bands that travel," Moyé continued, "and we need our own soundman who's familiar with our music because most of the bigger halls have rock-oriented engineers. Not many jazz bands require a twenty-four-track mixing board."

Then, too, few groups without electric guitars and keyboards fill the venues on the Art Ensemble's itinerary. The tour kicked off at the Minneapolis hall that served as the main location of Prince's rock film *Purple Rain*. Moyé said, "The reaction [was] good, as usual. Of course, people who like us come to hear us, but these halls have their own crowd, too. I can feel the difference between an audience that knows our music, recognizes the things we do, and one that doesn't. But both like us. In many places people come up to the front near the stage and dance."

Jarman concurred. "The myth and image of the Art Ensemble as a cult group is fading because of the realness of our diverse appeal, and the credibility with which we engage in so many different musical forms.

"The elements of our performances are not unique to black culture. We use face paint, for example, not as war paint but in place of masks, which are used in cultures of every ethnicity to subjugate the personality of the performer so he can more easily become a representative to the community. Masks and costumes make universal statements, and are archetypal symbols. We use Afro-American elements because they're closest to our experience, but it's an American experience, too. So even if we don't play rock, rock audiences understand us. So do traditional jazz fans, though we may not play much traditional jazz."

The Art Ensemble's studied approach has helped it endure. Though the Modern Jazz Quartet can claim greater longevity, no other improvising ensemble formed in the '60s or since has demonstrated the staying power or agreement of plan and action of the AEC. And the quintet has—despite its age, its reputation among some critics, its star status in Europe, its early '90s recording contract with the Japanese label Disk Union or late '90s contract with

Atlantic Records—remained principally untamed. They keep going, without regard to fashion.

Their theatrical presentation remains ritualized: Moyé and Favors daub themselves with bright colors and dress in something resembling Third World splendor. Goateed Bowie sits center stage, wearing a white research lab jacket and the mock-sober air of Dr. Hackenbush. Mitchell appears blasé in street clothes.

Instruments surround them. Mitchell and Jarman used to play more than twenty saxophones, clarinets, and flutes, as well as conch shells, glockenspiel, sirens, synthesizers, and kitchen pans. Moyé has enough hand drums to supply a tribe, and an expanded traps kit. Favors seldom puts down his bass; when he does, he's most likely to pick up and mutter through an amplified bullhorn. Bowie sometimes beats a huge parade drum. Yet their programs begin with a silent moment—as Jarman has said, "a prayer for unity and peace throughout the universe, then the sounding of a gong, which intones the spirit of music itself." Lead lines gradually emerge and themes evolve after some tinkering with bells, wood flutes, and the like. Then serious exchanges occur among the musicians, and the Art Ensemble members let spontaneity work for them.

"We have a phrase, 'Stoop and hit,' which means we'll see what we do when we get onstage," Bowie has explained. "We usually have some sort of outline of what tunes we'll play that we talk about five minutes before the show. We consider if we're playing indoors, where we can include more finely detailed work, or outside, where we need something to catch people's attention.

"But we always try to be creative and adventurous. We let the music lead. A beautiful march might come out of the sky. An unaccompanied solo might be programmed in advance or might happen spontaneously. The percussion might move into a sax solo, which becomes a bass-sax duet that leads into a particular song that develops into a free improvisation. We just don't know.

"If a song comes up that we hadn't sketched into the outline—well, there it is. There's nothing we can do to stop it or save the outline. We all feel and go with it automatically."

Working together for so many years gives the team its telepathic sense, but the Art Ensemble members seem by nature, design, and training to be particularly alert to each other's improvised nuances and mindful of the repertoire that fills their more than two dozen albums.

"We approach every concert with the same intense concentration," Bowie bragged. "Our senses are super-hyper, open to everything. When we're performing we're not watching the clock to see how much longer we should play, not counting measures—we're performing, working on a vibe, a feeling."

Each player actually projects his own feeling, but their characters balance and combine in flexible ways. Each contributes to the common repertoire, and their compositions affirm their strengths: Bowie favoring dramatically sweeping melodies, Jarman high-energy soprano sax features, Caribbean ditties, and coloristic instruments ranging from pitched, pressurized air horns to synthesizers. Mitchell insinuates both distance and commitment with an insistent, sour tone; Moyé has punch and polyrhythmic chops; Favors is soft but pivotal, his time sense as stretchy yet tough as sinew.

Prior to his withdrawal, Jarman believed their blend had "crystallized. We sound more to the point lately. Not less adventurous, but able to communicate through the music more clearly."

"You have to be around for a while to develop originality in this medium," Moyé added. "Time and talent are the main ingredients contributing to a unique voice."

In the '90s, the AEC sought to refresh its unique voice through collaborations with the Amabutho Male Chorus of Soweto and the proudly intractable pianist Cecil Taylor. In recording with the South Africans, the quintet failed to bridge the gap between far-flung improvisation and the choir's specific stylization; their concert appearances together in Europe may have been more satisfying. At least one track from the AEC's effort with Taylor deserves attention: in "Caseworks" Jarman and Mitchell play flutes, and Bowie essays a characteristic phrase, first to introduce, then to overlay, and finally to mistily waft away the pianist's prototypical motifs.

A Band of Reeds

Of other innovative jazz ensembles born in the late '60s–early '70s, only the World Saxophone Quartet has sustained as lengthy an independent career as the Art Ensemble. They might be cousins, considering the proximity of their midwestern birthplaces, their personal relations, the parallel trajectories of their careers, and the cordial relations between the larger organizations of which they're constituents. Some longtime observers will recall that once in the dead of a frigid winter the founding reedsmen of the WSQ, as members of the St.

Louis–based Black Artist Group (BAG), bused up to play a concert in conjunction with the AACM in an unheated University of Chicago auditorium. Everyone kept their coats on, and many musicians wore gloves while they played.

"The World Saxophone Quartet grew out of a situation in St. Louis where we played solos or duos or trios with different combinations of instruments," saxophonist Oliver Lake has explained. "That was a Midwest thing. The bebop-oriented musicians on the East and West Coasts didn't do it. If their rhythm section didn't show up, they didn't play."

The St. Louis founders of the WSQ—Lake on alto and soprano saxes and flute; Julius Hemphill on alto and soprano, too; and Hamiet Bluiett on clarinet and baritone sax (tenor saxist-bass clarinetist David Murray is originally from California)—didn't have that option. Gigs were so hard to get that the musicians would simply cope if the drummer didn't come. Indeed, the WSQ built its career on being drummerless until the '90s, when they made sure drummerlessness would be no problem. For *Metamorphosis,* the fourth WSQ release from Elektra/Nonesuch, African percussionists Mor Thiam and Mar Gueye of Senegal, and Chief Bey, who was raised in Brooklyn, added authentic rhythms on *m'beum m'beum, djembe, joum-joum,* and *asiko* to the reed section's blend. The African drummers continued to accompany the WSQ through changes that saw Hemphill leave and, first, Arthur Blythe, then James Spaulding, then John Purcell join the band.

"When the sax-quartet idea came up, it felt natural," Lake continued. "Each of us could carry a full evening as a soloist, so it seemed like it would be easy to carry a full evening as a quartet." By 1976, when the WSQ announced its establishment, the San Francisco Bay area-based ROVA saxophone quartet had already embarked on a similarly instrumented project. However, the two groups were far from the same.

ROVA's members—Jon Raskin, Larry Ochs, Andrew Voigt, and Bruce Ackley—were unknown as jazz players, and devoted to creating a unique ensemble identity with reference to exploratory forms of so-called new music. Each of the WSQ players had established his own reputation by 1976, when they were urged to form a unit by Edward "Kidd" Jordan, head of the music department at New Orleans Southern University.

Lake was a heavy spirit drawing on the inspirations of Eric Dolphy, Anthony Braxton, and St. Louis soulman Oliver Sain. Texas born, bred and educated Hemphill was the blues-rooted but ambitious composer-performer-producer of what was considered an underground classic, *Dogon A.D.* Bluiett was known for single-handedly stretching the baritone horn beyond its cool school and bop applications, notably in Charles Mingus's band. Murray was the great young tenor titan, a romantic stylist (and critics' darling) screeching as fervently as Albert Ayler and as gruffly husky as Ben Webster. Each man intended to take New York (hence, jazz itself) by storm, and their individual recordings—Lake and Hemphill on Arista Freedom, Bluiett on Italian Black Saint, Murray for a host of independent U.S. and European labels—had won followers.

In times past these four reedmen would undoubtedly have crossed paths as members of big bands which, in the '30s and '40s, toured the United States like baseball teams, trading and matching players who proved themselves in cutting contests and jam sessions. Big-band sax sections working in dance halls nearly every night were stable enough to interpret arrangements intuitively, to achieve identifiable ensemble subtleties, and to hone long-standing, if frequently friendly and mutually creative, musical rivalries.

The World Saxophone Quartet adopted formal wear for its initial performances to emphasize the nobility of its jazz lineage and suggest comparisons to the string quartets and wind ensembles of classical music. But its early repertoire was altogether looser than that of any sax section from the big bands or other chamber group. Charts written by WSQ members (principally, Hemphill) tended to offer basic guidelines following from through-composed passages.

As Hemphill told Leonard Feather in '81 for notes to the WSQ's Black Saint album *Live in Zurich,* "We know each other pretty well by now, so it becomes difficult for the listener to tell where the written passages end and the ad-libbing begins. I would say that in the course of any given evening from 60 to 70 per cent of what we play is improvised."

Even the most harmonically abstract, melodically interlaced, and timbrally thorny movements in WSQ concerts, though, resolved in gospel-related voicings and up-from-the-gutter swing. As the band refined its point of view, blend became its byword; contrast and counterpoint were simply two of its strategies. The four members shared one sense of breath, attack, and dynamics; until Hemphill departed in 1990, they became ever better attuned, though they often broke rhythmic lockstep for spontaneous interplay midpiece, and to allow space for solo statements.

Their early, Italian-produced albums generally pursued chamber music balance and short track times at the expense of expansive, raucous energy, but they still emphasized an original book of music. Contracting with Elektra/Nonesuch in 1986, the WSQ reevaluated its approach. Their first E/N release, *Plays Duke Ellington,* offered versions of classics that set melodic essentials within and close and dissonant harmonies. *Dances and Ballads,* a program of ten originals followed in '87; *Rhythm 'n' Blues,* covering soul hits by Gamble and Huff, Marvin Gaye, Otis Redding, and Junior Wells, in '88. It was a kick to hear the old favorites reconceived, but there was frustration within the band. Some of it was relieved when Hemphill left to pursue such ambitious personal projects as his sax sextet opera *Long Tongues,* which premiered at Harlem's Apollo Theater in November 1990, but entered a state of limbo when Hemphill's health failed (he died of diabetic complications in April 1995). Greg Osby, John Purcell, John Stubblefield, and Sam Rivers had subbed when a World Saxophonist was unavailable due to illness or double-booking; so had Blythe, who was inducted as the (first) official new fourth member.

"We [were] still playing the Duke Ellington charts," Lake commented, "with Arthur taking the lead parts, but we [didn't] record them again. We've talked about doing another 'masters' LP, maybe one of Monk compositions, but that's not definite. We'd really rather develop more of our own works and play them as standards."

Of course. Bluiett's "Hattie Wall" and "I Heard That," Lake's "West African Snap," Hemphill's "Steppin,'" and Murray's "Fast Life" are pleasing and memorable each time they're heard. Blythe contributed the title tune to *Metamorphosis,* the most consistently high-spirited World Saxophone Quartet album in a decade. The credit for that is in part due to the African drums.

"David Murray and I came up with the idea," Lake said. "Over the years we've wanted to do projects with other musicians, other instruments: Our gigs with Max Roach and his percussion group M'Boom were very good. In '89, the Brooklyn Academy of Music's Night of a Thousand Bands during the New Music America festival seemed like the perfect opportunity. Mor Thiam and I had worked together in St. Louis, when he was the resident composer for Katherine Dunham's dance troupe; Hamiet had worked with him, too. After BAM we did minitours and weekend dates with the drummers, and the recording went well."

"Katherine Dunham came to Senegal for the World Negro Arts

Festival in 1966," said Mor Thiam, a griot and rhythm master who leads his own Drums of Fire and sparked Don Pullen's ABC band. "I was a greeting musician at the airport, and she was struck by me. Later she found me through my government—I was with the National Ballet of Senegal—and invited me to the States. So I became head of the percussion department at Southern Illinois University in East St. Louis, right across the river from where the Black Artists Group was organized. I founded Drums of Fire, and recorded my first album with Oliver, Julius Lester, and Joe Bowie, John Hicks on piano, Phillip Wilson playing drums. They invited me to join BAG.

"I enjoyed this project. They're good musicians, ask a lot of questions, and want to come visit Dakar," continued Thiam. For *Metamorphosis* he wrote "Lullaby," dedicated to neglected and/or abused stepchildren, and "Su Mama Ah Zumu" for the South African people "who never know their future and struggle in pain to identify with the right leader." He said his composition "Africa" is the theme song of Senegal's national radio station.

Thiam's *djembe* is a hand drum with rivets rattling in three attached metal ears; his *joum-joum* is the drum with which royalty announces a war. Mar Gueye's *m'beum m'beum* is a short, hourglass-shaped, two-headed drum, held in the crook of the arm and played with a stick. Chief Bey thumps a pronounced bass on the big, open-bottomed *asiko*.

"Performing with the African percussionists definitely changes what the saxes play," Lake said. "They change the way we move through our concerts."

But they're not required at each WSQ gig; only the saxes are. "The saxophone quartet is a good vehicle for each of us," Lake thought, for Bluiett, Murray, the train of subs for Hemphill, and himself. All WSQ saxophonists lead their own groups and freelance with others. Yet Lake acknowledged that "the WSQ has a higher profile than any of us as individuals. It's great for each of our careers. We spend four months a year as the WSQ, and during other months fend for ourselves."

Members of the World Saxophone Quartet and the Art Ensemble, like Muhal Richard Abrams and Don Pullen, all reached that profit-making point where fending for themselves was possible. Though their works were singular, offering decidedly personal artistry, and not likely to be taken up by bluntly commercial enterprises, within certain sophisticated listening circles they'd become renowned. By the 1990s, each of them enjoyed a fairly secure life.

That isn't so for some of their younger associates, musicians who might be regarded, if they are known at all, as the ongoing avant-garde.

There are some former students of the AACM school, for instance, who continue to infuse the Chicago local of that organization with can-do enthusiasm. Kahil El' Zabar, who plucks an African mbira and plays hand drums, formed the Ethnic Heritage Ensemble with saxophonist Edward Wilkerson, Jr. and trombonist Joe Bowie. They've recorded and toured international festivals, but Kahil makes his living performing, sometimes unbilled, on West Coast–produced pop soul albums, and has won roles as a movie actor.

Wilkerson's own orchestra Shadow Vignettes appeared in the independently produced video narrative "Honky Tonk Bud," more like a cautionary Robert W. Service poem than a MTV-style music promotion short. His Eight Bold Souls (with '80s AACM president, double-reed specialist, and music educator Mwata Bowden) toured Canada, Japan, and the Middle East, besides playing at the Brooklyn Academy of Music during the New Music America Festival of '89. Wilkerson's gigs outside Chicago remain infrequent.

Acid-toned saxophonist Ernest Dawkins led his New Horizons Ensemble (with trumpeter Ameen Muhammad, one hand on his hip, blasting elephantine roars) in a set at the 1991 Leverkusen Jazztage which was preserved by the German CD label Open Minds. Drummer Reggie Nicholson, who's played with Sonny Rollins as well as Muhal Abrams and who provided the bluesy shuffles and tom-tom groove for pianist Myra Melford's outgoing trio of the early '90s, joined some older AACM members to revive the spirit, if not the charts, of the '60s Big Band at an Italian festival in spring of '93.

Then there's a thriving branch of the younger, not always black improvising community that's been moved by the generation of the AACM et al., though they're not members themselves. Making music with serious, though not humorless, devotion, they include Melford, raised just outside Chicago in the '60s, who's studied and recorded with AEC reedsmen Jarman and Henry Threadgill, and violinist Leroy Jenkins; pianist Marilyn Crispell, bassist Mark Dresser, and drummer Gerry Hemingway, longtime members of Anthony Braxton's studiously idiosyncratic quartet; Mark Helias, sometimes bassist with Braxton as well as the late drummer Edward Blackwell;

bassist John Lindberg of the String Trio of New York, reedsman Marty Ehrlich, trombonist Ray Anderson, guitarist Mickey Navazio, and pianist Matthew Shipp, who has worked in saxophonist Roscoe Mitchell's band.

No one of these musicians is yet crossing over to a general public, writing songs that are on so many lips that they get bought up for commercial jingles. None of them is making a fortune as a performer or recording artist—and it's fairly unusual for any of them to be courted by the sorts of not-for-profit American institutions that would project them to the arts-consuming elite. Their creations—and the work of legions of their peers—might be thought anachronistic, rooted in the big cultural bang of the late '60s, so avant-garde as to have no chance of being claimed by mainstream artists or audiences, so peculiar that they get put down by conservatives as less of an advanced front than a lost patrol.

Still, they are tenacious. They have survived, and even prospered. They have endured criticism and changing cultural tides, and their dedication has prevailed.

"As far as having achieved our goals, we haven't," Lester Bowie conceded during that panel held for the AACM's twenty-fifth-anniversary festivities. "There have been results, though, and we're not finished yet. This is only the first twenty-five years. We always understood this was going to be a long-distance run."

4 Birds of a Feather

Three musicians who worked, played, and lived in close proximity from the mid-'70s into the '90s represent entirely personal directions for future jazz. Though they're not self-avowed members of a single school, neither are their ideas mutually exclusive; they don't operate in a vacuum, they partake of the same milieu. Each built an international career from a base in New York City, and origins in the Left and Middle Coasts. They may not always be pals, but they've worked together and often shared contacts. Each is usually aware of what the others are up to.

Aloft in the Jazzstream

David Murray is out to *getcha*. "People think I haven't done this sort of thing," the reedsman said backstage at Lincoln Center before a much bally-hooed "Battle Royale" with fellow tenor saxophonists Joshua Redman, Don Braden, and George Coleman in August 1994. Despite having been widely hailed as the jazz savior of the '80s, this was the first time Murray was presented by Lincoln Center's jazz department, and he felt he had something to prove. "But I have. There was a European festival a few years back where I got up with Stan Getz and Johnny Griffin...Don't get me wrong, these guys tonight are fine musicians. But that was another *level* of tenor players, you know: stiffer competition."

So Murray's not afraid of a little head-butting; he just wants to triumph in it. Where does it come from, this bug infecting jazz musicians to be crowned over their peers? The ego victory is not quantifiable, as in sports, where statistics last, or in finance, where riches mount up. Jazz battles are more like gunslinging in the Old West; triumphs are temporary, and merely set up the winners as targets of up-and-comers' aim.

Murray did well at that Battle Royale; he and newly arrived Joshua Redman caught the crowd's favor, while purists hailed lesser-known Don Braden's idiomatic consistency and conceded that veteran Coleman had an uneventful night. However one scores the saxophone contests of the '80s and '90s, for sheer productivity and prodigious risk-taking, Murray is tops.

An example: Murray leaps in swinging his tenor saxophone on "At The Cafe Central" over Don Pullen's runaway organ on *Shakill's Warrior*—one of five albums featuring Murray issued during the 1992-93 season through Sony Music (formerly, CBS Records), either licensed from Japan's Disk Union (DIW) label or producer Bob Thiele's Red Baron imprint—and it's America's best-established jazz cult figure flying again! There goes his sound—up and out!

"Kind of horrible, isn't it?" Murray grinned wolfishly, twinkle in eye and tongue in cheek when complimented during one of his club engagements about that rip-roaring solo. "Feverish, you might say. *Baaad.*"

Shakill's Warrior is a quartet album of straight time, bluesy shuffles, memorable melodies, and hard-blown solos; a modest-enough concept, but the kind of album that, when done well, attracts listeners to jazz and is dug by aficionados for its grooves and inspired improvisations. *Shakill's Warrior* is done well. There's nothing glib about it, though it's among more than one hundred albums Murray has appeared on, usually as leader, during the twenty years of his professional career. With drummer Andrew Cyrille rapping an intro to his own portrait of a debonair "High Priest," guitar discovery Stanley Franks plucking single-note figures with aplomb, and Pullen in a thrilling soul-power organ mode, Murray conquers problems on *Shakill's Warrior* (named for his son's martial arts program) that have confronted him from the start.

"When I was in college in Pomona, California, I had a gig at a place called the Maharaja with an organ player and a guitarist—six nights a week," he recalled during an interview for the Japanese magazine *Swing Journal*. He and I have met several times: for *Down Beat* articles and Blindfold Tests, over lunch at the Harlem restaurant Sylvia's, in Manhattan jazz clubs and a Long Island arboretum concert, around the Chicago Jazz Festival, at Philadelphia's Painted

Bride, and at the bar of an Istanbul hotel. Murray has always been willing to chat.

"We were the opening act for a *smoking* belly dancer. The organ player, I remember, had a rhythm box." The funkiest drum machine invented would blow its memory chip trying to ape the perfectly hip rhythms Cyrille locks under the tunes of *Shakill's Warrior*. Still, how can a saxist outsmoke a belly dancer?

Or, does one draw attention away from the sideshow by blowing ferociously and bending harmonic rules to the breaking point? How best to create a popular music that also satisfies an interest in original expression and perhaps experimentation? Can young jazz musicians be both professional and wildly free, get their workouts and bring home the bacon? Murray and compatriots address these issues regularly.

Murray first attained visibility and subsequent cult status as a result of very good press notices attending his arrival in New York City in 1975. He was proceeded by his college professor and occasional drummer Stanley Crouch, who encouraged *Village Voice* columnist Gary Giddins to give him a good listen. Other culture journalists and opinion makers soon formed a chorus hailing Murray, a personable, articulate man with a sax sound identifiably his own. That in itself was a very attractive quality, after the era's surplus of John Coltrane wannabes.

But reams of positive profiles and reviews took Murray only so far. Due to a variety of arcane business considerations, most of his work appears on independent record labels with limited U.S. distribution. The Italian label Black Saint has more than a dozen Murray albums in its catalogue, as does Japanese Disk Union. Because of its styling, his music hasn't fit commercial radio formats—but then, hardly any improvised jazz fits that niche.

No, instead of reaching out to general audiences beyond jazz, Murray reconvened younger and older, black and white, North American and foreign jazz fans whose differing tastes had splintered their buying power. He displayed a fondness for singable songs and boasted a burly, relentless tone—both soulful, romantic virtues. He also returned to conventional head-solo-solo-head out forms after a brief era in which structural innovations were thought of as the jazz frontier. By swinging forthrightly, Murray was lauded for emphasizing jazz's original principles. He didn't deny that notice at the time, though now he claims it didn't do him justice.

"The critics may call me a neotraditionalist, but those older cats weren't playing at the top of the horn like I am," Murray insisted, "and they weren't hopping on the bottom like I am, either. Listen to what I'm trying to do; the older cats weren't trying to do that.

"Critics always compare me to Albert Ayler too, but I'll tell you the truth, man, I don't think I've sounded like Albert Ayler for one minute. I like what he did, but the reason I dedicated 'Flowers for Albert' to him was, I was walking down by the East River [near where the murdered Ayler's corpse was found] one day, I'd just finished talking to Sunny Murray [a drummer for Ayler, but not kin to David], and I started whistling that tune. I came home, wrote it down, and because of my conversation with Sunny Murray I dedicated it to Ayler. I never met the cat. That's as close as I've come. But everybody started jumping on the bandwagon.

"My experience in music comes more out of rhythm 'n' blues than anything else. Until I went to college I was one of the hottest r&b sax players around. Starting when I was twelve or thirteen, I had a fifteen-piece revue. For two years we worked schools—proms, assemblies, stuff like that. It was serious, though, no jive; I had a six-piece horn section.

"I had never even heard Duke Ellington's band. My band was modeled on James Brown's and all the r&b groups of the late '60s. I even went through a Jimi Hendrix phase, sitting on Telegraph Avenue in Berkeley, playing guitar. I was a really *out* kid; I'd get into things and I'd want to *become* them. I wanted to *be* Jimi Hendrix. It was fun, though, and it was weird at the same time."

What might seem truly weird about Murray is that after his decades of metamorphosis from r&b prodigy into resourceful freelancer, he's yet to secure the media-spread name or (more importantly) consistent level of opportunities that might be considered his due. He's the man who popularized the solo sax concert in jazz lofts, who set "free" vocabulary amid lyrical lines in conventional forms, who returned the bass clarinet to jazz action, who cofounded the World Saxophone Quartet and Clarinet Summit, who won all the critics' and readers' polls, and brought a circle of avant-gutbucket players (to borrow Jon Pareles's term) to the fore.

The fact that he's often overlooked has come through little fault of his own, unless his talent and musical comprehension are, as his detractors claim, simply inadequate. Well, he *is* another winner of Denmark's exclusive Jazzpar prize; maybe there aren't enough high-profile gigs in the jazz world. Maybe Murray will have to outlive the tenorists who enjoy today's best engagements, yet he's surely among

future jazz

those wishing good health and long life to Sonny Rollins! Maybe he'll have to go into seclusion or exile or develop scandalously destructive personal habits. Most likely, he'll just have to keep at it. Musicians in Murray's position can't coast; they must maintain their momentum, dream up and pursue ever greater ambitions, and hold to their killer schedules.

As an instrumentalist Murray, born in 1955, links the macho voraciousness of the sax's past and such of his forbears as Coleman Hawkins, Ben Webster, and Paul Gonsalves to the wider open harmonic range of the post-Ayler-Dolphy-Coleman-and-Coltrane present. He emits skeins of notes that crest in higher and higher waves, nonstop phrases that course through whole choruses with pulsating rhythmic vitality, and climactic squeals. He can affect an intimate whisper as well as crazy bird screams and deep, controlled belly tones. A very physical player, Murray embodies the lines of his solos by hunching his shoulders, hunkering into the modulations, kicking in time with a foot, and rearing back at the peak of a long passage. These moves aren't for show; they are part and parcel of his improvisations. But they do give his audiences vivid visual references, and that shouldn't hinder a successful career for the compactly built, casually handsome jazzman.

Murray tours the United States, but not with predictable regularity. More often than not, he and his confrères are on the road overseas. Here's a fairly typical sequence from his 1992 bookings: A week in the New York club Condon's with the twenty-piece orchestra he coleads with longtime associate Lawrence Douglas "Butch" Morris. Two days in Manhattan's Clinton Recording Studio for Disk Union, guided by producer Kazunori Sugiyama. Ten days of solos, duos, trios, or quartet work in the United States, including recitals at museums or other nonprofit venues, drop-ins at scrappy profit-seeking presentation places, and college-level clinics or lecture-demonstrations followed by concerts.

Then back to Condon's for another week, this time with his octet. Three days off (spent with his wife Ming and son David Mingus) prior to a two-week European tour—from which Murray flies home for a free outdoor JVC Jazz Festival afternoon concert at Damrosch Park outside Lincoln Center (his trio earns a standing ovation from some five thousand attendees). Return flight to Helsinki, on to Moscow, then Tokyo. In Japan he performs at the Zoa fest, the Pit Inn, and a fest in Ichigakigiwa; he also has a solo show. He'd like to spend more time in Japan.

"But since the Japanese sponsored my video shot in the Village Vanguard, it seems like they'd just as soon watch me on TV as see and hear me live," he said. Murray offers many such comments, accompanied by a twitch of his pencil-thin mustache, a frank stare, and a shrug.

He obviously loves what he does. He savors the action. "Practicing is one thing, but playing every night gives you an edge people who just practice don't get. Wynton is great now because he's had that opportunity," Murray stated, "like I have." Yet he complained, "I like playing this music, but I'm in it to make some money. I'm not as enthusiastic as I was ten years ago.

"When I started playing music, when I was a kid, I always thought I would be rich—and I swear to God, I still do. I always associated the saxophone with money. Dexter Gordon, Sonny Rollins—I'd look at their album covers, they all had suits on, and I'd think, 'Yeah, these guys are making *big* money.'

"I don't want it just for myself. I want enough so I can be happy, and all my friends can be happy. I want everybody working; I want the whole thing revised. That may never happen, but if it does, I'll be ready for it. Because the kind of money I'm making now, I could get a regular day gig and do about the same. But then my soul wouldn't be fulfilled."

Why can't he get the hang of selling out?

"It's gonna happen anyway." Murray dismissed his personal esthetic as though he could neither shake nor disown it. "The bands I've established prove I can only sell out so much. My octet was my idea to sell out. 'But *that's* far-out, too,' is what the major-label people told me. The octet's as far in as I could come!

"The sound, that's first," he responded, asked why he had so many ensembles. Economics matter, too. "When I started my bands I was thinking of sounds and my need to play with other musicians. My idea for my quartet originally was to do a nice album of standards and be working on the circuit that Stan Getz and Johnny Griffin make, because I believe my quartet will stand up against anybody's.

"And my octet"—which in its acclaimed albums *Ming, Home,* and *Murray's Steps* introduced a roster of players who continue to appear with him, and build reputations of their —"we're going to keep recording. I'm not certain what, but it will have a lot of twists and turns, leaps and bounds. It will be an extension. I see the octet playing festivals more than anything else.

"I'd like to play concert halls with the big band, and give Butch [Morris] space to do what he wants to do as well. It's our band: 50 per cent me, 50 per cent him—sometimes more. He's performed his conductions with others, but not with the kind of improvisers *I* hire.

"We've got renegades in the band. That's what Butch and I like: guys with big sounds who can read. There's resistance, sure. The guys have to be drilled to get their heads out of the music stands; then when they look up they want to *play*, not be directed. But they get the idea that Butch is the coach, even if it takes me shouting, 'Make like *he's* the one paying you.'

"I'd like to do more solo playing because that's one format I worked on hard for a long time. In the right environment I set up three microphones and play a three-personality thing. When I go to one mike, I play in one personality; at another mike, I play in another. Just to keep some excitement up and make myself seem like three people instead of one.

"See, man, everything gets more clear to me. I hit thirty and everything got clear as a bell. One thing that's changed as I've gotten older is the way I deal with musicians. In my twenties I had a hard time explaining myself in rehearsals to musicians who were my seniors. I always try to use my seniors because of the experience they have walking around with them, but being in awe of people—I'm done with that. It's easier now for me to cuss somebody out about my music. I tell them, 'Look, man, you're doing that wrong. Do it *right!*' Instead of going, 'Aw, man…'"

Murray wants musicians to play his themes—"Flowers for Albert," "Sweet Lovely," and "Lovers," among others—correctly because he believes they could find favor beyond genre limitations and across generations. He may abstract his original compositions (and standards) as though he's chasing ideas without caring where they take him, but he knows that's not the only way his songs can be played. He welcomes other interpretations *if* the songs are respected as written. And he scoffs at the notion that his own boundlessness proves he doesn't know what he's doing.

"Cats say I can't read my own parts? These cats must be crazy. I can play every part I have; I don't even have to read them—I *wrote* them. That's easy. My concept of soloing is that I can play any note on the horn on any piece, at any moment, because I feel that confident. Say a guy is talking about a C7 chord; I can play every note on my horn on a C7 because I know where to start and where to land.

"When I play a tune I've never played before, I'll spell out the triads on the first chorus. The second chorus gets more dense, and by the third or fourth chorus I'm playing what I really hear on it. I pride myself on my ability to do that, because if you listen to Bird and Trane and all the greats, that's how they did it. 'Oh, man, you played the wrong note on this change'—you hear that only from people who are on the periphery, because chances are they aren't going to play anything more than that, anyway. I don't pay too much attention to them. I know in the end nobody's going to be talking about them, they're going to be talking about *me*.

"I know they're not *always* going to be talking about me; I'm not expecting them to. This is my third time up since I've been in New York. I've been up three times, I've been down twice. When I first got here, the year 1975-76, I had a trio thing with Fred Hopkins and Steve McCall, Gary Giddins jumped on that. Then there was a lull, right up until I started with the World Saxophone Quartet, and that got it up again, to the high point for that group. Then, after I broke up with 'Zake [writer Ntozake Shange, to whom Murray was briefly married], there was a dormant period. I couldn't get work. I'd call people, I'd set up tours, and they'd get canceled. Okay.

"Now: Now is now. I know how it feels to be on the down side. Until 1982, when I started playing at Sweet Basil's a lot, I was coming back from a down period. Basil's increased my notoriety in New York. That was a period of growth. It's been pretty cool since then."

In his most recent period of growth, Murray has collaborated with well-regarded if purportedly noncommercial jazz artists including bassists Richard Davis and Reggie Workman; pianists Dave Burrell, Anthony Davis, John Hicks, and Randy Weston; blues-oriented guitarist James "Blood" Ulmer and the fluid electric bassist Jamaaladeen Tacuma. Murray has indulged his special affinity for drummers, having developed special relationships with the late Edward Blackwell and Milford Graves, Billy Higgins, Elvin Jones, Sunny Murray, Ralph Peterson Jr., and Ronald Shannon Jackson, among others. Producer/auteur Kip Hanrahan relied on Murray's impassioned sax to enhance the writings of Ishmael Reed on two volumes titled *Conjure* on his American Clavé label, and to offset the lusty vocals of Jack Bruce, Hanrahan's alter ego on *Desire Develops an Edge*.

Producer Bob Thiele, who promoted the later stages of John Coltrane's career on the '60s Impulse label, assigned Murray to record *Blues for Coltrane*, a tribute with McCoy Tyner, Cecil McBee, and Roy Haynes; an album of sweet standards credited to the Bob Thiele Collective, called *Sunrise, Sunset;* Tyner's *44th Street Suite* with altoist Arthur Blythe; and a project with Thiele's wife, singer Teresa Brewer.

"We did thirteen Tin Pan Alley songs, Teresa and me, with Grady Tate, Ron Carter, and Kenny Barron," Murray exulted. "Now *that* album's bad! It's gonna sell some. Teresa's popular with an older crowd and it shows me in a new light. You'll see!"

Murray works quickly. In six days in October '91, he recorded three complete albums at the Power Station for Disk Union, two of them anchored by pianist Hicks, bassist Ray Drummond, and drummer Idris Muhammad. On one, Murray played only bass clarinet, on the other, only tenor sax, and fellow tenorist Branford Marsalis joined him for two tunes. The third group of sessions had an entirely different cast: trumpeter Bobby Bradford, pianist Burrell, bassist Hopkins, and drummer Blackwell. Repertoire and mood were varied, without problem; these musicians speak a common language, whatever stories they choose to tell.

Murray's sessions are not, however, one-shots; they usually document notable occasions in long-lasting relations. Murray and Bradford, for instance, performed Bradford's suite "Have You Seen Sideman" as part of the 1992 JVC Jazz Festival in New York, honoring clarinetist John Carter. Carter, who died of cancer in 1991, was Bradford's partner, a major West Coast player and composer whose ultimate project encompassed five albums of linked compositions tracing the origin of black music in America and its development from a folk expression into an art form. Carter had his own style of sly licks, high whistles, and multiphonic squawks. He was one of Murray's first mentors, and they worked together in Clarinet Summit. Naturally, Bradford and Murray recorded the suite.

Murray composes for specific commissions more often than on impulse; he wrote seven new pieces before journeying to Denmark to accept his Jazzpar Award, which comprised, besides a handsome check, a recording session with Pierre Dorge's ten-piece New Jungle Orchestra. Subsequently he arranged Paul Gonsalves's famous twenty-seven choruses of Ellington's "Diminuendo and Crescendo in Blue" for forty-piece jazz ensemble. Murray said as a youth he learned only three jazz sax solos by heart, Gonsalves's among them. A winding staircase leading to great heights, its influence on Murray is obvious. Yet other, more modest music seems to inspire Murray to draw on his most personal reserves. The songs cut by his quartet on

Shakill's Warrior—including one piece by Butch Morris and four by Don Pullen—tapped some of his most heartfelt emotions.

"Every time I listen to that ballad of Pullen's"—"In the Spirit"—"I start tripping off my mother's funeral." Murray shuddered. "It almost doesn't matter *what* you play on an organ, slow as Don plays it. When he plays slow like that, it tears me up. When we recorded, I couldn't take it, I had to pick up the mood. I doubled the tempo in the second chorus of my solo—you can hear it." He took a deep breath and plunged on.

"See, my mother was an organist in church, and she was *serious*. I remember how she demanded that the church get a new organ. She'd drag me to her rehearsals each Wednesday night when I was ten, eleven years old. Sometimes she'd make me play my sax with her. She died of cancer when I was thirteen.

"Now, the organ's got a thing on it. If you play that sucker slow, it's going to mean *death*."

By unhappy coincidence, Don Pullen was diagnosed with his fatal illness the week he and Murray recorded a second volume, *Shakill's II*. Pullen died in April 1995, after recording *Sacred Common Ground* with jazz improvisers and Native American singers. Anyway, Murray meant death not as *finality*, but as the *ultimate*.

The Conductor's Vocabulary

Perhaps the combo format, specific personnel, particular intervallic relationships in the melodies, or the progressions of chords on *Shakill's Warrior* gave David Murray access to his ultimate level of expression and projection, the deepest dimension of experience he has reached and retrieved. But one of Murray's admirable qualities is that he doesn't rest on his laurels or depend on his art for comfort; rather, he rushes forth to embrace risk, challenge, and growth. That seems to be the basis of his collaboration with Lawrence Douglas "Butch" Morris. They met in California in 1971, as youngsters in drummer Charles Moffett's rehearsal band.

Morris was then playing cornet in the era's open-ended jazz idiom, though his sound had the coloristic sensitivities of a lyrical rather than technique-oriented brass virtuoso. He's heard pouring out lines of quirky melodic invention on obscure quartet recordings from '78: *Tricks of the Trade* (with tenorist Frank Lowe), *Let the Music Take You,* and *Last of the Hipmen*—the latter two with Murray. Morris wielded his cornet with Murray's quintet on *Interboogielogy*, with his octet alongside Olu Dara on *Ming* and *Home*, and with Bradford on *Murray's Steps* (all those on Black Saint).

Morris picks up his horn less frequently in the '90s, but when he does he's apt to spin the instrument backward and jam its mouthpiece into its bell, or turn it upside down to whistle across the holes at the bottom of the valves. He'll try anything his curiosity suggests. He's manufactured music boxes to showcase one of his jewel-like tunes; he enjoys the high-wire exposure of an a cappella cornet concert; he's played duets with J. A. Deane on electrically modified trombone and recorded atmospheric trios with keyboardist Wayne Horvitz (who uses advanced electronics) and drummer Bobby Previte.

However, since the early '80s, Butch Morris has liked best of all to enact a role he created for himself: improvising conductor. Audiences may now recognize him best from behind. His hair, thinning at the crown, rises in front to a dramatic peak; his thin shoulders tense; his left hand, and the baton in his right, lift to focus the attention of the musicians before him. He stands ready to make music from a few scribbled measures—or none at all—the quick wits of his players, and what appear to be charade gestures, the syllables of his language of conduction.

Long Road to a New Form

Morris didn't pull the concept of conduction fully formed out of the thin air; he's got a conventional jazz musician's background. He grew up in Watts amid music; his father, a career navy man, had swing and big-band records and liked to visit Johnny Otis's club in their neighborhood. His mother helped him at the piano. His older brother Wilber (now a bassist for David Murray and with his own quartet, Wilberforce), was originally a drummer who kept up with bop, '50s funk, and the new(er) thing. Butch's sister brought home Motown singles. At dinner together the family listened to a radio show that offered "bebop to boogie, rhythm 'n' blues and rock 'n' roll." Morris still links the '50s-'60s sound of Horace Silver, Lou Donaldson and Stanley Turrentine with greens, chitlins, and fatback. He followed the public school music curriculum, and benefited from dedicated teachers with high standards, including saxophonist Charles Lloyd, who taught a music appreciation class.

"Me and my father hit the daily double at the racetrack when I was about fourteen, and we bought me my first trumpet," Butch recalled with glee. He'd been practicing on a school-owned horn for two or three years already, inspired by back-porch player Walter Lowe. And though he'd heard Dizzy Gillespie and Clifford Brown, "I can't remember anybody that startled me more when I heard them on record than Don Cherry and Booker Little."

Morris made the school orchestra and after-class sessions; he wigged out on the Miles Davis-Gil Evans version of *Porgy and Bess,* and "before I got out of high school I'd taught myself flute, French horn, trombone, and baritone horn—I was still playing trumpet in the marching band orchestra, and studio band too—while at home I taught myself the mechanics of piano." Upon graduation he slid into a job at Grant's Music Studio in Los Angeles, copying big-band arrangements. He joined the army in August 1966 and was sent to Germany ("Now *there* was racism, concentrated to a degree that frightened everyone"); Vietnam, where he became a medic ("My mother sent me a flugelhorn one Christmas, and I used to practice in the ambulance"); Japan; and finally California's Fort Ord, where he decided to study physical therapy, prosthetics, and orthotics upon discharge.

Morris also got involved then with Horace Tapscott, whose influence in the black community of Watts parallels that of Muhal Richard Abrams on the South Side of Chicago. "It had crossed my mind when I was in the service that I was creating a personal way of improvising," Morris remembered, "and I had to find the environment in which I could improvise best. I wasn't a bebopper, I wasn't a postbopper, and I wasn't a free-bopper, so I had to create the environment. My development of it didn't start until later, but Horace in his band used to make little gestures that meant certain things for us to do that weren't on the page, and I started to think about how that could be expanded.

"In 1970, '71, I decided, 'This is it.' I started putting music down on paper, calling up cats, and saying, 'Come on, let's rehearse,' and they'd say, 'Oh, I can't, *groan*'—and I'd go physically *get* the cat because unless I did I was never going to hear how these ideas of mine sounded." As he became serious about music, he wearied of Los Angeles. "Sooner or later you come to grips with working and whether you have something to offer or not. You go where you can work and be recognized." Morris went north.

"When I was in college, studying conducting in Oakland, and I asked my teacher, 'How do you get the orchestra to go back to letter B?' and she said, 'You don't do that,' I knew I had a profession. But basically, I got the idea of conducting improvisation from Charles Moffett," the Fort Worth-born and -bred drummer best known for his association with Ornette Coleman.

"Moffett had a little club in Oakland where he used to conduct his rehearsals. A lot of people gathered together there: [trombonist] Ray Anderson, [saxophonist] Keshavan Maslak, [pianist] Curtis Clark, Moffett's young sons [bassist] Charnett and [drummer] Codaryl, David Murray. David was coming out of [saxophonists] Maceo Parker and Junior Walker—a strong r&b, blues, and church background—and not long after we met we realized we had some mutual feelings about music.

"Charles would lead his ensemble rehearsals with no music; he would just conduct, with a relatively undeveloped vocabulary of gestures. I knew it could be taken further. Now, Charles is an energetic cat, and what he did was musical, man. It was like: 'You, *play*. Now *you*, do what *he's* doing.' But he would never talk to us, it was all gestures. And I thought, 'Damn, this is some interesting music. This is great. I'm going to pursue this.'"

If Morris has a multifaceted musical imagination, Murray has straightforward determination and drive. When David traveled east to New York, Butch followed as his roommate. Morris enjoyed a taste of Europe when he took the opportunity to teach jazz and improvisation at the Conservatory Royal of Liège, Belgium; then he returned to New York and began a new life. His emergence as a jazz conductor dates to the debut of David Murray's Big Band, which the late Public Theater producer Joseph Papp encouraged him to form in '78.

Initially helping Murray compose and orchestrate for that concert, Morris soon stepped in front of the Big Band to "create music on the spot" with a gestural vocabulary he used to satisfy a desire for instant decision-making that few jazz arrangers (Gil Evans and Sun Ra *do* come to mind) have ever been able to indulge. Yet Morris applies a composer's sense of structure, a listener's perspective, and a jazz player's spontaneity to the musical impulses of whomever he confronts. He has become a man in the middle, between "jazz" and "new music," as he's developed an alternative to conventions of large group performance, improvisation, and composition that challenge the nature of those games.

Morris brought a jazz-inflected band into the Village Vanguard in the 1990s; he enjoyed week-long residencies with improvisers at

birds of a feather

the Whitney Museum of Modern Art at Philip Morris world head-quarters (on Forty-second Street, across from Grand Central Station), in Philadelphia and in Richmond, Virginia, and even longer residencies in Europe, Turkey, and Japan. His music responds to and generates interpretive movement: He's accompanied Alvin Ailey's American Dance Center, Diane McIntyre's "Take Off from a Forced Landing," and New York-based choreographers Cheryl Banks, Beppie Blankart, Yoshiko Chuma, Pooh Kaye, and Sally Silvers.

He has a flare for the dramatic too, having scored *Spell #7* by playwright Ntozake Shange; *Ghetto Follies,* a folk opera written by David Henderson, and pieces with writer Jessica Hagedorn. The just-over-a-minute-long "Crayon Bondage" on the anthology *State of the Union* is one of these. Hagedorn whispers, "I want to come...find you/Confine you/Confound you/I'd rather con-found/Than confine you/If I could just/Find you." Morris helped write the text; his cornet smears one well-placed tone at a time over motivic repetition of vibes, strings, and darker brass.

In the mid-'80s, Morris led his ensemble at large-scale perfor-mance events such as *Goya,* during which costumed actors enacted dramatic scenes, dancers leapt, and painters splashed oils on canvas inspired by "The Naked Maja" while crowds milled about the cav-ernous Cuando auditorium at the foot of New York's Second Avenue. Around that time, he also called the downbeat for alto sax-ist Jemeel Moodoc's Jus' Grew Orchestra, pianist Michelle Rosewoman's New Yoruba, and violinist Billy Bang's larger groups. "I see all my activities working together, but it takes a while," said Morris, who sports a wispy goatee. "First of all, change, diversity, and variety are central to my nature; and, second, I use them for my livelihood.

"I compose whatever my little heart desires," Butch claimed. "But I'm not meandering. I've got a goal: My whole idea is to cre-ate music for improvisers. I like to bring together people who might not necessarily play with each other, or who play in different styles and improvise in completely different ways. I rarely write, that is, *notate,* everything. I get tired of playing the same arrangements, so I constantly rearrange tunes to figure out their other harmonic and tonal possibilities. I'd hate to work with a band for three years and always play the same charts. I mean, even [Duke Ellington's theme song] 'Take the A Train' varied over the years.

"Most of my work has involved larger ensembles because that's where my heart is. I work a little differently with my own ensembles than I do with David's, because I'm more pulse- than tempo-oriented."

Morris's efforts hovering between unstated pulse and firm time signature are audibly evident on "Duet for Big Band" from the Murray album *Live at Sweet Basil Vol. 1* (on Black Saint). The sixteen-minute-plus track starts with tubaist Bob Stewart puffing four to the bar, and Billy Higgins tapping the rim of his snare drum in time. See Morris's right arm crooked over his head, his hand slightly clasped so his forefinger protrudes, flicking a pulse that slows the momentum? Fred Hopkins's bass slips from under the tuba; Butch points to the bassist with his left forefinger, alternates between Stewart and Hopkins, shifting their turns as though trying to catch one or the other off guard. He's also brought them back up to tempo and introduced a syncopation.

Next he opens his right palm, spreading his fingers for everyone to notice, and makes a cupping "gimme" motion. Almost at once, the eleven men launch their parts in a swelling, improvised arrangement of prenotated phrases that reflect each other, curl in on themselves, shore up, then slip away from sectional accents to etch a fully detailed, unpredictably constructed, but swinging and sturdy jazz edifice.

"There's a history for improvisers, a body of common knowledge among jazz musicians," Morris stated. "There's a whole repertoire of songs that have been used as a basis for improvisation, like the blues. We can just call a key, and it doesn't have to have a name—we can make music, right? Well, if I point to you, and you're an improviser, and as part of my vocabulary you understand that when I point to you, you're supposed to improvise—that's a beginning. You play until I ask you to stop. And if I hear something that you play that I want you to repeat or develop, I have a gesture I'll give you for that. If I want you to continue on that same frame on a longer curve, I have a gesture for that. If I want someone to do or emulate something that you're doing, I have a gesture for *that*. It continues to grow, my vocabulary for improvisers.

"I deal in terms of phrases because I think it's the phrase that decides what the overall music is going to be," he said. "First, it's the tone or sound, and then it's the phrase. I rarely tell soloists anything—that's their space—but in David's band, when somebody stands up to solo, the other players can't just put their horns on the floor and start dreaming, because I might call for them to do something at any time.

"If a soloist makes a phrase, especially if he does it twice, I might tell particular people"— Morris demonstrated his hand language— "'that phrase...I want...*now!*' Say two people are playing that phrase; I'll have them repeat it and build from that until what I've got is the trumpet and alto playing that phrase, and between their repetitions I've got the trombone and tuba playing something, and the tenor sax and French horn playing something a little beyond that. Then I start to juggle form. A lot of times I get very whimsical. I may tap out a rhythm and the player has to start in the middle of a chorus, playing that rhythm over the changes, while someone else has started at the top. And all of a sudden they collide.

"I have to figure out how to get the best from improvisers, put them in that light, then start to push them in another direction and see how flexible they are. A lot of improvisers are *not* flexible. They know how to improvise in a particular style, but they don't venture too far from that style."

Having taught this vocabulary to Murray's clique of jazz improvisers (some of whom have become aspiring composers themselves), after the Big Band's concert at the New York Kool Jazz festival of '85 Morris determined to concentrate on less tune- and solo-oriented, more suitelike and ensemble applications of his gestural direction, involving instrumental combinations of his own design. On February 1, 1985, at the Kitchen Center for Music, Video, and Dance, Morris created what he considers a historically important "full conduction, which is an improvised duet between ensemble and conductor based on subject matter, in which the conductor works out his gestures and relays them to the ensemble, and the ensemble in turn interprets the gestural information.

"*Current Trends in Racism in Modern America, a Work in Progress* was my first attempt to have a full conduction in the United States," Morris said with pride regarding the totally improvised piece for stylistically contrasting personnel including tenorist Frank Lowe, reeds player John Zorn, turntables manipulator Christian Marclay, percussionist Thurman Barker, pianist Curtis Clark, guitarist Brandon Ross, harpist Zeena Parkins, cellist Tom Cora, vibist Eli Fountain, and vocalist Yasanow Tone. *Current Trends* was released by the tiny independent European label Sound Aspects as the first issue of Morris's "semi-exclusive" contract; his next significant ensemble recording, *Dust to Dust,* was issued in 1992 on not-for-profit New World Records.

"The title of *Current Trends,*" Butch explained, "was a point of reference, subject matter for everyone to think about—not only the audience, but the musicians involved. And it was something that burned a hole in everyone's mind—especially the musicians', because when I called to ask them if they'd be a part of it, they all began to wonder what it was about.

"It was only important to me that they *wonder*. There was enough in the news at that time to let us ask that if some things [vis-à-vis racism] have changed, what have they changed to? I thought it very appropriate to have a conduction with that particular title because there are, in America and in the world, different trends of racism. And I use improvisation to comment on how I feel, how people feel around me, what I see, what people see around me, what I think."

Then he added, "For me, improvisation and composition are almost the same thing; I don't see them being separate. I don't know where my improvisation starts and my composition begins—they're one and the same."

Current Trends is not a easily listened to work, but then, its ostensible subject matter is the most difficult of our time. Opening with Zorn's squeal, turning thick and thin with ringing vibes overlaid by the strings of the harp and guitar, underpinned by Tone's groans, complicated by Lowe's growls and Barker's cymbal crashes, the piece corresponds to the unruliness of people at cross-purposes. There are both harmonious relations and bitter clashes. No duets or trios stand forth from the totality of the ensemble for long, just as every interracial exchange since slavery came to the United States has had a political, public context beyond any personal, private significance.

Other than the sudden eruption of a beat-box rap, there is no programmatic material—no quotes of "We Shall Overcome" or the unofficial but widely honored black national anthem, "Lift Every Voice." Nonetheless, *Current Trends* holds together as a concerto of compassionate if dissonant, flowing and simultaneously discrete encounters; it builds to a climax that's dramatically coherent, though apparently unresolved. It's a work like no other Butch Morris has yet created. Of course, repetition is not what he's about.

Indeed, "Technology will take care of history" is one of Morris's axioms. "For me the necessity to conduct spontaneous improvisation comes out of the need to hear a sound and see a particular form or structure happen in the *moment*. That's exciting to me. I think it's exciting to the musician-improvisers, and I think it's exciting to the audience. It's a once-in-a-lifetime opportunity, although I *do* think technology will take care of its posterity. I mean, a given improvisation is not something I feel has to be done again, but if it *has* to be done again, technology will take care of that."

Man of Many Guises

"I have never wanted to do one thing all my life," Morris said. "That is, the things I do with my own music, I've longed to do for many years, but I don't think of the range of what I create as much different than changing shoes. You know, you go out and buy five or six or ten pairs of shoes, and one day you wear this pair, the next day a different pair. But they all look like you. They all fit. They're all part of your personality. Hats, sweaters, pants, the same way. I don't look at music any differently. When I get into something else, I'm just changing a pair of shoes. And I love shoes."

If you look at Morris as a clothes horse, then know he's got a complete wardrobe, or a closet full of costumes from which he selects the proper disguise.

"If you see me as a cornetist-improviser, as a conductor, if you hear my music played by someone else, or view me as a composer for theater or dance, you're seeing pieces of a puzzle that are only part of a composite," he warned. The compound-complex Butch Morris doesn't want to be pinned down. Diversity even to the point of darting evasion is central to his charm. Note the title of the album he cut in 1982, his first under his own name: *In Touch...but Out of Reach.*

Though in the mid-'90s Morris performed at the Knitting Factory, at cellist Diedre Murray's Firewall Festival held at the performance space P.S. 122, or at the Nuyorican Poets Café, he spent less time at home in Manhattan's East Village as he found more work abroad, forging a network of individuals into fluid ensembles with orchestral instrumental resources and impact. He appeared at far-flung new music and multimedia conventions such as Istanbul's progressive Akbank jazz fest (Morris enfolded four of *ney* player Sulieman Erguner's traditional dervish musicians into a brilliant comprovisation); on tour in Japan he persuaded ritualized Taiko drummers to join him. In the United States, he conducted a gaggle of poets, and contributed music to Washington, D.C.'s, Folger Shakespeare Company's production of *Othello;* to *Hawk,* an urban crime TV drama starring his friend Avery Brooks; and to the soundtrack for Robert Altman's film *Kansas City.*

Perhaps flitting from project to project is a psychological necessity, not just an economic reality, for an improviser like Butch Morris; the plethora of projects keeps him fresh, and it's like nectar is to bees—a good excuse to buzz around. He'd welcome more financial security, as would anyone with child-rearing responsibilities (he has a son) and champagne tastes.

Yet Morris seems to thrive on uncertainty. Not knowing exactly what will happen next keeps up his interest. Uncertainty is a tool he holds over his improvisers, too. As some people respond heroically to danger, Morris's ability to establish then resolve chaos, and lead others through it, impresses both those who hire him and those with their eyes on his baton. All their ears are open to his swirling sounds.

He has some fixed principles. "We have to contend with who Beethoven was, with who Mozart was, with Duke Ellington," he said firmly, "with whomever you respect. If we're not reaching for their ground, what are we doing? A 1922 Louis Armstrong solo is going to last just as long as the best pop group there is today, and if I can't reach for something that powerful, I become useless.

"I want to use music in such a way that even if people are listening intently, there can be something going on that they're not aware of until it surfaces, and then they can remember that it was happening when they weren't hearing it. You know what I mean? I want the audience to get it, but I don't want it to just happen. Because all the musicality is over if it's simply given to you.

"Through my gestural vocabulary the improvisers and audience start to hear the music happen. You don't just hear the music happen, you *start* to hear it happen, and then all of a sudden, it *happens*.

"There's a great validity in having things well thought out," Morris conceded, "but there's an excitement about the other side too. I want to create something as powerful as my heritage and something very magical at the same time. If I'm not reaching for something as powerful as my heritage has been—" Butch lists Ellington, Fletcher Henderson, Count Basie, and Jelly Roll Morton among his predecessors as improvising, composing, conducting instrumentalists—"then it's not going to be meaningful in the long run. I want to create something as powerful as my heritage and something very magical at the same time.

"But I'm in no hurry. If I'm fifty or fifty-five before I get the opportunity to have a six-month residency with really good musicians—this would be my ideal situation—well, I'll only come out frustrated because by that time I should have too much work for any one group to deal with." Butch's eyes sparkled and he flashed a grin, as though he's not too worried about it. In 1993 Morris had assembled recordings of sixteen full-scale performances from San Francisco, Germany, Montreal, Bologna, Antwerp, Istanbul, and Florida State University, among other sites. In 1996 they were issued as *Testaments,* a ten-CD set with the conductor's extensive written commentary, handsomely packaged by New World/Crosscurrents. By the end of the '90s he'd established standing ensembles for his conductions in Belgium, Berlin, Istanbul, Tokyo, and Great Britain.

The Circus of Applicable Truths

"You can't really talk about one thing without talking about everything. Then you know you're talking a real truth," said Henry Threadgill, friend and neighbor of Butch Morris, multi-reeds player (featured in a rare sideman role on a David Murray octet date), composer, improviser, band leader, AACM associate—a man who, wherever he goes, projects a swift, incisive sense of being.

"I hate to talk just about music. Because if you're really talking about something, it applies in every category, across every line. Then you're talking about *something:* a real idea, a real generator. Like gold, silver, a mineral, the water, the air. You know you're talking about something, rather than about things, impressions, people, and that whole area. Ideas. Real ideas. There are concrete truths at the bottom, you know."

> A very ordinary man works a ho-hum job and leads a humdrum life. He lives alone and enjoys no satisfying relationships at work or in his personal life.
> —from Ilyse Kazar's synopsis of When Life Is Cheap and Death Is Taken for Granite, an Imaginary Film, libretto by Henry Threadgill

Threadgill walks about in the East Village as he did in Chicago, where he was raised, and no doubt does in Goa, India, where he lived with his wife for part of the year at the end of the '90s: limber and loose of stride, in bright, self-styled clothes, alert, sometimes impatient, ready with his greeting, mind flush with music. In the fall of '93 he was about to release an album of compositions played by cherry-picked instrumentalists from New York's elite nongenre talent pool, a complete contrast to his earlier album of the year by Very

Very Circus, in which he stands at the point of two electric guitars, two tubas, and rock-solid drums. That release, *Too Much Sugar for a Dime* (Axiom), featured his longtime colleague violinist Leroy Jenkins, a pair of male Venezuelan singers, Middle Eastern oud player Simon Shaheen, and others as guests. It followed by six months a live Very Very Circus album documenting a nationwide tour of out-of-the-way venues—from schools to prisons to truck stops to coffeehouses—that Threadgill booked and financed himself, helped by the Lila Wallace Reader's Digest Fund.

"That's my *will*," Threadgill said, frankly. He moves so fast that he's sometimes invisible—which is to say, the press doesn't know how to regard or cover such activity. The out-front qualities of his music seem to render it too provocative—or perhaps Henry can be too particular, cause too much trouble—for the regular jazz club circuit, though it's a sound he's purveyed for twenty years, based in gospel, the blues, parade marches, serious study of how they all come together as well as what's beyond. Threadgill makes a fair living; he scrapes by. "All musicians live a creative life," he said. "Artists, period. I don't know how *anybody* survives. It calls for a lot of imagination." He's got that, and the will with which to override limits and concepts the nameless world would impose.

"I became a musician because I loved music as a kid," he explained. "Music is my game. I didn't grow up with any boundaries on music. I grew up in a ghetto in Chicago, and there was music everywhere. My grandmother took me to churches where there was music, record shops had speakers outside so you walked down the street hearing music, bands played—and still play—at the Maxwell Street flea market. Even at grammar school, teachers played records during rest periods, good music we would cool out and sleep to.

"There was never any talk of *this* kind of music or *that* kind of music. I grew up with hillbilly music on the radio, Polish music on the radio, Tchaikovsky, gospel. Radio was exciting; there was Serbian music, Mexican music, stories. We listened to all of it. And I heard music live. I would hear polka bands, then turn around to [bluesman] Muddy Waters or [gospel singer/guitarist] Rosetta Tharp, then go hear a choir from Rumania. We listened to it all, and we heard it in the community.

"As a kid, I wanted to learn how to play all this great music, the way these great people had been doing it. It wasn't in my head to have a Mercedes or fifty thousand dollars a year; I wasn't sophisticated enough to be thinking like that. To grapple with the music was enough. And I haven't really lost that initial thing I came to music with, that interest I have. I don't need anybody to support me in that idea anymore. I can go to the grave with my ideas. I can go on through."

> The man forms a belief in the existence, somewhere, of sincere human exchange. So he sets out to confirm this faith in the potential for love and understanding. Every subsequent encounter ends in his being abused, his idealism scorned. Every person and institution he deals with disappoints his faith in humanity.
> —from *When Life Is Cheap*. . .

"I learned through trial and error," Threadgill continued. "And some help from some good friends, and years and years in musical institutions. But I didn't get too much out of institutions, I must admit. I'm very grateful to have been able to be there, but I got more outside of them. I went to all the music schools—universities, colleges, conservatories—all around this country, on the university level for eleven years, partly on the GI bill, partly on my own. I was constantly studying at these places, taking every course in music they had to offer. That was my approach; I was never interested in a degree, I was interested in the *catalogue*. That never made any sense to me—do this for four years, and you have a degree—because I said, 'No doctor would ever operate on me after only four years of study; how can you be a musician in four years?'

"Here's something I want to say: It's been put out in some quarters that so-called jazz musicians don't have classical backgrounds. Now, this must be about musicians who are younger than I am, because it's impossible not to have a classical background if you're my age. There was no such thing as a jazz program or any jazz schools then. I played Prokofiev, Poulenc, and Hindemith sonatas when I was a flute major; when I was a piano major I played Beethoven sonatas, so I don't know what this crap is about only a couple people out there being special, classically trained musicians. It's a lie and a fallacy. Outside school I was in blues bands, but people wouldn't let me sit up with orchestras if I didn't know how to play Mozart and the *Brandenburg Concertos*. They weren't into any tokenism, they wouldn't be passing me on no color basis. I had to *deal*.

"I started out as a kid with piano, and when I got really interested in playing I went to saxophone, then clarinet—that was still a very accepted thing to learn then. I was lucky enough to have a teacher who got me into a big band, a reading band, and taught me what the second tenor part was. Just like in a choir: How does the alto support the soprano? What role are you playing besides just singing your part? In these schools now, everybody knows so much, but only something specific. They don't make mistakes, and that's bad.

"That's right: No mistakes is bad. I'd hate to have learned how to walk without falling; I'd probably not know *how* to fall, and if I fell, I'd kill myself. You never learn how to jump out of an airplane if you never fall.

"My first professional experience was traveling with gospel music, church musicians, and evangelists. I was into that for a couple of years, then I came back to the secular community. That's when I started playing with blues bands. That was the first place I could play, and I had to learn to play with them. They taught me. That's some highly sophisticated music—both the emotional basis and the technical basis too, because the execution of every note is a highly sophisticated event.

"Howlin' Wolf was my greatest hero, my favorite. I didn't know him personally, but I loved those people. I used to play in blues sessions on Sunday—jazz sessions on Monday—at the Blue Flame, and everybody would come to the bandstand to play. Most of the AACM cats had that kind of background: Leo Smith came up to Chicago playing with Little Milton [Campbell], Lester Bowie, John Stubblefield, they know all about this. If you came up in the Midwest, you had rhythm 'n' blues background. That was the heart of most of your work, and you played at it for long hours.

"But one reason I stayed in that so long was that the traditional [jazz] guys didn't want me to play with them, didn't like the way I played, because I wasn't playing bebop the way they were. They said I didn't know what I was doing, and those cats would leave you on the bandstand playing by yourself. When that happened it would make me question my understanding of that music. I wouldn't take the rejection for granted, it had to be looked at. Why? I asked. It certainly wasn't about the feeling of what I was playing. What would generally be the case was they manipulated the licks, and I never wanted to do that. I wanted to *say* something.

"When I was a kid we used to listen to Sonny Rollins; he did-

birds of a feather

n't sound like he was playing somebody else's licks. Gene Ammons was one of my biggest heroes; I didn't hear Gene Ammons playing no Johnny Hodges licks, or Sonny Rollins licks, or Charlie Parker licks—his stuff was coming out of Gene Ammons. On the street the guys would be playing those licks, and they were good at it; the reason I wasn't was that I wasn't practicing them.

"I was trying to get through the material, the structures, and the forms and the harmonies. To me, it seemed like *they* were all manipulating the same thing, but *I* was fishing. At least I knew *where* I was fishing; I had a clear understanding of form. I'd say to myself, 'If I keep my main pulse on these forms, I'll know what to do at the next juncture. Between here and there I might have problems, but I'll know what to do when I get there.'

"I had my first association with the AACM in Muhal Richard Abrams' Experimental Band in 1962 or '63. I was still playing in the blues places and working with marching bands, with VFW post bands. I used to make a living playing parades in Chicago in the summertime. I could play two parades a week and pay my rent and everything else. The jobs would come out of the union, and somebody might give me a big job, like a circus gig for the night. But with the AACM, I was into the circuit I really wanted to be in. I didn't so much want to get out of the blues—the blues was good, is *still* good—but I knew where I wanted to go.

"In the AACM what was happening was an expression of what I was about, and of the moment. I knew that it expressed the times, it was all intricately tied up with everything I saw about me: the revolution in America, God is dead, America shooting down its kids, the war, the questioning of traditional philosophies, Coltrane going on to an emotional base of music. I knew where I was supposed to be. I was tied into that moment. I didn't reject that moment. I didn't look back. Look back to what? There was nothing for me to look back to. My life was going on. I'm young."

And so in the late 1960s, Henry Threadgill became who he's becoming now, who he's been all along: himself. "I don't try to play what Charlie Parker and them played; they lived through that social period, and I didn't. I learned how to play a lot of what I'm playing by studying that music as I was coming up, but I didn't have the emotional background, I didn't understand the significance of that life to try and express what Charlie Parker and his peers were expressing. They all came out of that same context, expressing that time. It's ridiculous for me to try to play that time. Yes, I played the music of Scott Joplin, you know [on *Air Lore* (RCA/Bluebird), with bassist Fred Hopkins and drummer Steve McCall as the trio Air], but I had to transpose it to this moment, still.

"I've always been a composer. Basically, about 90 percent of the music for Air—I wrote it. And that music is *written*—down to the drum parts. There's nothing vague about it. What I was doing with Air was a scaled-down version of what I'm doing now. It had to be done with smaller instrumentation, so it was a harder job, more complicated, than writing for seven musicians. I'd have to allude to things. Because we had only two hands apiece, and the instruments give up only so many tones at once, I had to devise ways to imply another tone quickly, and shift, and be back in place. Here [with larger ensembles], I just stick that tone on another instrument. Before, I had to make the implication; now, I can state the fact.

"One thing I've been working toward is a larger orchestral sound that gets away from the traditional big-band sound. I had a very large palette in the Sextett [his seven-piece band: trumpet, trombone, Threadgill's reeds, cello, bass, two traps drummers]. Just with the drums alone, I had twelve pitches; two floor toms, upper toms, snare drum, floor bass drum, and concert bass drum. I had two percussionists, that's six tones apiece just on the drums, so that's part of my entire palette. A number of people have asked me if there's been overdubbing on my Sextett records, but I'm still trying to accomplish the same thing through other means. I have on my agenda to study electronics, but I haven't finished with acoustics yet.

"Writing is a special thing to me; I haven't been able to write enough because the vehicles aren't out there. People say, 'Oh, it would be nice if you wrote something for orchestra.' Well, that's okay, except I don't write music to sit on the shelf; if I can't hear it, there's nothing for me to learn. If I just wrote stuff I completely understand, there would be no reason for me to be writing; I could just be *manufacturing* music, since I'd know what it's all going to sound like.

"But writing is a daredevil experience, you always have to go further; that's what every great writer did. There's not a great writer who ever existed who didn't keep taking chances. Beethoven took those chances. Duke Ellington. Alban Berg. That's why they remain great composers, and that's how they kept opening up new harmonies, new forms, new concepts. Because if they kept voicing things only the way they *were* voiced, not stretching out the binary and ternary forms, we wouldn't even be talking about them today.

"I compose through the laws of nature," Threadgill claimed. "There are ways to compose that have to do with the way that life exists biologically and metaphysically. There are laws that are operating like the laws that make the sun come out, that bring the rain. I observe the laws of acoustics, for instance, and I submit it all to my heart and my head. I don't just subscribe to a methodology. I think my approach is in line with that of people I've been fond of and studied with, like Muhal—and that's not coincidence, that's the actual fact of the transference of information.

"Of course, there are things that are notated and some things that aren't. This music we're playing comes from an improvisational base, but so does classical music: All the great composers were improvisers who could play, who could sit down and make up music on the spot. *Collective* improvisation, though—that's what the AACM was about, and we're still with that. But that's not all. Evolution has gone on.

"One thing that happened when the music changed from the last period to the present is the shared repertoire disappeared, and a new collective repertoire did not take its place. The community of musicians in New York, they don't know my compositions. Even if they might have heard something on record, liked it or disliked, most of them don't know how to play it. You have to understand the makeup of the piece and what the improvisation involves if you're going to play '80 Degrees Below' [one of his compositions]—*or* a Haydn piece, or 'Donna Lee.'

"And I don't just work in the traditional improvisational methods that occur in traditional jazz. There are no limits to improvisation. If you're going to put a limitation on improvisation, you might as well forget about it. Charlie Parker would never have gotten to where he did if he'd accepted a premise or limits, nor Coltrane. What Ornette did was beautiful, too, opening up the whole arena again—though a lot of people, even some musicians, haven't caught up with that yet."

They will, he firmly believes. " 'Blood' Ulmer told me something Ornette used to tell *him*. He said, 'Jazz is the teacher, and blues is the preacher.' I added, 'But time is the *reaper.*' You can't stop it. There is a destiny that is in the genes and molecular structure of things, that *has* to happen."

Can one commit oneself to destiny? Threadgill thinks so.

"I'm really excited right now"—as if he ever weren't—"because I find I'm stretching again. I feel like if I work, I'm going to be able to peel off another layer of skin. It's extreme, but my life has been extreme, and I love it. Ever since I was a kid, I've been interested in change, the extremism of it.

"Change is good. It can hurt, but it's still good because it's evolution. My greatest fear is the fear of not being able to go along with change, of becoming stylistic and set. There are a lot of people who don't believe in evolution, who would like to see things remain the same. And those are the people who don't want to see our music become accessible and strong and turned over, the way pop music is turned over. Because this music makes people *think*."

> Unfailing, he persists in his mission, convinced that an island of goodness lies somewhere amid the corruption. In a final conflict his unyielding belief meets up with some hard-core human malevolence. The world does not conform to his interior reality. He vaporizes out of the world as we know it, but continues eternally in his mind's quest after its own truth.
> —from *When Life Is Cheap* . . .

5 Guitars and Goals Beyond

There's been little positive comment *or* critical outcry about the ever-greater influence of guitars in late-century jazz, maybe because in its battle since the mid-'60s to survive against better-selling divisions of pop music, jazz has sent its guitarists forth as slightly disreputable knights-errant. "Go ahead—get the gold, platinum, double-platinum album," jazz has said to its only instrumentalists who've seemed capable of performing that job.

They may stand somewhat outside jazz's inner circle, they may have closer links with truly popular music than jazz elitists care to allow, but guitarists' choice of instrument immediately helps in this quest. The ax is the most commonly owned musical instrument in the United States and an enduring symbol of (especially) raw youth's infatuated self-expression.

For decades the electric guitar has been regarded as a novelty in jazz dominated by trumpeters, sax players, pianists, and drummers. Jazz musicians characteristically associated the guitar with folk forms rather than art bands, though from the 1920s through the '60s guitarists including Lonnie Johnson, Eddie Lang, Django Reinhardt, Charlie Christian, Oscar Moore, Herb Ellis, Barney Kessel, and Wes Montgomery gained attention. In the past three decades the electric guitar, with diverse special effects and attachments, has been barely tolerated among players upholding so-called straight-ahead "acoustic" traditions. Some have come to realize that while it *is* capable of deafening volume, that volume can be controlled, the better to reach an audience. Electric guitars are, after all, also able to convey the softest subtleties—depending on the sensitivity of their players' touch.

The guitar can be both a cutting solo voice and useful, *provocative* accompaniment. Its dual nature has been recognized since Danny Barker joined Jelly Roll Morton, well before Freddy Green anchored Count Basie's rhythm section. If, disregarding its past, rock 'n' roll relentlessly promoted the guitar as representing sexually vital musical energy—well, jazz listeners can't be blamed for expecting, seeking, *demanding* that guitar music dazzle, soar, and sting.

As the guitar itself is a force jazz must confront, its commercial appeal has a double edge of challenges and traps. Masterful guitarists have differed so much in their approaches that they've revised defining characteristics of jazz.

The Yorkshire Avatar

In 1969, a twenty-seven-year-old British guitarist emerged from the enervated, psychedelia-eclipsed European jazz, blues, and folk scene to meet three American soulmen, all associates of Jimi Hendrix, at the rocky frontier of instrumental music. The guitarist John McLaughlin's *Devotion* (originally on Douglas), reissued in the mid-'80s sans cover art portraying the bearded, fur-clad Yorkshireman as he might look in a funhouse mirror, or to himself after eating opium, opens with organist Larry Young's Leslie-swept chords, drummer Buddy Miles's splashing cymbals, and a lazy guitar figure hovering over an inexplicable mix of bird trills and tambourine. A thudding drum break, then electric bassist Billy Cox strides four notes forward, three notes back, and McLaughlin rises like a hawk from the marsh, worrying one string swift as wings against air, aiming for an envisioned peak, pulling the giddy listener along behind.

So much has happened since then…yet *Devotion* remains a milestone of future jazz as a liberated flight by a then-little-known virtuoso who sustained, without vocals, more than sixteen bars of vocabulary at considerable remove from conventionally swinging or boppishly altered blues-based jazz. His early music cut a groove more wicked than hot or cool; it often gained momentum from dynamic odd meters rushing toward urgent resolve. Sure McLaughlin knew how to play the blues, if rather more self-consciously than a native bluesman. His melodies seemed to transform some Teutonic, virtually Wagnerian—or Norse? Celtic? Hindi?—

motives by exhibiting the ferocity of the attack of, say, Chicago bluesman Elmore "Dust My Broom" James. But his harmonic forays, his plunge outward after distantly linked notes, were daring if certainly preplanned, very well informed, polished, confidently accomplished; his phrasing was taut, determined, and rhapsodic, his solos impassioned yet not necessarily emotional, as they launched from rapt concentration into almost physically gratifying explosions.

The dramatic fervor of McLaughlin's saber-slash guitar was in contrast to his stage demeanor. He projected utter humility and integrity. Amid late-'60s decadence, extremism, quasi-sensuality, and political harangues, McLaughlin appeared in holy white with shorn hair, honest body language, and no verbal rhetoric, wielding a cranked-up, double-necked electric Les Paul solid body or a lovingly crafted acoustic instrument (as on *Devotion*'s follow-up *My Goal's Beyond,* which balanced solo renditions of some piquant standards with a long modal group piece dedicated to guru Sri Chinmoy).

The guitar is McLaughlin's lifelong implement of devotion; a beautiful, round-bottomed acoustic Ovation lay in its open case on the bed of his hotel room one day in New York City while he was on a Warner Bros.-sponsored tour behind his 1984 album *Mahavishnu.* "I feel nervous without a guitar," he explained. The man is articulate, handsome, and stylish, in well-cut casual clothes, with a strong, direct handshake and gaze, and full gray hair. "It's part of my body. I've felt that way since I first picked up a guitar when I was eleven years old. That same day I was taking the guitar to bed with me, so that gives you an idea what I feel about it."

His dedication fairly quickly bore fruit: McLaughlin was a powerful instrumental force within months of being brought to the United States by drummer Tony Williams to form the trio Lifetime with organist Larry Young. Jazz star Miles Davis immediately spotted his next protégé. Post-'60s jazz fusion issues in the wake of the Davis-McLaughlin collaboration.

"Miles became kind of my father," McLaughlin said, "especially after he asked me to play on *In a Silent Way* such a short time after I'd arrived in America. I used to see him a lot. I'd go over to his house all the time, every day, with my guitar, and we'd talk about the music. He'd ask me, 'What about this? What do you hear here? I've got a couple of chords like this; what would you do with them?'"

McLaughlin became Miles's foil—his musical answer and reactor, confidant and contrast—as had saxophonists John Coltrane, Cannonball Adderley, and Wayne Shorter, pianists Red Garland, Bill

Evans, and Herbie Hancock before him. For the rest of Davis's life, up to and including his last public performance in Paris reuniting with band members of his past just before his death in 1991, Miles called on McLaughlin for counterpoint and solo extensions on spacey, atmospheric tracks (hear *Big Fun*), flat-out rave-ups *(Jack Johnson)*, frankly goofy outings *(You're Under Arrest)*, one-of-a-kind programmatic works *(Aura)*.

From May 1967 on, Davis tried to create an electronically enhanced and/or modified, emphatically rhythmic, broadly accepted yet often otherworldly musical concept that broke with features of jazz instituted by swing bands and bebop combos. Davis was frequently quoted and blamed for seeking the mass audience that found "social music"—repetitive, predictable, emphatically rhythmic funk, for instance—functional and appealing.

Davis toyed with guitars in his groups prior to McLaughlin, briefly employing George Benson, Joe Beck, Bucky Pizzarelli, and Sonny Sharrock, but it was around McLaughlin—before Sri Chinmoy dubbed him Mahavishnu for the Hindu god of sustenance—that Davis's ideas cohered. Their recordings, like those earlier of Davis with John Coltrane, have been studied, absorbed, popularized, and disseminated by a successive generation of musicians. Davis was commander-in-chief of jazz-rock-fusion, directing his forces by dint of charisma and nuance through sprawling studio sessions that were subsequently edited by producer Teo Macero; the Mahavishnu Orchestra (recorded by Columbia) was McLaughlin's elite shock troupe capturing young ears not with the conventions of black jazz but with the rambunctious angularities and distortions of progressive *rock* guitarists—Hendrix, George Harrison, Eric Clapton, Jerry Garcia, Carlos Santana, and Frank Zappa among them.

Like those players, and his Brit rock contemporaries Jeff Beck, Jimmy Page, and Dave Mason, McLaughlin could be loud to excess. But he sustained core jazz values, pledging allegiance to its heritage (he cited bluesman Skip James and '50s guitarist Tal Farlow as early favorites); to technical virtuosity at the service of musical substance; to imaginative exploration of compositions through improvisation; to a general openness toward ideas and dedication to the spirit of search that Coltrane had mandated for postbop musicians.

"Coltrane had a tremendous influence on me," McLaughlin volunteered. "He's a man I revere, a mine of inspiration and encouragement. I continue to draw from him; my debt is profound because he was a great example of manhood. There are not many; Sonny Rollins is another. They are among the reasons I got involved in spiritual life."

The earthly reward for McLaughlin's music was adoration by hoards who might otherwise remain ignorant of jazz. The first Mahavishnu Orchestra—with violinist Jerry Goodman, keyboardist Jan Hammer (later composer of soundtracks for TV's *Miami Vice*), drummer Billy Cobham, and electric bassist Rick Laird—progressed from playing college coffeehouses to large theaters to enormous stadium shows, and quickly issued three albums that secured their listening audience. Live, the ensemble seemed to concentrate on the serious work of musically inducing transcendent consciousness. Then the band seemed to burn out, as wildly enthusiastic if less than discerning audiences demanded ever more epiphanies for encores.

McLaughlin's music shifted toward Western classicism when violinist Jean-Luc Ponty joined his Orchestra; the MO's settings, already heavy with guitar sustain and keyboards, became yet bigger when arranged to include a community of their friends (on *Visions of the Emerald Beyond*) and the London Symphony Orchestra conducted by Michael Tilson Thomas (on *Apocalypse*).

Then McLaughlin turned away from popularity, and survived. He convened a lively, delicate acoustic quintet called Shakti to play adaptations and interpretations of traditional South Indian music.

"I don't play classical Indian music," McLaughlin insisted. "That would be presumptuous. I've studied its theory and practice. I was lucky to have lessons concentrating on rhythmic theory from Ravi Shankar, and I studied vina, flute, and alap. I know the music well, I understand what's happening in it, and I play the way I play.

"I'm able to play with them [Shakti's Asian members: violinist L. Shankar, tablaist Zakir Hussain, percussionist T. S. Vinayakaram, and R. Raghavan on mridangam] in my own way and they like that. Because I'm *not* a classical player, they don't know what to expect. I'm not playing exclusively by their rules, though I understand them. I play as a Westerner, from an Occidental background. That's one thing that makes it interesting."

Shakti lasted, formally, four years; Shankar remained for Mahavishnu's short-lived electric One Truth Band, and Hussain has remained among McLaughlin's gang of percussionists, as he's distinguished himself among all Westerners by collaborating with contemporary virtuosos who expand on traditional musics from the Asian subcontinent. Also during Shakti's run, McLaughlin applied his facility to albums with Santana *(Love, Devotion, and Surrender)* and Larry Coryell *(Spaces,* on Vanguard), leading up to the flamenco-fusion of *Three Guitars* (Verve) with Paco de Lucia and Al Di Meola.

A decade after McLaughlin swept his laser-light guitar through the esoteric mists and jungle-machine rhythms of freely improvised fusion on Miles Davis's *Bitches Brew,* Davis himself was completing a five-year seclusion, and his coterie's spin-off bands—including Weather Report and keyboardist Chick Corea's Return to Forever—were chided as old and in the way. McLaughlin wasn't immune. The cosmic consciousness he'd once represented among pop cognoscenti gave way to a secular cynicism, typified by Britain's new-wave songwriters. During those new-wave years, McLaughlin championed high-tech: specifically, a Synclavier guitar synthesizer in a reconstrued Mahavishnu Orchestra.

"I love the electric guitar," McLaughlin asserted while touring to support the eponymous first release of that band—as regenerated after half a dozen years—on Warner Bros. This was our talk in '84. "It's irreplaceable. But for other areas it's a little narrow, misses a certain depth. So, for me, the Synclavier guitar is a revolutionary instrument. It's infinite, as far as sounds are concerned, allowing me to create sounds that are my own.

"There are, of course, presets that are flutelike or brasslike, but there are also sounds I've created via computer that are very personal, that belong to me and have become my voice. I don't adopt these sounds arbitrarily and gratuitously. It's what I can do with them that's really important.

"What does one of these sounds say to me? What does it touch in me? How do I feel about it? What can I do about that? What can I *give* to that?" These are his questions, and his recorded answers are inconclusive.

On "Radio-Activity," opening *Mahavishnu,* his guitar screams like Thomas Pynchon's missile arcing across the empty sky; on "Nostalgia," it approximates a goatherd's lissome pipe, reedy high and full blown low. On "When Blue Turns Gold," it's hard to distinguish between the guitar-synth and Bill Evans's flute (throughout most of the album Evans plays tenor or soprano sax with a throaty vocal quality that offsets McLaughlin's sounds).

McLaughlin's unadorned, crisp Les Paul Special-tone on the uptempo "Nightriders" offers relief from the abundant electronically glinting sounds of keyboardists Mitchell Forman and Katia Labeque, and bassist Jonas Hellborg. That track and another kicker called "East

Side West Side" support McLaughlin's contention that his '80s MO was "a little…*crazy*."

Crazy—unpredictable? intuitive? high-energy? wild—after all those years? What would McLaughlin like the kids who'd never known his first Mahavishnu Orchestra to hear?

"I hope they're going to hear the tradition behind us," he said without hesitation. "I believe nothing is contemporary unless you can feel the tradition behind it."

What of "the tradition" does he, has he, employed?

"I've had my jazz discipline. Without discipline, I wouldn't know what I was doing. You have to have a discipline, whether it's classical Western or classical Eastern or jazz or rock 'n' roll—though you don't need much theoretical background in harmony or rhythm for rock."

Mahavishnu, Left Behind

If deep theory isn't necessary in rock, a tight tie with one's audience is. McLaughlin's Mahavishnu Orchestra of the mid- to late '80s failed to forge much of a new one, was cut loose by Warner Bros., and eventually disbanded. When McLaughlin and I spoke again in 1992, he sat behind a desk in a borrowed office with an auspicious view in the New York City headquarters of Polygram Records. "I think my audience has become a little older, like me," he acknowledged. "To an older audience, high-volume ultrarock concerts may be events to remember more than relive.

"The Mahavishnu Orchestra—that was great twenty or twenty-two years ago," McLaughlin proclaimed. "But that was another era. You may remember very well—the Vietnam War, the '60s—it was another world. We were all part of it, and the music went for it and I went for it. But now, the way I am today…"

He paused long enough to consider what of the past he meant to uphold. "I want to be true to myself and to the music. As long as I keep to that, I feel I'm betraying nobody.

"There've been times when business pressures were brought to me—not always but yes, sometimes. You're taking risks and that's part of the deal. If you're going to follow your instincts, you've got to assume the risks, which I'm very happy to do. Thank God I'm able to continue to live and work as a musician; what more could I ask for? The idea of going to play for some twenty thousand people, though—what does *that* mean?

"There are two kinds of success you can have: One is musical, the other is commercial, and we should not confuse them. Think of Charles Ives. I went to London to hear the New World Orchestra conducted by Michael Tilson Thomas play Ives's Fourth Symphony, a staggering piece, and you know Ives never heard his piece played? Not once! So let's keep perspective with regard to artistic music success and commercial success. As a commercial success that symphony was a dismal failure, but I think we have to 'fess up that the man who composed it was a genius.

"I don't compare myself to Ives, but I consider myself pretty lucky."

He has, luckily, heard, performed, and recorded his *Mediterranean Concerto* for guitar with Tilson Thomas conducting the London Symphony Orchestra; as we spoke, his second symphonic commission was progressing toward debut.

"The stylistic barriers are really falling now," he stated. "Particularly amongst my contemporaries, my friends; several are very interested in getting me to write for them. The violinist Guidon Kremer? Yo-Yo Ma, the cellist? We all played together recently on a French television show. They don't really improvise, that's not part of their training, but they're very keen to learn anything, and if I write something for them in my genre, they'll play it."

Little more has been heard of McLaughlin's Synclavier, but he's toured Western and Eastern Europe, Japan, Australia, Latin America, and the United States playing a basically amplified acoustic guitar in trio with bass guitarist Dominique Piazza and percussionist Trilok Gurtu. In the mid-'90s he retired that personnel to satisfy the glint and grin he'd beamed as a lad styling himself "Johnny McLaughlin, Electric Guitarist" on his first business card. Again, he took up his solid-body electric, to travel with young grits 'n' greens organist Joey DeFrancesco and Parliament/Funkadelic power drummer Dennis Chambers.

McLaughlin also recorded exquisite duets with classically oriented pianist Katia Labeque, with whom he had a long personal relationship; in the '90s he issued an overdubbed solo acoustic appreciation of the late pianist Bill Evans, and a trio recording of Coltrane compositions, abetted by Trane's drummer Elvin Jones. He is still committed to the ideal heralded by the title of one of his earliest recorded compositions: "Follow Your Heart."

"I believe if you listen to Shakti or my *Belo Horizonte* album or

Three Guitars or any of my others, it's just guitar. I'm a guitar player, that's what I am primarily, that's what I'll always be.

"I like to write music, but I want to be a better and better guitar player just as I want to be a better person. I want to be more articulate, able to utilize space better, to play silence more profoundly. There are many things left for me to do, much work to be done.

"When you play music it's your life that you're talking about, that's expressing itself through music. That's why music's very rich, because it comes from the life of people. And there are things spoken in music that cannot be said vocally, or any other way, for that matter. We must keep the horse before the cart—nothing can replace work in music, and discipline—at least, these are *my* musical parameters. But when I'm listening to music I want to feel the person's life, the character of the individual or individuals making music together.

"I think we learn everything from other people, everything, including philosophy and what we think. I need to be inspired in my life, and for me, all great musicians are spiritual people. In fact, everybody's spiritual, really, and music is the language of the spirit because music speaks from the hearts of the player to the heart of the listener. And no, we don't care what language, what culture, what nationality. Music doesn't pay attention to any of those things.

"That's why music is so great. Music, globally speaking, is the spiritual language. Everybody loves music, everybody wants to listen to music—so who doesn't have a spirit?

"My work in music is a work of the spirit; it's a development of my spirit and the development of myself as a human being," he continued, though he said he preferred to be more discreet about his spiritual and religious inquiries than he was when he first took his Hindu name. "These words 'spiritual' and 'religious' can be very easily misunderstood. But what I really feel in my heart is that music is higher than any religion. If that's heretical to half a dozen religions in the world, it's what I feel. We don't know if there's a God, but if there *is* a God I think music is the face of God."

The Greatest Love of All

McLaughlin and guitarist George Benson are contemporaries, born in 1942 and '43, respectively. Both rose from obscurity in the '60s to fame in the '70s; both then established musical territories in which they'd operate for decades to come. Miles Davis is one common point of reference; both played with pianist Herbie Hancock, too. Yet they've lived in vastly separate worlds.

A youth who sang blues, gospel, and popular tunes, accompanying himself on guitar, in neighborhood taverns of his hometown Pittsburgh, Benson advanced to working with the best organ bands; from the time he was signed away from that circuit and Brother Jack McDuff's band by talent scout John Hammond of Columbia Records, he came on strong. Benson's fingers were nimble, his rhythms catchy and upbeat, his sparkle engaging, down-home, evidently genuine.

His material was corny? But through the '60s into the '70s he led tight, bluesy units, fully commanding their rhythms, soloing like a horn only better, with the in-sync efforts of worthy sidemen (organist Lonnie Smith, baritone saxophonist Ronnie Cuber, multi-reedist Joe Farrell, and guitarist Phil Upchurch, among others). Benson stepped out fiercely as a soloist on some of the funkier sessions led by other jazzmen in that era on the distinctive CTI label, though he most often tempered his edge on his own somewhat more plushly arranged, pop-jazz-slanted albums, produced by Creed Taylor, who earlier made the great guitarist Wes Montgomery—Benson's idol—a crossover star by bedding his plummy tone in quasi-orchestral tracks.

Then (and now) jazz purists disapproved of Taylor, whose CTI and Kudu productions prefigured the '80s and '90s jazz-lite by concocting hit-oriented albums for critically approved players including Freddie Hubbard, Hubert Laws, Stanley Turrentine, Milt Jackson, and Randy Weston. CTI and Kudu also launched or boosted the careers of Grover Washington Jr., Bob James, Patti Austin, and Esther Phillips—unabashed pop-jazz straddlers. Yet Benson sought renown as an instrumentalist at CTI. He didn't sing at all, applied himself to crafty, though sometimes merely trendy, material, and took his challenges seriously.

By 1976, Benson had moved to exploit his more contrived pop talents. His aims changed when producer Tommy LiPuma recast him as a smooth, ingratiating balladeer, singing Leon Russell's "This Masquerade." Upon the subsequent vast radio play and resulting peak of worldwide popularity of this tune, Benson remade himself as a pioneer of jazz-pop (black-white) crossover, a suave cousin, perhaps, of Stevie Wonder, descended from Billy Eckstine, a nephew of Nat "King" Cole.

Now Cole's considerable gifts as a jazz pianist are commonly unknown to the vast audience that cherishes him as pop singer, actor, television show host, American icon. Similarly Benson's single "This Masquerade" from his album *Breezin'* and his follow-ups ("The Greatest Love of All," an anthem, and disco-designated numbers including "Into the Night" and "Love X Love") lifted him up and away from his hard-won jazz credentials.

At Home

It was autumn 1987, and Benson was puttering about the Synclavier-equipped, twenty-four-track digital recording studio built into the lowest level of his home, set directly on top of a brook burbling down a ridge in New Jersey's wooded palisades, across the George Washington Bridge from Manhattan. He stopped fiddling with the equipment, sat down to talk, and said he's never left the music of his roots. He still drove his Mercedes across the Hudson to Harlem to jam with his long-ago boss, organist Jack McDuff, and to sit in unannounced and scat with singers Jon Hendricks, Al Jarreau, and Bobby McFerrin at late-night sessions in a Village club. For the most part, he said, it's better he keep word of such activities from his public.

I'd seen one of these unadvertised performances—at a Manhattan benefit concert organized by Newark jazz radio station WBGO-FM for terminally ill trumpeter Woody Shaw. Benson had walked onstage at swank Sweetwaters, with a few words redirected the rhythm section that was playing, then unleashed immaculate guitar lines, atwist with details—complex, commanding, several-chorus solos with grabby, finger-snapping introductions and thrilling, funky resolutions. He was unself-conscious, unencumbered by responsibilities to a nonjazz audience or format-minded radio folk or record producers.

That performance alone had convinced me his jazz chops could be turned high; I've seen him several times in the years since. At the first of George Wein's jazz festivals staged at Saratoga Springs, New York, Benson had focused and galvanized an impromptu finale with tenor saxophonist Dexter Gordon, wailing "On Broadway." At Wein's JVC Newport Jazz Festival in 1997 Benson and band had kept a significant audience enthralled while a dark, wet squall passed through the surrounding bay and threatened to downpour on the fest field.

I'd also seen Benson perform glibly and shallowly—in suburban arenas, and also in Carnegie Hall, where he simply sang his greatest hits and maintained a dazzling smile. In 1987, when we spoke, Benson's most recent jazz efforts were *Collaboration*, an album featuring guitar duets with his protégé Earl Klugh and one to be released with the Count Basie Band, arranged by its sax-playing-leader Frank Foster, Bulgarian-born Angel Rangelov, and British arranger Robert Farnon.

He had other jazz in hand: From the swivel chair in front of his gleaming new control board, Benson called up rhythm tracks he'd recently recorded of pianist Herbie Hancock, bassist Buster Williams, and drummer Grady Tate. He picked up his Ovation guitar, plugged it in, hit a "play" button on the console and improvised along with the tape. Notes streamed from his fingers, his fretting hand casually, affectionately petting the guitar's neck. When he set the guitar down he spoke for publication:

"I'm a guy who's versatile; all my life I've had to be in two places at once. As a commercial artist I've been expected to do things, like, 'We want you to sing, George.' So I sang.

"At first I said, 'I did that when I was a kid, and I never made any money singing. I had a big name, and people thought I had money, but I never made any money.'

"I mean, this fellow had said to me, 'You sing for me and I'll give you fifty-five dollars a week.' Fifty-five dollars a week—back then I'd do anything for fifty-five dollars a week! So I left school in my last semester. My teacher had told me, 'George, you've got to make up your mind: You either want to play music or go to school.' I said, 'No contest. I'm gone, man. Are you asking me to give up a job that pays fifty-five dollars a week?'

"I left and started working with this band. I sang, though I believe I was really hired to play the guitar, because there were very few guitar players in Pittsburgh at the time. But I couldn't play enough guitar to last a night; I didn't know enough songs, and I had hardly any improvisation at all. This was when I was seventeen years old. Then by the time I was nineteen and on the road with Jack McDuff, nobody outside of Pittsburgh knew I sang at all.

"See, when I was eighteen I'd met this saxophone player Larry Smith. We were playing r&b songs and he was playing bebop lines like Charlie Parker and Sonny Stitt. I said, 'Man, what's this stuff you're playing? It doesn't fit what *we're* playing'—which was some raunchy stuff. He said, 'I listen to Bird.' Bird? He said, 'You don't know who Charlie Parker is? You better come in my house.' I'd just driven him home; I came in and he put on Charlie Parker with strings playing 'Just Friends.' That was it. I heard a musician talking to me in a beautiful language.

"That was the first time music ever came over me like that. Music's always been music, but it had never communicated like that unless the person was actually saying the words and I could under-stand what they were saying. Charlie Parker, man—it was like he was telling an incredible story. I learned to sing his solo from 'Just Friends' note for note and started going to jam sessions.

"But in my town the jazz people hated me because I was pop-ular for my singing. When I started coming to the jams they didn't like it at all. I couldn't play any jazz music. I'd really come to learn.

"Well, one night a friend told me, 'Jack McDuff is at a club on the other side of town and he's looking for a guitar player.' I said, 'I can't play with Jack, what he's doing is much too advanced for me.' He said, 'George, you never know till you try.' So I went out and sat in with Jack McDuff. What Jack was impressed with—and it's a knack I've always had—is how I made *him* sound.

"A lot of improvisers, when they stop improvising, that's it. What Jack liked was that when I played behind him *he* sounded good. So he didn't really hear me improvise. I wasn't playing anything; I had no chops, no ideas. But he told me to come to his hotel room the next day. He called his manager and said, 'I found this kid who's incredible, and only nineteen.' He took me on the road with him—and fired me the first night.

"I couldn't play with him, not even the melodies, they were so unorthodox and different from what I knew. In Jack's arrangements, the guitar played the second or third parts, never the melody; the horn played that. I didn't even know what chord changes were. He said, 'I don't think you're going to be able to make it with the band, brother; I'll try to find you another gig.' But he couldn't find any-body else to take my place, and as the weeks went on, I learned. I stayed up all night to learn.

"How do you become a man with facilities overnight? You can't. I had to circumvent; I had to devise a way of playing the gui-tar that made it sound like I *could* play. Jack would show me the songs one note at a time; it took hours, and then I'd go home and figure out how to play it fast. And every night he played faster and faster. Eventually I did it; I learned all his charts.

"When his manager heard me he said, 'I like what this kid does to your band. He gives you a commercial quality.' That was because I was bending strings. No jazz guitar player was bending strings in those days; everybody was trying to be cool like Miles Davis or Jim Hall or Wes Montgomery, not like Charlie Christian. Well, they took me into the studio to record, and Jack had a smash album. Every record I was on as a sideman was a hit—that's what made me in New York. I cut hit records with Hank Mobley, Freddie Hubbard, Stanley Turrentine, Lou Donaldson. They all had hits because I made them sound good.

"To make somebody sound good, you've got to find a spot, some place that's your own, take it over and say, 'I'll handle this. You got *that*? OK, I'll handle *this*.' The other guys say, "Okay, yeah, I'll handle *this*.' So you got that going on [Benson sings a rhythmic lick], and some excitement [he sings a way-out guitar line], and Freddie's gonna go [he imitates a Hubbard trumpet phrase]. I want to make that sound like the greatest thing Freddie ever did.

"'How do we make this song special?' For me, that's what's happening. It's a privilege to have a spot to improvise in a song that's cooking with some great musicians, but it's not everything. I don't have to be the soloist in order for the song to be great. If I'm playing behind Benny Carter or Miles Davis, man, that's already greatness."

How did Benson compare himself to elegant veteran Carter and the ever-innovative Davis? Through his instrumental abilities?

"The guitar's popularity has helped make me what I am today; it's done more for my career than my voice would ever have done. Singers come and go. There are very few Nat Coles and Billy Eckstines and Frank Sinatras. The voice is something that's current: You put out a record; if people like what's on the record, they buy it, and then it's forgotten—unless it's a great song, and I've been fortunate in that respect. But the guitar has given me a solid place in history. It's given me a great identity, a place in the musical world. For that reason, I feel an obligation to guitar lovers.

"And that's the reason I built this [he gestures to encompass his three-room studio]—so that I can get my ideas down. This is how I started, before I did the *Breezin'* album [with "This Masquerade," on Warner Bros.], back when I was making all those guitar albums. I had a little studio where I could go and try things. I'd listen to myself and criticize myself and find ways to improve what I was doing. I'm getting back to that now.

"The guitar makes me feel good. If I play something on the guitar, it will be a while before anyone else can really capture it, figure it out. Musicians examine each other so we can benefit by what each of us is doing. When I hear someone play something good, I get my ax, and finally I learn it so I can say to them, 'Hey, man, that's an incredible way of approaching that particular sequence of things.' I'm sure other players do that with *me*.

"The biggest enemy I have is not playing every night. You have to play; when I was playing every night, there wasn't enough room in one night for me to play all the ideas in my head. But along with ideas you have to have the facility to play them; you've got to keep your chops up. I play a lot around here, but there's nothing like bouncing off the drum licks live, bouncing off the whole band. After I've played live for three days, I scare myself—because I don't know where those ideas come from. I say, 'Now, why did I play that? That's not what I meant to play, but it sounds okay. Why?'

"I play guitar by ear—all day, when I have the chance—and I listen for things in the air, trying to imagine musical scenarios and what I can do to enhance them. I play a lot of notes, by nature. It's like I'm nervous and have to be doing something. Of course, music is a therapy for me. It makes me feel good when I'm down. Those years I barely made a living, I was happy anyway because I had an instrument and something I could do with it that was different.

"Now I have to play for about three days solid before my flow comes back. After that, I'm raring to go. Just run some chord changes by me!"

Benson's album *Big Boss Band*, finally released in 1990, had neither Frank Foster's version of B. B. King's "Every Day I Have the Blues" nor Rangelov's arrangement of the Thelonious Monk classic "'Round Midnight," which he'd played for me. It drew mixed reviews from jazz critics, moderately favorable response from his public, and some radio exposure, too—but didn't effect a change in the repertoire of his stage shows. I called him some months after its release, more than two years after our initial interview.

"It's a strange thing," Benson said. "People talk about 'Why don't George play more guitar?' But it's difficult finding those great instrumental songs that make the difference"—that is, the difference between a radio hit and a critically acclaimed but modestly selling instrumental.

Was it always so? His forthright if hardly experimental jazz playing made a best-seller out of *White Rabbit,* a Creed Taylor production on which Benson covered the Jefferson Airplane's titular ode to pill-popping, as well as "California Dreaming," a Mamas & Papas song already appropriated by Wes Montgomery. During his CTI days Benson also essayed Miles Davis's "So What?," Luis Bonfa's samba "Gentle Rain" (on *Beyond the Blue Horizon*), the Beatles' songbook *(Another Side of Abbey Road)*; "Here's That Rainy Day," "In a Mist," "People Make the World Go Round," Freddie Hubbard's "Straight Life," and Coltrane's "Impressions." Surely songs are still being written.

"Creed was a good instrumental producer, but we're talking about selling one million records every time out," Benson responded.

Oh, he was upholding high standards. Had any jazz instrumentalist achieved such sales security?

"Grover Washington used to do well, and still does," he replied. "*Winelight* was his biggest LP; the vocal by Bill Withers on 'Just the Two of Us' helped it out. Kenny G's gone double platinum, with Smokey Robinson on some of his songs…"

The answer: Not unless there's singing. Security is song.

Benson had always known a hook when he heard it. He'd gained his early audience with instrumental renditions—bedroom classics—of soul standards including "The World Is a Ghetto" and "It's All in the Game." He'd brewed up "Sanctuary" with Miles, "Will You Still Be Mine?" and "Easy Living" with Jack McDuff. He worked breezy, tricky figures, as in "Body Talk," with oh-so-smooth exuberance.

"The jazz album that everybody's crying for—you think I don't want to do it?" Benson was incredulous. "It's foremost in my mind. I'm mentally committed to it.

"But you know," he said in a confiding tone, "there are some people who don't know I play guitar. They only know me from singing 'Give Me the Night' or 'Love X Love' or 'Turn Your Love Around.' And when they see me playing guitar, at first they say, 'I didn't know he could do that.' Then they say, 'Wait a minute, is he going to play all night or *do* something?'"

Those people may represent the largest segment of Benson's audience, but he faced a reported one hundred thousand listeners eager to hear his grittiest jazz and blues with organist McDuff and saxophonist David "Fathead" Newman at a Chicago Jazz Festival of 1986—and was greeted with ample applause. Benson said he'd enjoyed that all-instrumental set but questioned its drawing power.

future jazz

"After we played," he referred to his peer all-stars, "*my* band came out [for its usual set] and satisfied *everybody*."

"Words communicate better," he insisted. "Women fly to the store to buy a vocal, especially if they're home all day listening to the radio. That's been my experience. And I always like to put romance in my songs because romance is never going to fade. All my favorite cats did that. Wes was so great because of the beauty of his playing. That element, mixed with blues and funk, gives you the most powerful music.

"Everybody loves the blues. I try to add some beauty, some *pretty*, to it, as Nat Cole, Sam Cooke, Ray Charles, and Charlie Parker did."

Instrumental jazz could be big, Benson observed. "We've got to use the powerhouses to get people out to hear it. The Sonny Rollinses, the Wynton Marsalises, me. Then show off the most powerful new young talent. And hype them. The emcee should come onstage full of stories to tell the audience who the artist is, what he can do, to make them watch the artist from the start.

"You know what sells a record?" Benson asked, ready to tell. "A record is going to sell when you put something on it somebody wants to hear. For all the producers' good intentions, it's not going to sell if they make me sound like somebody else."

True enough: People had proved over and over they wanted the real George Benson. Who is he? A recording star? Improvising guitarist? Singer? Jam-session leader? Commander of the dance floor? A man who would be two places at once? Can anyone do that?

Sure and Steady Earns Its Place

Advanced instrumental abilities and good studio skills needn't be burdens for jazz players. Neither do a busy touring schedule and the opportunity to record regularly mean a musician has to dig himself or herself a rut. John Scofield is a case in point.

He was Miles Davis's front-line partner for a productive period in the '80s; Scofield is heard to advantage on both the underrated studio and live tracks of Davis's *Decoy* (Columbia Records, 1983). But by the time he hooked up with the trumpeter, Scofield, who'd studied at Boston's Berklee School of Music, had already recorded a handful of well-received sessions, including several with his trio comprising electric bassist Steve Swallow and drummer Adam Nussbaum. Earlier still, Scofield had been showcased on albums by

Jay McShann, the Kansas City pianist who'd brought Charlie Parker to New York in the '40s, and with Charles Mingus, Chet Baker, Gary Burton, Dr. John, Bobby McFerrin, and Wilson Pickett, among others. While with Miles, Scofield also contracted with ambitious, independent New York-based Gramavision Records.

Electric Outlet, Scofield's first Gramavision project, was based on an additive process in which he assembled quirky riffs and counterpoint over bluesy chord progressions, guitar track by guitar track. Synthesist Pete Levin was spare, supportive, and self-effacing; alto saxist David Sanborn and trombonist Ray Anderson added spice via riffs and short solos. The interlocking parts were more interesting compounded than they would have been individually, rather as though one of the contemporaneous "minimalist" composers such as Philip Glass had toyed with thirty-two-bar song structures and rhythm 'n' blues licks.

"*Electric Outlet* was an overdubbed record," Scofield remarked one sunny afternoon in the comfort of an informal patio he'd created on the roof outside his apartment in the Manhattan artists' building Westbeth. "I'd always wanted to try that. I was working with Miles, and I'd just gotten one of those four-track home demo setups. So I put down bass parts, laid in the drum machine, and said to myself, 'This is the way to do it!' I was really into the process, and I still like the idea of stacking stuff up. But there's nothing like getting a feeling from live players.

"I think the more you record, the better you get at being able to do in the studio what you do on a good night in a club. It's hard now because we're seeing these magnificently sculpted records from the pop world that are labored over for years. It's a temptation to make records like that—little gems. But I'm trying to get spontaneity in there, too."

Spontaneity, anchored in unassuming confidence, is not in short supply on Scofield's records or performances; one pleasure of seeing Miles during their time together was hearing the trumpeter prod him, and the guitarist fire back idea-generating responses. Scofield never seemed in competition with Miles or awed by him, but rather offered rhythmic propulsion and open ground for improvisations, as no one had since John McLaughlin, a decade before.

Flash isn't Scofield's style. Onstage, as in life, Scofield appears to be thoughtful and talented, with a taste for genuine fun as well as an acceptance of real responsibility. Sco' secured his status as a family man during the years he stalked the stage with Miles, the quintessential jazz loner.

In the years after Miles, he still sometimes walked around while squeezing off his thick gauged wire lines—but more often stood in place, bending and swaying slightly from the waist and knees, giving form to his phrases. Scofield wears suitably fashionable clothes, but pays much more attention to his bandmembers' efforts than to costumes. He signals his intentions with nothing more than a glance. His career is fueled by the ongoing popularity of a choice musical vocabulary: the bluesy feel, classic forms, and backbeat energy he recalled from his teen years in the '60s, with its soundtrack of soul hits from Memphis's Stax artists, Allen Toussaint's New Orleans' kin, the Chicago bluesmen marketed by Chess Records, early Motown, and the best Atlantic Records productions.

"Rhythm 'n' blues is what we're talking about," he said. "I keep hearing its influences in pop music. There's *always* been crossover between jazz and r&b. Think about Horace Silver, Cannonball Adderley. Or look at late '40s and early '50s r&b records—they have Connie Kay on drums. Who's more of a jazz drummer? Johnny Griffin played some of the tenor solos. R&b was always connected with jazz. There's some difference, sure, but it was always like the same thing."

Scofield is inspired by and adapts that soul sound, rather than imitating it. His themes, characteristically hummable, often include tricky syncopations or stop-time breaks before their sly returns. They're also casually, naturally funky. Where'd he get these blues?

"From the radio, hot damn, right off the radio," he boasted. "My parents weren't really into music. The music of my people—who knows what *that* is? The Connecticut Sound is not a big part of my thing. What is the Connecticut Sound—the sound of Prudential-Bache insurance? 'I woke up this morning, and both my cars was gone / I got so upset, I threw my martini on the lawn,'" he quotes comedian Martin Mull's "Suburban Blues."

"No, I learned from records and the radio and the few live bands and musicians I met. The music from as early as I can remember was rock 'n' roll, r&b, and folk music, then jazz when I got a little older. And that's the background of everybody I know, whether they're from the ghetto or wherever. They learned from the media, and the few good musicians they'd meet.

"I didn't meet any good musicians until I was eighteen or so; I didn't meet any jazz musicians in Connecticut, that's for sure. Except for Dave Brubeck. I used to go to his house and play with his son Chris, the trombonist who still plays bass in Dad's band. Dave was really nice, and gave free records to any kids who were visiting and were interested in the music. But Dave wasn't really accessible to teach a young guitarist about jazz. I just sort of picked it up.

"In New York, there are incredible guys who get it together really young. Like Jackie McLean and Sonny Rollins, who used to go to Bud Powell's house and Monk's when they were teenagers. Or, today, Marcus Miller and Omar Hakim, both from Queens. But if you live in suburbia or the country, you meet just a couple of musicians before you're old enough to move to the city. And those musicians don't have to be great, because when you first start to play you're not ready for Bud Powell anyway. Some guy who's interested in music and has the right records and shows you, 'If you play this scale and this chord, it should come out right; try it'—he's important too."

Scofield appears to treat all the musicians he encounters as important, or at least worthy of respect, and those with whom he works are regarded as full-fledged collaborators, helping shape his sound. The drummers he chooses (among them, Marvin "Smitty" Smith, Dennis Chambers, Bill Stewart) always provide a solid bottom and telling accents. He depends on bandmates such as tenor saxophonist Joe Lovano (in his mid '90s quartet) and soul-jazz innovator Eddie Harris (on his '94 Blue Note *Hand Jive*) for solid, signifyin' contributions. He takes his own sideman chores just as seriously, offering original, creative, musical ideas behind Joe Henderson on his Miles Davis tribute *So Near, So Far* (Verve, 1993) and revision of *Porgy and Bess* (Verve, 1997), braiding his sound with guitarist Bill Frisell's in bassist Marc Johnson's quartet Bass Desires and with Pat Metheny on *I Can See Your House from Here* (Blue Note, 1994).

Despite his lengthy discography, Scofield's work is mostly at its best live, whether in sophisticated city nightspots, roadhouses in secondary markets, prestige concert halls, or jazz fests everywhere. In concert, his music is by turns piercing, lyrical, reckless, and contemplative, depending on his mood, his colleagues, and the audience. When he's hot—inspired beyond his usual consistency—he can rock a house with R&B vocabulary, jazz acumen, and what-the-hell spirit. Does that make his music jazz?

"There's not one bar of traditional 4/4 on *Loud Jazz*," he said in 1987, in reference to his then-most recently released Blue Note album. "It's all electric and mostly funk-oriented. But I meet people in the hinterlands who've never heard Charlie Parker and yet think my music is jazz. They think any instrumental music with guys taking solos is jazz. I kind of go for that.

"I'm aware of the so-called pure jazz tradition, very much so, but I like the fact that to their ears there's jazz—which is guys blowing, and there's classical music—which is written out and you can tell it's not improvised. Then there's pop-rock, which is everything else that has words.

"I had a Jamaican cabdriver who was telling me he was in Kingston when the first reggae bands started. He says, 'Man, did you know the first reggae bands played jazz?' I don't know anything about reggae and I wondered, 'What does this guy mean by jazz?' He meant players blowing over a groove. He was talking about the Skatalites. I heard them, eventually, and that's what it was: Parker nuts playing over a reggae groove. That's sort of what our music is. Only there's another vernacular that's come about from guys who've been influenced by jazz, who've been deeply into learning standards and changes and phrasing, but have also always played in other kinds of bands."

Scofield said, "If I had to play all night on rock beats number one, two, and three, I'd get bored. I want elasticity. What I learned playing with Miles is that you can swing more on certain rhythms. What Joe Zawinul writes always has swinging-type bass lines, and you can express yourself over that. There's more shuffle to it than to straight-ahead rock-type stuff."

Knowing what he likes, he finds concerts and club dates the crucial tests of his compositions. "Only about a third of the material I've written seems to hold up, so I want to play it live. And it takes me a long time to figure out what's going to work. The obvious stuff gets boring. Stuff I think won't work because it's too tight, I find a different way to arrange."

The recording industry sparks his creativity. "You have to make a record every year just to stay in business, so I'm always thinking, 'What the hell am I gonna do next?' There's the exotic point of view: You know, go to Bali, play gamelan music, put it in your stuff. That can be pretty jive. But you don't want to make the same record over and over. Even looking at bebop: Except for Bird with strings, Parker was always making the same record. Of course, he was a great genius, and it's not boring, but idiomatically he was always working in the same context."

The context in which Scofield barnstorms has its own fatal flaws. "The fusion curse," he called it. "What I hate about fusion music is the gymnastics. We're often playing to audiences who want to hear fast and loud and don't know from anything else.

"Excuse me, audience, but there are a lot of people like this. And I have to watch myself. Because when you're playing, and you want to play fast, sometimes you're saying, 'I can get those kids at that table to be on their feet jumping up and down if I go nuts. Let's nail 'em!' And that's a real cheap thrill." Scofield half-seriously credited his sometimes producer and bassist Steve Swallow with keeping him on the right side of bad taste.

"These kids are just waiting for that. They say, 'We heard Chick's Elektric Band and they blew us away!' Or, 'We just heard Al [Di Meola] and it was wicked awesome!' They identify with our band. I'm a guitarist, coming out of blues. Which is where Eddie Van Halen and those rock 'n' roll guys are coming out of, too, whether they know it or not. I've never been that good at doing fast stuff; luckily, it doesn't come easy to me. Now, someone like [drummer] Dennis Chambers is a chops phenomenon. On his solos he destroys the drums. But he also has inbred musicianship. So it's exciting, and it's not so calculated."

Scofield sharpened his point. "You can't define hard-and-fast goods and bads; there are some show-off guitar players I really like and some subtle guitar players I really *don't* like. But think of the bar scene in *Round Midnight*," the Bernard Tavenier film about an American jazz saxophonist in Paris. "Those people are there to hear poetry in the broadest sense. We're not playing for that audience but I think the bulk of people who come to hear us are looking for something like poetry, too.

"We're an alternative to other kinds of fusion. Our idiom is an open field. If I were to play bebop guitar—well, it's a pretty big field, not to mention the history that's gone down. But there aren't so many bands that use the elements *my* band uses. And people really want to hear us, which is nice.

"I've got to say: I've chosen this. I'd be lying if I said financial responsibilities don't move me, because if I'm going to make my money playing music, I have to have people come to the gig. But I'm really trying to stay pure and do what I want. I'll find things I want to do that appeal to the audience too. But I always pick stuff I like, especially on the gig.

"You see, it's so easy to make a record you can't listen to again, which I haven't done. But on the gig, when I've driven all day and the only good thing about my day is playing that gig, I can't get up there and do something I don't like."

Does band leadership ever feel like an albatross?

"Oh yeah. It was fun to be in Miles's band because there was the band—and the star. We could talk about Miles behind his back, complain, we got shuffled from place to place...But we didn't have any part in the decision making regarding the music. I like having a band and being responsible for what goes down. It makes it worthwhile, but it's not as much fun. It's more work.

"I don't know how much longer I can do it. But I don't see myself doing anything else. A few years ago I used to think maybe I could be a studio musician and grind out jingles, but you have to know the current sounds that are making pop hits so you can play what's on that *other* cheeseburger ad. You have to be into it completely, and I couldn't do that. Teaching is difficult—satisfying, but incredible frustrating. Maybe I'll end up doing that, but I'm too selfish. I'd rather spend the time figuring out what I'm going to do. That leaves the road.

"Playing, that's supposed to be the main stuff. You can interact with yourself"—overdubbing and such—"but it's a one-way street, and after a while, it sort of stops. The main thing to me is playing with other people, the weird interplay and all the subconscious stuff that occurs.

"Maybe we're looking at a future where instrumentalists are rare," Scofield speculated. "Because what are you gonna do? You want to be a professional guitar player, but there's no place to work. There are about a tenth of the live gigs there were fifteen years ago. I don't know; some people are pessimistic about the future. And society has got to come to grips with this incredible technology—computers, that's what we're talking about. Something with artificial intelligence that can get a great sound right away. But I don't want to be pessimistic. It would be nice if, with all this technology at our fingertips, great music came out."

Is synthesized music what people want?

He paused for a moment. "I want people to like what I do, for survival's sake; otherwise I can't play gigs. But sometimes I don't think about that at all. And I think I'd like to *not* think about that. Right now I'm thinking about playing certain music, about how to get that together, and not about whether people will like it or not. I'm doing this thing with upright bass, and drums, and no synthesizers and not as many backbeats, per se (there's going to always be a beat). I'm doing it for musical reasons, for me, because I want to change. If I was thinking about the public, I'd probably go more in the other direction. But I think that my public is really jazz fans, people who simply like music. You lose some, you gain others.

"I don't think about radio airplay either, because my music does not get on the radio. Did you know that? These records I've made with all these elements of r&b and pop don't get on the radio! What gets on the radio is something else. I don't understand it. I don't *want* to understand it. I don't want to sit down with market analysts who say, 'Maybe if you do *this*, you can get your stuff on the radio.'"

Why resist such advice?

Scofield sighed. "I've played some standards for years—'Softly as in a Morning Sunrise,' 'Just Friends'—and I like to play these songs that are sort of in me. I feel I have something to say in them.

"What we're talking about is improvisation, right? Not just playing the songs, but playing that leads you into improvisation. A lot of the Tin Pan Alley stuff is harmonically great to play on. These sets of chord changes are America's finest. The chord changes, the harmonic things, are excerpts from the past two hundred years of classical music. The chords to 'All the Things You Are' are classic harmony examples; they move like so, and there are a million lines you can play through them. Once you learn them, they're fascinating and become addictive. Like blues changes. They're classic in that sense.

"But what we think of as the most popular tunes of the last fifteen years don't necessarily have those harmonic situations. It doesn't make them better or worse, but I don't think they're universal vehicles for musicians to improvise on. There are a couple of songs out there that are harmonic: 'Just the Way You Are' has nice changes, but I don't want to sound like I'm playing in a lounge band. Stevie Wonder and Michael McDonald write harmonic stuff I like, but when I think of Stevie Wonder's songs, only Stevie can do them, seems to me."

Scofield realized something besides harmony has changed since the glory days of the American songbook. "Those tunes from the '30s and '40s, and the show tunes, they were sheet music hits. There were eight million recorded versions of these. They were songs people sang every day. What's on the radio now isn't what you sing every day, or play on the parlor piano."

What's a restless guitar star to do to refresh himself?

"I keep thinking that I'm just going to play better on the guitar, and that's what's going to be different." Scofield won't go acoustic, though in 1997 he switched labels and released *Quiet* (on Verve). "I'm really an electric guitar player. I've gotten a sound that I like, finally. Did you ever notice that when these electric guitar players play acoustic guitar, they all sound the same? Except for McLaughlin—he's got an incredible sound, and his acoustic music *pours* out of that instrument."

Scofield resented the market's pressure to constantly come up with something new.

"My idols seemed to be able to make record after record of their jazz, and it was okay," he stated with only a trace of irritation because he actually knew McShann, Mingus, and Miles operated under equally frustrating, if different, market constraints. Then he summed up his situation.

"I don't know if I'm going to do anything new in my life. I would like to, yeah, because all the stuff that I admire is new and different. But isn't it really about taking everything that you're made of, everything you ever heard, and for some reason it comes out different?

"If you listen to Charlie Parker's music, you can hear these rococo things from classical music, blues, and everywhere put together in this genius way. The same thing with Ornette Coleman: For some reason he wasn't scared to free the music up and go on instinct. But the melodies and everything else he uses came from the older music, when you really analyze it. You've got to say, though, 'Who would have thought of putting it together like *that*?'

"For some reason these guys were strong enough, felt brave enough, were individuals enough to do it their own way." He is too.

Blood on the Facts

"I lived in Detroit for five years before I came to New York," recounted James "Blood" Ulmer, nestling his guitar in his lap, leaning into the microphone at the New York National Public Radio news studio. "For about six months I played at a club called the Blue Bird there, where the owner was very much in love with jazz. At the end of my gig he said, 'Listen: You can play the guitar, so I want you to take this money and go to New York and find Miles Davis. Tell him I sent you to play with him.' I said, 'Good, give me the money, I'm ready to go.' He did, and I came to New York. I never found

Miles. But I found Ornette Coleman! And he said the *natural* way I play is harmolodic!"

This was news to Blood, who'd spent his Blue Bird years chomping at the bit, taking chord dictation on the bandstand from organist Hank Marr, waiting for a chance to solo at a stretch equal to the horns'. He absorbed and gladly accepted Coleman's notion that his natural way was something special, and he's clung to it ever since.

At the Knitting Factory on New Year's Eve 1994, guitarist Ulmer played like a bear roused from hibernation—growling lyrics semi-intelligibly, hulking about heavy-limbed in front of his black rock band, swatting out clotted lines and chords anchored in a twanging drone as though funk would clear the way for springtime. It's not Ulmer who's been napping; rather, the United States is asleep on him.

After five years without an album on an American label and with three fresh recordings available in '94, Blood should have been blinking in the light and basking in the glow of newfound fame. On *Blues Preacher,* his Japanese Disk Union (DIW) album released in the United States by Columbia Records, he attacked pop forms with the determination of a working man. For *Harmolodic Guitar with Strings,* until 1998 available on DIW as a Japanese import only, Blood posed as an improvising composer, his relatively free style formally under-scored by violinists Gayle Dixon and John Blake, violist Ron Lawrence, and cellist Akua Dixon Turre—the Quartette Indigo. With his fourth Music Revelation Ensemble album—featuring saxophon-ists Sam Rivers, Arthur Blythe, and Hamiet Bluiett, bassist Amin Ali, and drummer Cornell Rochester, also on Japanese DIW—Ulmer redeemed his promise of a jazz with explosive energy, reconceived harmonies, jostling improvs, and offbeat syncopations.

But Blood has remained on the fringe of popularity and at the fore of future jazz for a while now. His 1978 recording debut as a leader, the clangorous *Tales of Captain Black* (Artists House) with Ornette and Denardo Coleman and Jamaaladeen Tacuma, became out of print and impossible to find. Blood had a good run on Columbia in the early '80s, self-producing *Freelancing, Black Rock,* and *Odyssey,* and worked with bassist-producer Bill Laswell on *America—Do You Remember the Love?* for Blue Note in '87. He's con-tinued to thrill audiences in Europe, from which come some of his orneriest albums, including *No Wave* (live from the Moers Music fest) and his street jazz masterpiece, *Are You Glad to Be in America* (on

Rough Trade, a DIW reissue), with a front line of David Murray, Oliver Lake, and Olu Dara—drummer Ronald Shannon Jackson pounding humongous rhythms behind.

Celebrated obscurity is okay with Blood. There's a twinge of pain in it, perhaps, and he doesn't make star money, but he owns a building, bought at a bargain price in the 1960s, in Manhattan's now-fashionable Soho district, so he's got some security. In youth Ulmer worked the black American chitlin' circuit, backing singers and organists. He knows the pathways of a music career are unpredictable. Having already come a good distance from his birthplace of St. Matthews, South Carolina, he trusts he'll end up someplace, if not necessarily where he thought he was going. He'll roll with that.

"The role of the guitar used to be limited," Blood remembered from his pre-Coleman blessed days. "You took one or two choruses, then the horn player took about twelve and you played backgrounds. Made me want to get my own band, so I could do what I wanted to as a guitar player.

"Mainly, the guitar had to play the piano part. I never felt it was a full guitar part. If you follow a piano chart, you play chords in thirds. You can play sevenths, but you only got four fingers.

"If I had nine fingers, I could have played bigger chords, thirteenths or whatever. But Hank Marr would be playing standards and calling the changes to me—'Eleventh chord, ninth, flatted five-seven, major seven'—and I'd have to condense that down into three or five notes. And everybody else was improvising.

"I thought improvising was a very wonderful thing to do, like a salutation or praying to yourself," chuckled Ulmer, who also goes by his Muslim name, Adamu Mustafa Abdul Musawwir. "It got so I wanted a chance to do that, to play a very, very long solo."

Blood abandoned his old style upon being "initiated" by Ornette—whose concept of divergent unisons makes solo and background distinctions irrelevant—and he got the chance to really stretch out when he met drummer Rashied Ali.

"Rashied was in the zone about playing free, and I hadn't played free with nobody before. So I had to figure out how to prolong my solos, and find out what the guitar itself does. It's a rhythm instrument like a piano, but it's *not* a piano. The piano is so big, it makes a lust'rous, cushy sound. I wanted to find out how to play my three little notes and get a big, full sound.

"I did it playing from the drone, really designing a tuning system. If I wanted to play in D, I would take the lower E string and put it on D. So when I play the D I can play that, get a whole new sound from the drone, and it will be more equalized into the key. I can play all the notes—it could be D minor or D major or D major 7 with a minor five, or...

"My original concept of tuning to the drone was to change each string to the same keynote. You could call that diatonic harmolodic tuning. You tune up to the note, to the sound. But after getting into that for a while I learned how to get what I want from the original tuning, which is basically all fourths, and use five strings for the guitar and one for myself.

"Since I've got two Es, I use one of those for *me*. One for me, one for the guitar. I give it the harmolodic approach, and maintain the drone, and am still able to play all twelve notes in a chromatic scale. Which is a little different than playing in the key, because in the key you have to stick to the eight notes of the key, but in the drone, you can have the drone that rings like a key, and you can also play alternative notes. You know what I'm saying."

Maybe yes, maybe no—anyway, you hear what Blood's *playing*, which is a line of nearly infinite possibilities, outrageous dissonances and blues inflections wedded to a drone like that against which Indian sitarists play. Blood will discuss his system in detail, demonstrate on an instrument at hand, theorize as he continues. But his basic message is "You are allowed to play all the notes." He recommends *Odyssey,* his trio album of 1983 with Charles Burnham on violin, as a most successful result of the method. *Odyssey* sounds like a rocking blues raga hoedown.

"Rock 'n' roll is far out because it goes for the fullest guitar sound possible and heads for *more,* even if they have to use two or three guitars to get it. But the thing about rock is, the music is not as advanced as the words. I like the music part," insisted Ulmer, whose voice can be effectively sweet—if never light—and plaintive, as well as a hoarse roar. "I like words too but I put them in perspective. Singing is singing, and playing music is playing music to me. I've been singing songs, and it's much different than playing guitar.

"When I started playing music I was singing all the time, but I left it out for a long while. I don't really think nothing should be left out; if you can do something at all, you should do it. You don't want nothing laying around, hanging dust on it. You got to find a use for everything you have.

"To me, there ain't but two categories of music: When you're singing and when you ain't. If I'm going to a gig to play music, and don't have to sing, I'm more relaxed. If I have to sing, I'm more upset." He had a wheezing fit of laughter, then straightened up. "The categories of jazz, rock, punk, funk—I think people do that to market the music, but I don't think it's a real thing players do in their heads.

"They used to call my music all kinds of things—punk, funk, harmolodic, jazz, fusion—and I can see why. Before, I tried to do everything at once. I would have the band play one song, and we'd say we wanted to go ten degrees into the audience's mind while we were playing. We wanted them to experience every kind of twist we could put on them. I'd say ten degrees like if you were talking from one to ten…And if I played ten different kinds of songs, or ten different approaches to a melody, you'd listen and might come out humming one or two. If I'm playing only one thing, a person either likes it or doesn't like any of it.

"But now I want to separate the styles of my music, I don't want to play all mixed up. If I'm feeling all songs [with words], I play all songs. If I make a record of songs, I don't add instrumentals, or long drum solos, and nobody is telling a story. Same way in the harmolodic music we play—everything is totally harmolodic. Now I don't do but three things: I do records of songs [i.e., *Blues Preacher*], I have the Music Revelation Society that plays harmolodic music in instrumental form, and I write music, such as the string quartet music with guitar."

Blood's most telling song on *Blues Preacher*—deeper than the hooky "Let Me Take You Home," ringing truer than the concluding "Angel" (which he sings in duet with his longtime partner/ex-wife Irene Datcher)—claims even in its title that "Jazz Is the Teacher (Funk Is the Preacher)."

"If you play jazz you can learn a lot about music," Blood explained. "It's a very technical form of learning how to play music; you almost have to go to school. In fact, you have to go to one school or another, such as playing with somebody a lot, to learn how to play jazz. Because jazz is involved. It's about chord changes, modulations, and you have to learn it. If you can't learn it, then you can't play jazz.

"And funk is the preacher, appropriating preaching style, where the statement is felt in the words. That's what straight funk is."

What of blues?

"Well, I like gospel because I like spirituality more than I like blues," Blood said. He was a member of the Southern Sons vocal quartet in his boyhood. "My family was tripping out on spirituals, and spirituality got to mean—to me—coming closer to what you think is the truth, instead of how something sounds. To be spiritual is to be truthful with something. A blues musician can be spiritual if he's truthful with the music."

Another gulp of Blood Ulmer's spiritual truth?

"I have the same audience, it seems to me, wherever I go. I'm not hooked up to no commercial audience, but every place I've played seems to know my music. Because I make a recording somewhere every year, sometimes two or even three. Somebody hears it. They're the ones who like my music, who come and hear me play.

"I'd like to play in America again, like I did in 1981, '82, '83, '84— but something happened, seems the money dried up. If someone is really thirsty for something, they probably go get a drink, don't you think?"

Whatever people thirst for, whatever artists offer them.

6
Wynton Marsalis Restarts Us

Discussing pop music and his own ambitions, Wynton Marsalis is led astray from his main course of thought, and suggests...

WM Let's start again.

HM I'll ask you questions from that point where you say we went astray. Did you play with hometown friends in New Orleans?

WM Yeah, I played with everybody, I did every kind of gig you could do, went to all kinds of rehearsals, played in the community band, in the civic orchestra, in music parades, in the funk band, and what little jazz I could—which wasn't much.

HM What made you decide you had to really concentrate on your instrument?

WM When I was thirteen I started listening to music. Clifford, Miles, and Dizzy. Boy, Dizzy will make you practice.

HM Are you still in Juilliard?

WM No, they banned me from the school. Just playin.' I left about two years ago, when I went with Art Blakey. Every conservatory in America should change its curriculum, start including American music and quit using people like Aaron Copland as their true example of what American music is like.

HM How should they teach real American music?

WM The people who know about that would have to sit down and think about it, like they figured out how to teach Bach. It could take fifteen years, or one thousand five hundred years; the music will stay the same because it's documented, on records. And if you know how to listen to the music, you can hear the period of its creation in it.

HM When you play classical compositions, do you interpret them as they were interpreted in their time?

WM It's not important. The times are different, but the music's the same. The drama in the music is the same. The *fortes* and *pianos* and *crescendos,* those Italian words nobody understands, that's what the real music is, and it's the same.

HM When you play a composed piece, aren't you bringing something of your own to it?

WM When you do anything, you bring your own feeling to it. Everybody does that. Even people who express no emotion: They're expressing the emotion of *no* emotion.

HM When you compose, are you trying to express a particular idea?

WM No, an overall feeling. It's difficult to translate music into language, because music is its own universe. You're just trying to write or play *music.* And there's so much going on, especially in jazz. Because jazz is the most precise art form in this century.

HM What does the precision attach itself to? Where can you hear it?

WM The time. What the jazz musician has done is such a phenomenal feat of intellectual accomplishment that people don't believe it is what it is. What the musicians have figured out is how to conceive, construct, refine, and deliver ideas as they come up, and present them in a logical fashion. What you're doing is creating, editing—and all this as the music is going on.

    This is the first time this has ever happened in Western art. Painting is paint*ed.* Symphonies are writt*en.* Beethoven improvised, but by himself, over a score. When five men get together to make up something, it's a big difference.

HM But when you create with your band, there's a thoroughly understood idea of what's going to happen in the piece.

WM No. There's a language of music present, but how that's going to be used, how something will be used to achieve whatever effect you're after, we don't know what that is. First thing is, we don't have set chords all the time. We don't play on modes, ever. Whatever chord Kenny [Kirkland] plays, that's what chord it is. If Jeff [Watts] plays a certain beat, the piece becomes in that time. The form has to stay the same, the structure must be kept, but our understandings are very loose. We understand the logic of our language.

HM Jazz has its own language. Do new words enter the language?

WM The music has so much history...but of course, all the time. I hate to use the word "jazz" because it's so imprecise. Improvisation itself is a misunderstood language, and a vast one because so many people have contributed. Like Ornette, what he was doing twenty-five years ago, phrasing all across the bar lines like nobody's ever done—people still can't do that today. And it's not old, because nobody has figured out how to do it except him.

HM Do these people's innovations lead you to your own innovations?

WM No, because you already have your own innovations in your mind. When you start out, you play because you have a feeling about playing and you love music. You automatically have innovations in your mind, but you can't come up with them because you don't know enough about music to do it. You want to play like yourself, but you have to go through everybody to get to yourself. Otherwise, it's like inventing the wheel when people in New York are driving cars.

HM Are other musicians more or less tolerant than you about what is jazz?

WM Oh, they all know, except maybe the musicians in high school. Everybody just tempers what they know to make it seem like they're the hot stuff. We all do that; we're all the protagonists of our own plays. Whatever camp someone's in, due to deficiencies in technique or concept, they formulate their concept to make them seem like they're doing the right thing. But the right thing is what's going to *last*.

HM You've thrown in with what you think will last?

WM You throw in with what you think about life, in music. You study to know what music is, because if you don't know what it is, you can't play it.

HM Do your records represent the music you *know*?

WM Not really. *Think of One* (Columbia) is my best record, but I've just made two records. Two records [as of this interview, April 24, 1984].

HM Was *Think of One* made the traditional way, or did you take advantage of the studio?

WM No, we played. Our problem now is, we can't find a studio that's big enough to play in, so, though our engineer does a great job, the records don't sound as good as they should.

There are a lot of problems with jazz, man, that people just don't understand. Misconceptions. Like that musicians are all,

"Hey, baby, wha's happenin'?" Like that jazz musicians can go to Europe for respect. Or Japan—it's not like it was, maybe twenty years ago. Now the Japanese are going toward the pop culture thing. They like the music, but Americans understand jazz better than any other people. Because the music is about America. It's the most American music.

7 Modern Maturity

Sage of the Jazz Age F. Scott Fitzgerald's famous comment "There are no second acts in American lives" doesn't apply to artists in jazz today. Several of the best bright innovators who established themselves one short jazz generation ago have honed and held their edges without compromise, found satisfaction without burnout and continued testing themselves, creating all the while, even if they've had to sometimes regroup from the setbacks that hit everyone whose so-called career—that is, real life—lasts long enough to matter.

Twenty-year veterans of the marginally commercial American music wars include saxophonists David Murray and Henry Threadgill as well as record producer/auteurs like Bill Laswell, Kip Hanrahan, and Hal Willner; crossover sensations such as singer Cassandra Wilson (whose blue light dawned brightly after she'd spent a decade in New York), and sixty-something sax survivor Charles Gayle, regaling audiences internationally with bloodcurdling wails of urban extremes. Prominent postfusion, pre-Marsalis (1975–84, say) artists with moderately high-profile gigs/albums/influence in this milieu—who betray no signs of letting up into the '90s—stretch alphabetically from Geri Allen to John Zorn. They're not all based in New York, either. Not by a long shot.

"Keeping an edge in midcareer is a real concern," says James Newton, a Californian who since the late '70s has let rip with an unlikely but incisive ax: his supple, sophisticated flute. Influenced by the multi-instrumentalists (and particularly daring flutists) Eric Dolphy and Rahsaan Roland Kirk,

Newton arrived in New York through the David Murray network; after a dozen years of high-level transient jazz life, he became a tenured professor at University of California-Irvine. He participates in education-based residencies and composes on commission for accomplished ensembles internationally. His music has many dimensions—he writes for ensembles, not just himself—but he's compelled by the flute. As if it were a wand? a pen? the fast flow of an inner voice? Newton's heard on some dozen fine CDs of the '90s, among them his *Suite for Frida Kahlo* (Audioquest), pianist Fred Hersch's *The Russian Collection* (Angel/EMI), and drummer Andrew Cyrille's *X-Man* (Soul Note).

Spirit, Heritage and Tradition

"When you're younger, 'the career' is something that has a lot of luster," Newton says. "I wanted to be well known, travel widely, and record as much as possible. I'm forty-one now [in 1995]. My children are thirteen and seventeen, difficult ages. I want to be around rather than on the road. And the music that means the most to me is that which has spiritual value and reflects my heritage and tradition."

His breakthrough album was *The African Flower,* a vivid Ellington/Strayhorn homage, issued by Blue Note Records in 1986. Newton says his Blue Note contract was "voided" when he followed up with *Romance and Revolution,* versions of Mingus and Ornette Coleman works unlikely for radio airplay. In years that followed, his projects comprised a first symphony (premiered in Germany) and solo piano pieces. His record *Gumbo Ya Ya* (Contour Records) was all flute overdubs and electronics inspired by the sounds that hooked him: "African rhythms, Jimi Hendrix's *Electric Ladyland,* Miles *Live at the Fillmore East,* Herbie Hancock's Mwandishi bands, and Sun Ra, who *always* pushed the envelope." Newton works with the Bay Area's active circle of Asian-American improvisers, and besides more conventionally constituted ensembles, has a collective group called Flute Force Four, with Henry Threadgill.

"The way I feel about playing the music of Mingus, Dolphy, Ellington, Strayhorn," Newton says, "is not so much from the point of being a revivalist—more along the lines of playing music of these great composers. Most Ellington you hear is one of twenty standards. People aren't playing his longer music, or Mingus's, and as a composer I feel it's tragic to see these great works just laying down. That's number one.

"Number two: I set myself the goal of one day being an excellent interpreter of these composers. That's why I play this music along with my own. I'm trying to show the relevance the music has today, and use some techniques used in today's music, such as multiphonics, with the flute. I do that just as when Mingus took Eubie Blake's 'Memories of You' he reharmonized it and used more modern changes.

"With Ellington, or Strayhorn, or Mingus," says Newton, "you don't have to do too much with harmony, because it can't really get any better than they did it. But you can do different things with orchestration, tempo changes, and such.

"On *African Flower* my orchestration had to be radically different because anybody who sets himself up with a big band reorchestrating the music of Ellington or Strayhorn is up for a colossal failure. It can't be orchestrated that way better than they did it themselves. I orchestrated it for a small group with a totally different timbral palette—flute, cornet, alto saxophone, violin, vibraphone, piano, bass, drums, percussion, voice, baritone voice, bass baritone voice— and tried to keep the spiritual and the rhythmic essence of the music.

"At the time we approached *African Flower* I think there was only one other recording of the title track, by Gary Burton, outside of the Ellington-Mingus-Roach original [on *Money Jungle*, Blue Note]. 'Strange Feeling' by Strayhorn had never been done by anyone but Strayhorn and Duke. I chose some other pieces that are played a fair amount, but 'Sophisticated Lady' was the only *really* popular one.

"I also spent a lot of time studying Monk's trio date of Ellington because that's Monk showing how he grasped different elements of Ellington's music to do what *he* was doing. I hope you can hear the Harlem stride pianists—and I tried to show how much the trumpet plunger specialists Ellington wrote for, like Tricky Sam Nanton and Bubber Miley, influenced what I try to do on the flute."

Trumpet plunger specialists, influencing his flute? "I borrow different things different people are doing," Newton says, "and mix them together. Like with multiphonics, which is two or more sounds being created at the same time. There are lots of different ways to approach it.

"One is through fingerings, as is mainly done in European music, contemporary classical music. My thing is to use multiphonics to get more weight, more *meat* out of the flute, and to add a harmonic vocabulary and a timbral vocabulary to the flute. I've found the most interesting way to do it is to use my voice in conjunction with different fingerings. My fingers might create two sounds in my playing, and singing I get another two sounds.

"When I listen to the brass plunger players, their plunger movements to me are expressive language. It's talking. The opening statement in Ellington's 'Harlem'—Cootie Williams plays '*Wah-waaah*,' calling out, 'Harlem.' As far back as the drums used in West Africa, there have been tonal inflections in musical language. My work is a direct connection and correlation with that.

"I've got about a four-octave vocal range without my falsetto. The flute range is three octaves and a half. I've been working on combining those two ranges, and on the tones that happen as a *result* of the combinations of the two things interacting together."

Though a standout instrumentalist, Newton's not all alone taking this direction. Among his notable colleagues is one Robert Dick, a flute de/reconstructionist whose innovative techniques and intense interpretations have their roots in a radical critique of conventional conservatory practices and a fascination with sounds initially emphasized by electric guitar amplification. Newton, too, is ultrasensitive to conservatory flutism that's cold to the point of quantification, or science.

"Science is definitely part of this music, but there's also the important element of ritual," he asserts, "where the spirit takes over and creates another set of possibilities that don't have anything to do with science. They have to do with spirit. It's something much deeper, something much more *inner*.

"A lot of modern artists today are grappling with mixing science and the element of ritual, but there's a certain point where science has to stop, because it only goes so far. Ritual can go beyond imagination. A lot of times when I'm using my voice and playing the flute, I know how to control the different tones, but something will come inside, a feeling will happen that *creates* a feeling, a different feeling I know only from the stage. And it changes everything. Sometimes I lose the feeling of my body, totally. It's like the top of my head is blown off and my fingers are moving—something's happening, but I don't know *what's* going on.

"That does not happen every night. On a tour once with a Mingus Dynasty ensemble, I was amazed that it happened six or seven times. Before that, I hadn't had that feeling in almost a year. When it does occur, it shows me how *right* that music is for me to be studying."

"It's different when I'm composing. Sometimes then my thought processes are really together. I'm trying to feel every note that's written. There's a feeling of tranquility I get sometimes when even if I'm writing for something as thick as an orchestra, a whole forty or fifty seconds of music will come to me, clearly. I'll hear it totally orchestrated.

"That's rare, too. You have to work for every little bit of what usually comes. Every once in a while you get a gift like that."

Newton considers. "When we talk about the spirit lifting, I realize now that that happened for me for the first time in the Baptist church. The female voice, especially, seems to have a sonority in it that pushes a button for this experience to occur, this manifestation of holy spirit. When it happens when you're playing the blues, you might not exactly think it's the holy spirit! Maybe it's a little something else or a combination of a lot of different things, but it's a very similar button, anyway.

"In African-American culture the separation between secular and sacred is very thin," he goes on. "A lot of the same intervals are sung in the churches and the clubs. It's the text, but even beyond all of that, it's just an approach to life. It wasn't conscious, but the more I think about it, I realize my church experience when I was young has a lot to do with my choices in what I play. The female voice is still my favorite instrument, whether it's Sarah Vaughan, Kathleen Battle, Heather Harper, Jessye Norman, Mahalia Jackson, Ida Cox, or Ivie Anderson—who's still my favorite voice. And don't let me exclude Betty Carter.

"Even when I'm traveling, I'm studying. When I'm at home, I'm analyzing every day. I listen to music three, four, five hours a day, every day. And practice flute, among other things I have to do. But it's like you're building a fire. If you don't keep putting wood on it, your flame dies. I have to keep working on what I'm doing to feel like it has some validity. There have been nights when I fall on my face: Like this week, I felt only two nights out of five so far have I played decently. The other nights I feel like I played horribly. I just keep working on it, and I know it'll get better, and my percentage will, I hope, get higher."

One Brecker Brother

Above a Chinese grocery just off the Bowery, saxophonist Michael Brecker shows off an eighteen-inch-long black tube of metallic, matte finish, like lab equipment. It's an EWI—Electric Wind Instrument. Two plastic-coated straws, a long finger length, run from the tube's top to a cloth-covered spool that grips a misshapen-looking sax mouthpiece—sans reed. Into this Brecker blows.

The EWI is a prototype. Brecker is a premier tenor saxophone soloist whose brief breaks on Paul Simon's hugely popular records are surely more widely known than his fuller statements in what are relatively mere cult favorites: McCoy Tyner's *Infinity;* Pat Metheny's *'80-'81,* or Herbie Hancock's *New Standards,* for instance. Of course years back Brecker starred in the '60s jazz-rock ensemble Dreams, in the '70s disco-jazz band Brecker Brothers with his trumpeter-sibling Randy, and the '80s fusion supergroup Steps Ahead with Mike Mainieri, et al. But now he's thinking forward.

"This is your basic small MIDI studio, and there's nothing particularly unusual about it," Brecker says of a sun-parlor space, doored off from the loft's grand piano and visitors' seating. His Selmer saxophones live here, at the ready and in travel cases; a tenor sits out, with gleaming presence. Other equipment includes Yamaha, Oberheim, and Casio keyboards; a six-voice Oberheim "expander"; Akai 900 and 612 samplers; multiple sets of speakers; an old but essential Tapco mixer.

The EWI, the most recent addition to Brecker's gear, was invented by Nile Steiner and built for Brecker in the mid-'80s. Akai planned a model for the consumer market, but the device has not yet stirred much interest.

Brecker is a quiet, bespectacled man with a somewhat reserved, perhaps cautious, air. After thirty years' experience, he's still advancing his skills on his main instrument, and it's like he thinks it's dangerous: He titled one '90s album *Don't Try This at Home* (Impulse!). Brecker has been a pro New York studio musician since his teens, adding sax behind such performers as James Taylor, Joni Mitchell, and Cameo. He has encountered many advanced electronic inventions over three decades and learned something about them rather than simply set them aside.

"I've been through various phases of trying to electrify the tenor, trying to alter the sound so it would blend better with electronic instruments," Brecker explains. "There have been times, particularly in the Brecker Brothers, when we were very *very* electric and I almost couldn't get through the wall of sound with the sax.

"Plus, the tenor's range is low, so it was hard to compete—if that's the right word. When I'm playing with very loud instruments, especially a loud bass, I feel them sympathetically vibrating my instrument—which makes it hard to get a good sound. I start overblowing and everything gets vibrated out.

"I used some cheap boxes because that's all that was available at the time, and I found a few things that worked. There was the Funk Machine, kind of an envelope generator, which fit—but on some level I always hated messing with the sound of the sax. Because we spend so many years learning to get a good sound, it's upsetting to distort that sound. I eventually stopped using that stuff, especially playing with Steps.

"We [Brecker, Mainieri, bassist Eddie Gomez, drummer Peter Erskine] began Steps as an acoustic band, as fusion refugees. We added technology gradually as technology appeared. You know, there's been a technology boom in this decade"—'80s to '90s—"and it doesn't seem to be slowing down. Technology has become fascinating all over again, in a much deeper way.

"As Steps [established in '79] become more and more electronic, I found myself in the same boat again. Then the EWI appeared, and it's like an answer to all my desires. It's a wind-driven synth with an eight-octave range, touch-sensitive and extremely expressive, and it's very satisfying to play."

To demonstrate, Brecker holds up the EWI and emits what amounts to a chorus-length of agonizingly modern percussion—high-pitched, hollow-bottomed, hiphop rhythms on garbage cans. What jazz needs: a tongue-in-cheek drum machine.

"That sounds stupid," he mutters. "I was just using that for writing some rhythm tracks." He dips into his filebox of computer disks, and finds something better.

Eight brass rollers are affixed to the tube's underside, where the octave key is on clarinets; thumbing them and also pumping two attached foot pedals, Brecker blows a steady airstream with no more effort than two straws need to bubble soda. Out of the EWI comes a dark burble that boils up into a piping cry. At the same time he has triggered an orchestra-dense background moving contrary to that piping line. How?

"Oh, I don't know," Brecker answers, puckishly. Of course, he *wants* to tell.

"The basic unit that Nile made is not programmable, but it consists of two oscillators and some gorgeously warm filters, which are manipulated manually. The Akai will be programmable, with a microprocessor, and will send out sixteen MIDI channels. I've got a

MIDI wind-driver that Nile adapted for the EWI. He found by taking the output of the sampler and feeding it back into the filters of the EWI, you could have a lot more control over sampled sounds, so it seems like the sounds are being *breathed*."

Understood? What it comes down to is sonic potentials—of timbre, say, or extreme registers, or dynamics, or use of "found sounds"—way beyond those available from any single instrument, although musicians *have* been known to suggest impossible things. And these sounds *are* all caused by the players' physical activity. Could electronically extended gear offer a musician *too* many choices? Brecker shrugs and sighs. "It's up to players to find their own way. This may not be everyone's way.

"After playing the EWI for a time I have almost a craving to play an acoustic instrument, and vibrate air myself, creating a sound that's maybe more in nature," he says. "I love the EWI because it's capable of so much, and I probably wouldn't enjoy it if it wasn't as expressive as it is, but it's also freed me up on the tenor, because, quite honestly, I'd been feeling trapped. I've been playing more tenor since I got this than I had been; I practice it every day again. I'm not happy playing just one or the other. I've gotten used to playing both."

On "Itsbynne Reel," opening *Don't Try This at Home*, Brecker uses the EWI to produce a double-reediness like bagpipes that twines with bluegrass star Mark O'Connor's fiddle, then veers off to quote Eddie Harris's "Freedom Jazz Dance." After a rhythmic switch, Brecker's extended EWI statement gains the thickened keyboard-like timbres Joe Zawinul popularized while in Weather Report—a sound that's a time marker till Brecker grabs his tenor sax and unfurls a melodic line that starts in a steely tone and pulls up with a wrenching human cry.

Trombone for the Cyber Age

Robin Eubanks wanted to be the next known trombonist. Jazz has had a few, including Kid Ory, Jack Teagarden, Tommy Dorsey, Glenn Miller, J. J. Johnson, and Bill Watrous.

While in his early thirties during the late '80s, Eubanks's debut record *Different Perspectives* from JMT, a German label with uneven U.S. distribution, attained high chart positions in *Billboard, Radio and Records,* the *Gavin Report,* and *Cashbox.* All instrumental but varied with mellow commercial funk, swinging standards, and two hard-edged, odd-metered compositions, the album followed on Eubanks's stint as music director of Art Blakey's Jazz Messengers, coincided with his frontline role in bassman Dave Holland's quintet, and underscored his association with alto saxophonist Steve Coleman. Eubanks was among the crew of composer-performers in Coleman's loosely conceived M-BASE association.

In an interview for radio that I conducted Eubanks flashed a boyish grin, and not one pretense about his talent or doubts about the course of his career. His confidence was based in part on family background and experience: His brother Kevin was the guitarist leading the *Tonight Show* band after years of his own albums on Blue Note, GRP, and Elektra Records; their mother was a piano teacher; their uncle is pianist Ray Bryant. Robin's résumé boasts a modernist's session schedule of work: dates with the Talking Heads and Patti LaBelle, stints in Broadway pit bands and ensembles run by Sun Ra, McCoy Tyner, and Abdullah Ibrahim.

Comfortably commanding on his signature instrument, a Bach 42B 'bone with a large bore and low note trigger, Eubanks also played keyboards and MIDI percussion on *Different Perspectives,* which he recorded in June 1988. Given his adaptability, appreciation of polished production, and breadth of tastes—Eubanks followed Led Zeppelin, the Mahavishnu Orchestra, and Motown in his teen years—why a 'bone?

"It happened back in '64, when I was in fourth grade," Robin recalled. "These guys came to my class playing Christmas carols. On the trumpet I could see all the fingerings, on drums I saw all the players' actions, but on trombone I could see only an arm moving back and forth. It was really mysterious, and my curiosity got the better of me."

During his after-school lessons, Eubanks learned to love the trombone's lower frequencies, its close ties to the overtone series, its overall distinctive sound. "It's not the kind of right-out-front sound trumpets have, and not the very focused sound of saxes either," he said. "I hear the trombone as the most expressive of all the wind instruments. Like a string instrument, it gets the microtones between the half steps. It has a dark, very robust sound—kind of like Paul Robeson—and the capability to be piercing in the upper register. You can play it really soft, or loud. It combines the best of everything.

"It's a medium for me to get out my ideas. Ideas I can't express in words, I can express tonally, and the trombone is the instrument with which I can do that."

Among the recordings of Eubanks expressing himself are Blakey's *Not Yet* (Soul Note), Holland's *The Razor's Edge* (ECM), Coleman's *World Expansion* (JMT), and Marvin "Smitty" Smith's *Keeper of the Drums* (Concord), but his own album demonstrated that, besides a blowing sound, Eubanks had developed a personal style of using computer and MIDI technology to advantage. Electronic music, he said, never scared him—nor has electronic gear.

"I was always into energetic, high-powered fusionesque stuff. I don't process my trombone now much, but in the mid-'70s I used a Crybaby wahwah and a phase shifter to emulate sounds I heard in funk and fusion. I've got a Canadian Pitchrider 4000, a pitch-to-MIDI converter so the trombone can go through any module and will end up as digital information. I have a Mirage sampler, a Casio CZ 1000 keyboard, all the drums I need with a Korg DDD1 drum machine and an Alesis drum machine. I trigger the drum machines with a DW 5000 trigger pedal and Roland Octapads so I can play it like a drum kit. My drum technique is functional, but I have a lot of respect for percussionists, so I called what I did on *Different Perspectives* 'MIDI percussion.'"

Eubanks continued: "I run DKT KCS software through my Atari ST 1040 computer. I usually split my keyboard into an acoustic bass in the left hand and a keyboard in the right, then I sequence everything to the computer—lay it down, overdub melodies, and save to disc. I write arrangements that way; since it's all in the computer, I can hear everything at once, edit it, and *know* what will work instead of just *hoping* it will sound right when we play it.

"It's also faster to compose on the computer. Before, I used to have scraps of paper all around with ideas that I'd sing into a tape recorder. Now I may get an idea that's only eight notes but I'll store it, and then a month later I'll get another idea that connects to something I saved. I *like* the computer. The more I use it, the easier it gets."

He believed computer facility helped him craft his first album for three different slices of the jazz market while retaining idiomatic authenticity and expressing a personal style. "Traveling as a sideman in different bands, I was in a position to gather information all the time," he said, "so I approached my project from an international marketing perspective. Japanese jazz audiences are traditional and prefer straight-ahead stuff, so I put the ballad 'You Don't Know What Love Is' and my trombone choir version of 'Walk-in" on *Different Perspectives* for them. Europe seems wide open to anything, so

'Taicho,' with the Octapads producing wood-block and timbales sounds, and the title cut were set for that market. The United States is, I think, the most commercial of all the countries I've been dealing with, so I put Stevie Wonder's 'Overjoyed' and mellow tunes like 'The Night Before' and 'Midtown Funk' on for the U.S. market. I hoped to get around criticism that the album's too diverse by making the funk tunes the funkiest you ever heard, the straight-ahead stuff sound like you just dropped the needle on some '60s Blue Note record, and keeping the music on a level of excellence so it's not like I'm dabbling in something I don't know anything about."

Eubanks's plan worked well: He's further displayed his breadth on subsequent albums—such as a two-trombone project with his friend Steve Turré. Besides being a gifted trombonist, Turré is a Mingus and Latin music expert, past leader of the *Saturday Night Live* television-show band, ringer in the Lincoln Center, Carnegie Hall, and the Dizzy Gillespie—founded United Nation jazz orchestras, and a specialist in mining the purely acoustic musical properties of conch shells.

Broad Shoulders, Tender Heart, Open Ears

Saxophonist Joe Lovano has a sound. It's a broad-shouldered, hairy-chested, tender-hearted sound, able to bear responsibilities in big bands as well as in trios, in long-term collaborations as well as in spontaneously convened ensembles. It's a sound equally applicable to companionably interactive play and true passion without forced intensity. Lovano's sound on tenor sax especially, but on alto and soprano saxes, flute, gongs and drums, and the clarinet family, too, has gradually become a keynote of the '90s.

Joe now seems to be heard everywhere: in John Scofield's quartet, in Paul Motian's trio, in Charlie Haden's Liberation Music Orchestra, the Village Vanguard Monday Night Band and the Smithsonian Institution's Jazz Masterworks Orchestra, with Dave Holland and Billy Higgins at a memorial service for revered drummer Ed Blackwell, and on such of his own ambitious Blue Note albums as *Celebrating Sinatra* (reinterpreting Ol' Blues Eyes' repertoire sans kitsch) and *Rush Hour* (with handpicked chamber orchestra soloists performing newly commissioned Gunther Schuller compositions). Joe has recorded distinctive work with regular members of his core group *(Universal Language)*, sets that feature his blowing *(Quartets: Live from the Village Vanguard, From the Soul*, and *Landmarks)*, or his collaborative abilities (*Flying Colors*, with Cuban pianist Gonzalo Rubalcaba, *Tenor Legacy* with fellow tenor saxophonist Joshua Redman). Lovano's sound is the sound of compassion, of fully earned accomplishment, and dependable professionalism. No wonder in the bottom-line decade Joe Lovano is the man.

"I'm just trying to play, to find myself, and get next to my sound," Lovano says, earnest and soft-spoken about the mission he's taken for life. Thoughtful, modest, in the early '90s having just turned forty, Lovano has jazz in his blood. His father, Tony "Big T" Lovano, was a tenorist (with whom Joe recorded the satisfying *Hometown Sessions* in 1986, not quite a year before he died), a central figure in the organ combos and progressive bop sessions of the Cleveland scene. Joe's uncle played horn, too, and his brother Anthony is a drummer. Music is a legacy from their Sicilian family, but jazz—*modern* jazz—is the special love of its American generations. Furthermore, Joe's wife Judi Silvano is an engaging jazz soprano with precision diction; on *Universal Language, Rush Hour,* and *Celebrating Sinatra,* her wordless lines wrap around Joe's themes and discursions like silk scarves on a Maypole.

Joe worked at jazz in his teen years, studied at Berklee College of Music, and since arriving in New York in the mid-'70s has applied himself nonstop to the real seat of jazz traditions—bands led by organists Lonnie Smith and Jack McDuff, herdsman Woody Herman, and the Mel Lewis Jazz Orchestra, for starters. He naturally moves into musical situations that are genuine and substantial, taking him closer to the answer of his big question: "Who is Joe Lovano?" Music frames his investigation.

"I've primarily focused on tenor as my main voice since I was twelve years old, but I started on alto when I was a kid," he says. "Playing with Blackwell during the last few years of his life really brought that back to me."

Drums and drummers are also vital to him—as they are to any jazz player, but so much so that Lovano practices on traps he keeps set up in his Manhattan loft (which has been a gathering spot and jam session scene for myriad jazzers of his acquaintance). He counts among his "most important associates" Detroit-Cleveland rhythmist Lawrence "Jacktown" Jackson and drummer Bill Stewart, whom Lovano met while serving simultaneously on the faculties of New Jersey's William Patterson College and New York University in the '80s. He reserves his greatest praise for Blackwell, best known for drumming with Ornette Coleman's circle of improvisers. Blackwell also recorded with John Coltrane, Eric Dolphy, David Murray, and Archie Shepp, and throughout *From the Soul* profoundly underscores Lovano besides attending to Holland and pianist Michel Petrucciani, two musicians he'd never previously met.

"He was a treasure in music, and an inspiration to me," Joe lauds. "Musicians like Blackwell, who are completely original and have forty years of recorded music in their lives, get me deep into who I am.

"I've played in a lot of bands, and I always try to find something new with the people who are right there at that moment. That's what keeps music fresh for me," he says. "Playing with people who are their own players, like Blackwell, taught me how to find myself. I've been with Paul Motian since 1981, and joined the Mel Lewis band in '80. Being with both those drummers for ten years has been fantastic. It's grounded me in an awareness of interplay, of being creative with the *other* people, rather than just playing my horn.

"To be an honest musician, you play from your history. As your experiences grow, the music comes out. All my favorite players developed like that. Of course, we play from the history of the music around us, too. But *your* history, what *you* experience, is what really comes out if you can get deep inside yourself, the music, and the personalities of the people you play with, and don't just treat your instrument like a technical thing."

Nobody's likely to accuse Lovano of being a tech-head. His mastery of his horns and reeds, the perfection of his intonation and articulation, the fluency of his fingerings and phrases is unquestionable, but so is his commitment to playing feelings rather than licks or chops. The point is that Joe's experiences give him new ideas about expressing those feelings, rather than simply refining his cold skills. Even his years in big bands emerge in personal ways, as became evident with the advent of *Universal Language*.

"Doing stuff with Carla Bley—I toured with her in 1983 for a year—and Charlie Haden's band, which I joined in '87, and with Bob Brookmeyer in Mel's band, has helped my ensemble writing to come out a little more," Lovano explains. "*Universal Language* features a little larger ensemble with Judi's soprano voice, trumpet by Tim Hagans, Kenny Werner on piano, Jack DeJohnette on drums, Charlie Haden and Steve Swallow on some pieces together, and Scott Lee playing bass, too. It has directions and influences from all the periods of my musical growth.

"Charlie's band and Carla's band were really fun because they were looser, more open. You not only had to play your part as written but there are places in the music to create your *own* part. Those are concepts I'm putting into my music.

"The whole idea of playing in ensembles and blending with other horns is the most important thing of working in big bands, I think. A lot of the great players from the history of jazz had that one thread in common, that they all played in bigger groups with five and six saxophone players. They were all in each other's faces. They didn't want to sound like each other, you know, and they'd say, 'Oh, yeah, you thought *that* was bad? Check *this* out!' They had that attitude, and that's how I grew up, playing with my dad, playing with Woody's band and the Mel Lewis band.

"I think young players who don't have that experience miss something in their playing. They just stand there and play by themselves, they don't play with a sense of ensemble. I want to have that ensembleness in my playing even when I'm playing a duet with somebody," Lovano emphasizes. "In my solo projects, when I accompany myself on percussion as I'm playing tenor, there's some of that too. I'm playing with an ensemble attitude even when I play alone. That definitely comes from playing in big bands."

Solo projects where he accompanies himself on percussion— gongs and rattles et al.—while playing tenor? Oh, yes, some of *Universal Language* is like that. As a Midwesterner growing up with a tenor saxist for a dad in the '60s, Lovano was privy to Sonny Stitt, Eddie "Lockjaw" Davis, Harold Vick in Shirley Scott's band, Dizzy Gillespie with James Moody, and records of classic horn men like Lester Young, but there were also more experimental ideas in the air.

"I heard some of the solo records of Roscoe Mitchell and Joseph Jarman that I really dug," he says of the Art Ensemble of Chicago's reedmen, "and solo works of Anthony Braxton—they were improvisers, they were *playing*. Albert Ayler"—radically free-spirited tenor saxist of the '60s—"was from Cleveland too, and he had a lot of followers. So I was around some of those pioneers of free jazz as a kid, attending some of their concerts.

"I never heard Albert himself, but I grew up on the music of Coltrane's bands, Miles's bands, and Ornette's bands, and the players who played with them through all their different periods," he elaborates. "The way Billy Higgins and Scott LaFaro and Charlie Haden played, and Philly Joe Jones and Max Roach's band with Clifford Jordan, and Art Blakey's bands—they're all part of my history. You might say you hear something in my playing with Scofield that comes out of Ornette, but remember: All those bands were digging and influencing each other, too.

"That was a beautiful period for creative music, given the interplay among all the players in those different groups. All the things Sonny Rollins did, Wayne Shorter, Dewey Redman, Don Cherry, Freddie Hubbard, Bobby Hutcherson, Eric Dolphy—every record seemed to have *personality* in it. Jazz is a very social music, it's a lot about your contemporaries and how everybody feeds off each other. I know Coltrane played how he did because of how Sonny was playing down the street. I really try to feel that now. Here Jackie McLean is, playing at the Vanguard, while I'm with Scofield at Sweet Basil. That means something to me that's going to be in my attitude all week.

"And the Brecker Brothers at the Blue Note—it's a different kind of music, but the energy is there. Their band is really arranged. They get into different aspects of interplay within the solo spaces, though it's not as open a concept as what we're playing with John. Still, Mike's created a voice for a generation of musicians. I've always dug his playing. He's a good friend of mine. And it means something to me that he and Randy are playing during the same week I am.

"See, I want to play some *modern* jazz. I feel that's the music from the period that's really inspiring to me. And I mean *today's* modern. It's got to do with the way I play and the way people around me improvise together, but it's a growth from what modern jazz *was,* and modern jazz from the '60s to me was a growth from the history of jazz to *that* point. It didn't stop there. I think it still can carry through.

"I want to play in bands that project *tomorrow* but *are* today, *really* today. I'd say the Motian trio plays some modern jazz. Bill Frisell is a complete improviser, one of the most creative players today. The trio has developed the most incredible repertoire of music, standard tunes, and a lot of Monk, Paul's compositions and some of Bill's and my own. Paul plays with a complete sense of adventure amd exploration, letting every sound and everything around him come through his playing into the music. That's what improvising is, for me. It's listening and reacting.

"One thing I want to put together in my playing is the collective inspiration from the history of jazz up until today. So I'm not just playing a style of bebop or fusion or hard bop, or re-creating a period of swing—but instead incorporating what swing means to me. How bebop comes through *my* language, how the Modern Jazz

Quartet's classical approach and really hard swinging blues come through *my* playing.

"When you're young, you focus on some things you like," he knows. "That's how you play, that's the world you try to live in. But as you grow as a player, you start to combine all the different attitudes, if you're open to that. I want to grow and change and develop my ideas with everything that inspires me.

"I've always been cross-generational, but I'm speaking of international influences too. This last year I've played in Chile, I've been in Europe a bunch of times, played all over Japan and Hong Kong. The different flavors of the countries and their people—if you let all that influence you, your music can go anywhere. That's what Duke Ellington did, and look at all the beautiful music he gave us. To respect different cultures and let all peoples into your life to influence you is a rich thing—it filters in through *my* music, for sure. I don't ever want to lose that. That's why I love living in New York City."

It's not for everyone, nor can every good player immerse himself or herself in *every* aspect of performance and presentation, as Lovano has. Partially funded by National Endowment for the Arts jazz grants, he's staged two "these are my influences/this is my music" concerts, parleying the one in Cleveland into an evening presented by the annual Tri-C Jazz Festival and eventually broadcast over National Public Radio.

"As a musician, you have to create your own gigs," Lovano believes. "Musicians and artists have to be really involved in what they're doing. Then it will mean something. And I think if you are involved in the whole presentation of what you're doing, rather than waiting for the phone to ring, you're going to be able to do more things you wanted to do.

"Chick Corea's done that. Jack DeJohnette's like that, too. The deeper you're involved, the deeper you're going to play. It inspires me, especially when I get things planned and then see them running smoothly." He laughs.

"Personally, I want to try to get deep inside myself through music. That's it. It's a deep love my father had and gave to me. He did warn me of the pitfalls. He was a barber as well as a musician. His situation was always changing: He'd be playing around town five nights, two nights, three nights. I saw firsthand that the money was always light, that you had to deal with all these sad cats, club owners or whoever...But somehow, he'd always take his horn out to play down in the basement and all that other stuff would go away.

"And for me, that's what I wanted to do. I'd hear my dad practice when I was a kid, and all I wanted to do was create that sound myself.

"It's a hard life out here. You have to be strong, you have to be organized, you've got to be on top of a lot of stuff. But I think the musicians who are really involved in their careers and the directions they go in are going to be able to live a life in music."

For Lovano, "a life in music" is better than a worthy pursuit. It's a dream he lives.

The Radical Professor

Pianist Anthony Davis, in spring 1996 awaiting the end of the semester at Harvard University where he lectures on "Jazz since 1960: Freedom and Form" and conducts a seminar on "Composing for Improvisers," concedes that teaching does cut into his performing and composing time. "But then ideas build up and I get eager to write," enthuses Davis, who has composed the operas *X—The Life and Times of Malcolm X, Tanya,* and *Under the Double Moon,* as well as scores for the Pulitzer Prize-winning two-part drama *Angels in America: Perestroika* and *The Millennium Approaches.*

When we spoke Davis was taking a brief break from pouring his energies into an opera based on the Amistad slave ship uprising, commissioned by Chicago's Lyric Opera Company, due to be premiered in November 1997—but he was most of all relishing spontaneous jams in class with guest lecturers soprano saxophonist Steve Lacy and clarinetist Don Byron, his too-infrequent duet gigs with James Newton, appearances with drummer Bobby Previte's band and concerts with his quintet comprising singer Cynthia Aaronson Davis (his wife), violinist Mark Feldman, bassist Mark Dresser, and drummer Gerry Hemingway.

"I haven't worked in a club in a while," laments Davis, with not too much woe. He came up in New Haven's lively mid-'70s scene, then cut albums of unconventional improvisation on the India Navigation and Gramavision labels. "You know what I miss?" Davis asks, and answers without a pause, "The three sets a night. They say it's exploitative, but after a one-set concert I've just warmed up."

What troubles Davis most, really, is not his graduation from playing clubs—he's kept his edge sharp, anyway, thanks—but the disappearance of his recordings from store shelves. Since Gramavision was sold to Rykodisc, even *X,* recorded by his fourteen-piece improvising ensemble Episteme, the Orchestra of St. Luke's, and original cast members in 1989 but not released in its elaborate two-CD box set until '92, has become hard to find.

"It's frustrating." But Davis shakes the frustration off and hastens to add, "I haven't pushed my quintet, but now we've got a body of music to put out, so I'll be shopping it."

Looks, Deceiving

Davis maintained a modest lifestyle, sharing a sparsely furnished apartment that looks down Forty-second Street to the Hudson River from a tower of the artists' cooperative Manhattan Plaza with soprano Aaronson and their two cats. Fresh-faced, in his early forties, still bushy-haired (though his once-outrageous Afro had been trimmed), and ready to chuckle at a memory, an audacity, or a favorable score for his favorite basketball team, Davis seemed more like a man of comfortable accomplishment than a provocateur of music theater.

But that's what he's been at least since the mid-'80s and the final development of *X*, a full-scale, three-act dramatic opera about the challenging black man whose factual, symbolic, and philosophic significance still sparks impassioned debate among politically aware youth and august intellects. *X* was Davis's first such grandiose effort, though he'd been working up to it for a while.

Its uncompromising story was developed by Anthony's brother Christopher; the powerful, plainspoken libretto written by their cousin, poet, novelist, and journalist Thulani Davis (wife of the Art Ensemble of Chicago's Joseph Jarman). With support from a host of public and private foundations, cooperation from the Shabazz family who survived Malcolm X (known just prior to his assassination as El Hajj Malik El-Shabazz), the consultation of experienced dramaturge Rhoda Levine, the services of the New York City Opera under conductor Christopher Keene, a superb cast—and the gratifyingly effective enfolding at the very core of the score of deep improvisations by Davis's long-standing ensemble Episteme—the work was quite stunning upon its world premiere at Lincoln Center in autumn 1986. Be it noted: This was one year after the Gershwins' American classic *Porgy and Bess* was finally presented by the Metropolitan Opera of Lincoln Center! The Davises' daring new *X* posed the possibility of similarly grand reach, toward an opera—and opera audience—of today.

Spike Lee's unrelated, big-budget Hollywood film *X* brought even more attention to Davis's subject, and just as the movie opened in the United States, Gramavision released the opera as a recording. Anthony hadn't just been waiting for that to happen, as he explained over tea at his kitchen table.

"I've been teaching a history of jazz class and an Afro-American composers' seminar covering both classical and jazz composers—William Grant Still, Ellington, Jelly Roll Morton, a bit of Joplin—at Harvard. But *X* is still very present for me. I've looked at the work again and had opportunities to do concerts of portions of it. It's alive, and it's really fun to see people be interested in something I did several years ago. I'm still proud of my accomplishment: it was a milestone for me. And I'm very optimistic I'll be able to do the opera in Europe and Japan as well as in America again. Then I'll have a fresh look at how we might stage it.

"This was my first piece, so it was about learning how to do an opera—dealing with issues of structure, the role, for example, of instrumental music in transitions. Rhoda Levine was fantastic helping me with that, and became part of the creative team that began with Chris and Thulani. But I think the movie liberates us. When we did *X* in 1985, there was so much information we had to give people in a way that in opera is very difficult to do. I remember my producer in Philadelphia asking questions—'The Fruit of Islam, what's that?'—because he didn't have a frame of reference. Now people know so much more about Malcolm X that we might be able to do a much more expressionistic version. Which would be very interesting because I think the music takes you in that direction itself.

"In the recording we went for musical expression, primarily. We had to make decisions about how much to include things that are there for the choreography and staging and such, which I'd let the music cover. We had to edit some music out to fit the opera on two CDs, too. The overture was originally much longer—I shortened it by starting with the very end, which brings you headlong into the opera—*Bang!* I thought that would be effective because one purpose of the overture was to underscore this Brechtian idea of showing the cast and giving a miniplay as they become their characters. But there's a lot of thematic material in that overture. When I do it again, I'll do a version between the two lengths.

"Also, when we were at City Opera we felt we didn't give enough information about the vision of Malcolm—or El Hajj Malik El-Shabazz—after his visit to Mecca. For purposes of the drama, after his visit to Mecca you want to go very quickly to his assassination. If we do it again, I might set some of his later vision to music.

"In the movie Spike never used his name El Hajj Malik, which I thought was a curious decision because if you're going to talk about his metamorphosis, that's its culmination, and it's just as symbolic as 'X.' But *that* was a dramatic decision. People have to understand the difference between drama and real life. Sometimes you make artistic decisions to streamline something as an interpretation or for purposes of dramatic structure.

"But one thing that's fun with opera is that you're so detached from real life to begin with—the form itself is so absurd"—Davis flashes one of his characteristic sly smiles—"that it gives you freedom. We were dealing with Malcolm X, but it didn't matter if it sounded like him or looked like him, because just the conceit that everything is sung *already* demands a leap of faith. There's always the problem, dealing with figures in contemporary life, of competing with people's opinions or what they know. I think we always have to see that it's an artist's interpretation, and ask how well the interpretation works."

On CD, the so-called jazz elements performed by Episteme blend more smoothly with the through-composed orchestral sections than in the stage production.

"I was pleased with the recording because my intention was that the music be more seamless, that you'd get to this place and say, 'Wow, I go *there!*' Also it was recorded in a way that helped achieve that effect. It would have been easy to record this as a jazz record—put the drums in a booth, and so on. But I thought it was important to hear it as one esthetic working through different styles or idioms.

"I taught a course in American opera at Yale a couple years ago; I do these courses so I learn about stuff. I'd never listened to Samuel Barber's opera or even Menotti's before this course. I learned about things done earlier, before *Porgy and Bess*. People don't know that William Grant Still wrote six operas, that James P. Johnson wanted to write one, or that Duke Ellington planned two operas. Or that there were black composers who helped Gershwin in his research of *Porgy*.

"In part, the black composers then wanted to prove themselves equal to the form—but, also, they were all involved with theater. Ellington did several shows, revues for the most part. He always had ideas of doing Broadway shows too. He saw opera as a way of telling the story of jazz, its development, perhaps; he had ideas of what opera *should* be. 'Black, Brown and Beige' was originally supposed to be an opera. The thought of turning opera into an African-American form was on the mind of a lot of composers. It's natural to me they'd look at it as a possible creative outlet."

Naturally, as a child Davis was aware of, if not versed in, opera.

"My grandfather was a big fan; he liked only opera and gospel music, nothing in between. I wasn't *really* exposed to opera until I was in college. I knew Weill's *Threepenny Opera* as a kid, and I'd heard musicals—I had a record I liked of *Stop the World I Want to Get Off*.

"I'd get parts to sing in musicals in prep school, but my brother Chris was much more into that than I was. When he first had the idea about doing a piece on Malcolm he used the term 'musical,' because he's a theater person. I was the one who thought of opera.

"I got into opera by studying philosophy. When I was at Yale, and even before, I was a Nietzsche nut. I read *The Birth of Tragedy* when I was in high school. Nietzsche's idea of combining the Apollonian and the Dionysian—here he was trying to define Wagner and German music, and I thought, 'Oh, that's like jazz, that's great!' I had the idea *then* that one could forge a new kind of music, a new opera, based on American traditions. I kept it in the back of my mind as something to explore.

"But basically I was into jazz. In college and after I was consumed with learning bebop. I was in the house band at the Midtown Motor Inn in New Haven; they used to bring in [saxophonists] Jimmy Heath and Phil Woods, so that was part of my education. And I was beginning to play with musicians my age—[trombonist] George Lewis, Mark Helias, Gerry Hemingway, [drummer] Pherroan ak Laff. Pherroan and I played with [AACM trumpeter] Leo Smith, who was living in New Haven, and [saxophonist/painter] Marion Brown. Mark Dresser, who knows [trombonist] Ray Anderson, and the Rozie brothers, [saxophonist] Rick and [electric bassist] Lee, and [vibraphonist] Jay Hoggard—they were all there. Ed Blackwell was real important; he was at Wesleyan University in Connecticut. I played in a trio with Helias and Blackwell, then in quartet with them and Hoggard. We recorded for India Navigation.

"I was always interested in telling stories with music, too, so I began writing suites based on science fiction novels back then. When I moved to New York City in the late '70s and started working at the Public Theater, I did some music for theatrical productions with David Murray and Michael Gregory Jackson for Ntozake Shange— 'Where the Mississippi Meets the Amazon' was one—and with

Baikida Carroll too. I also did music as background for some of Thulani's poems, which gave me the idea of setting her words for X.

"Thulani's poems were always very bluesy. The language of Ntozake and Thulani and Jessica Hagedorn was very connected to jazz—they were all interested in the music. And so many bands were playing at the Public—David [Murray] and James Newton and George Lewis, we were all in each other's bands. It was a fun period that I don't think has been that much talked about.

"My early suites stand by themselves, but a lot of my later work turned out to be studies for opera. The piano piece 'Middle Passage,' 'Hemispheres' with Episteme [commissioned by dancer-choreographer Molissa Fenley], and 'Walk through The Shadow' were definitely studies for X; they were incorporated into it. I'd keep working the same piece over, developing new ideas to extend it rather than writing new pieces all the time. Musicians would make fun of me: 'Why you keep playin' the same piece?' I'd say, 'Well, I'm not done with it yet.'

" 'The Wayangs, Number Four and Number Two' became parts of my second opera, *Under the Double Moon*. I don't know where *Tanya,* my third opera, came from. Maybe it returns me to my jazz roots. I worked with a tight ten-piece band on it, and it's sort of my tribute to Charles Mingus.

"He was one of my ideals as a composer when I was growing up. I was always intrigued by his sense of harmony, rhythm, the tempo changes, the abrupt turns—and his sense of structure was incredible. He was so gritty too. *That* really interested me."

Once Davis made the shift to opera, did he miss playing, improvising?

"I do miss it, yeah, and I'm starting to do it again. I'm touring Europe with James Newton and [cellist] Abdul Wadud in March; I hope we'll record over there. I did a club date at the New Music Café with Mark Dresser, Gerry Hemingway, and Mark Feldman, and we're going to tour with Cindy—Cynthia—singing next October. I haven't had much time to play because of the writing and teaching schedule I've had, but now I've got some time, so we'll do it."

Are composing and improvising like one for him?

"I think so; improvising is how I get to compose. It helps me. Composing helps me improvise, too. They're two parts of the same thing. I don't like to play in my operas, though, because I need to see the whole thing. [Marilyn Crispell and Clyde Criner play piano on the CD of X.] "For *Tanya* the theater was too small to have a pit, so the band was behind a wall, the conductor was on a video monitor in front of the band, and the music was amplified, projected. I wouldn't have seen my piece at all if I'd been playing.

"When I write, I think up some of the players I work with: This is for J. D. Parran, this is for John Purcell, and this is for Marty Ehrlich [all reedmen]. Casting the band is as important to me as casting the roles—it's the same sort of personality thing. This gets to be a struggle; whatever opera company I'm working with has to accept that I want outside musicians. It's more expensive. That's one of the problems with getting X done again. I need ten improvisers, and that's daunting for some companies.

"If it makes it a little more difficult to do my work, it's also partly what makes my work unique. Classical music has tried to make the language so limited that the parts are all interchangeable. Financially that's sensible, but I don't think it's interesting musically. And dealing with the individuality of the performer, the player—that's part of the esthetic I'm bringing, which comes from jazz.

"They're not even used to the composer telling them what singers he wants, but when I go into an audition I say, 'I want to hear them do *this*.' For me, a singer's experience with jazz is very important. During *Tanya* this mezzo said, 'How do you want this part phrased?' I'd written very specific rhythms. I said, 'Well, really, it's out of Billie Holiday. She taught me more about writing for the voice than anyone else, and that's what I'm trying to do!'

"This mezzo knew the reference. The performers are way ahead of the institutions. I did X in concert with the Chicago Symphony last November—the whole first act; act 2, scene 1, and 'We Are a Nation.' I got them to hire some AACM players as improvisers, but several of the symphony's players also came up to me and said, 'Oh, we're very excited about having a chance to improvise.'"

Cynthia Aaronson was within earshot; her husband mentioned that she sang the Patty Hearst role in *Tanya* (as staged by the American Music Theater Festival, an annual event in Philadelphia), and, when they perform together, "Some Springs," Anthony's settings of some of his cousin Thulani's poems.

"I'm classically trained as an opera singer." Cynthia spoke for herself. "Anthony's music is a stretch when I have to sing over something that's improvised. The counting, the rhythm is much more developed than anything else I've done. I *wish* I improvised; I just panic, getting ready to do it. But J. D. Parran's writing a piece with improvisation for our autumn tour, and I'll try.

"I'm listening a lot. My mother listened to Ella Fitzgerald when I was young, so it's in there somewhere. But if you don't grow up doing it, you think everything you do is going to be stupid." She appeared to shiver slightly. "I know it's part of what Tony wants, for classical musicians to be trained to stretch out and improvise."

"I think the orchestra should learn to improvise, too," Anthony insisted. "My idea of education would be: You go to Manhattan School of Music, you study opera, and you study Billie Holiday, just to get the rhythmic thing and that concept of phrasing in your voice. It's so sad education can't bring in the whole American experience."

Is that what he's trying to bring into opera?

"Well, *Tanya* is sort of a weird take on our popular culture. Beginning with a Mingus-esque ballad overture, it's very eclectic. In one of Tanya's dreams, she imagines her father is Fidel Castro and her mother is Betty Ford—they're having an affair—and Fidel's aria is almost a Tito Puente salsa piece. I had a great time writing it. The character Cinque is this bass-baritone, I made him really sexy. I did a Brook Benton takeoff in it, [singing], 'And the funk goes this way/ And the funk goes that…You've got to sift through the ashes/And feel the heat.' I had all these freaked-out Symbionese Liberation Army people in it. I just tried to shock, every minute—*Boom! Whoa!*—moving from thing to thing.

"The idea was to divide the stage into two worlds, the closet world and the so-called real world, and you don't know which is which, as Patty/Tanya goes back and forth through the closet. The idea was that everyone has a Tanya in their closet, some other self. It's more in the form of a music-theater work than an opera because of the playfulness and the jazziness of it, but it's operatic in that it's through-composed and sung all the way through too. It has some really funny things, like an aria I wrote for Cindy—'Who will play me in the movie of the book of my life?' —that's like a parody of Peggy Lee."

Cindy said, "He's got grooves in that aren't 4/4."

"That's in 11/4," Anthony stated. "One of my tricks is to write accompaniment in one meter, and the vocal lines in straight 4/4. It sounds weird because of how things are turning around. But I think people would really be interested in *Tanya,* and that it would work as a recording too. It's frustrating that things take so long to get through the stages from composition to theater production to record distribution because I find my works influence other works, and then people haven't heard what I did before they were done. It would be great if *Tanya* were recorded.

"The language is part of the problem," he explains, "because the libretto by Michael John Laquise has a lot of profanity in it. It belongs there because that was part of the SLA at the time." With great glee, the composer delved directly into the libretto's profanity.

"See, Tanya as Patty goes out to lunch with a friend, and her friend is teasing her, saying, 'You sure like to eat, but your legs are so skinny.'" Then all of a sudden Patty turns on a dime, she gets really angry, she becomes the SLA person. She sings, 'You're a fucking piece of dogshit/You're a fucking fascist piece of dogshit/Did a poodle/shit you out its fucking asshole?'

"The music I wrote to set that was really fast, in waltz time, so it's really goofy. And in her culminating aria, where she accepts herself as Tanya, she sings, 'Blow the motherfuckers/Away!' And underneath it I put this almost Miles Davis groove. You feel the sense of the groove with the sense of the drama too. That was a lot of fun."

Anthony *is* rather subversive, you see.

"Yeah, to me that's what's fun. Jazz has always been subversive. When I read about Charlie Parker and Dizzy and Miles, they had that subversive quality, too. That's part of it. The irony, using the music as subtext that doesn't necessarily play with what you think is happening."

As though Miles had charged into his Juilliard classes after he'd spent the night playing with Bird—Davis wants to infect the music schools with some revolutionary, arguably dangerous, elements.

"It has to be done," Anthony Davis says with a nonthreatening smile. "The difference between what we do and the Third Stream [proposed by composer Gunther Schuller] is that we're not trying to change jazz by taking it into this other arena; we're taking what was classical music in America, which was fundamentally European-based, and making it a truly American form. That's a much more subversive idea to me."

No Generation Gap

Geri Allen and Hank Jones are both elegant pianists, sharing the deftness, flexibility, and devotion to the cultivation of musical skills found in jazz's greatest exemplars. There's some forty years' difference in their ages, but that pales next to their shared interests in composition, improvisation, leading combos, serving as accompanists. Not so incidentally, they're both from Michigan. Because she's so aware of her roots, Geri Allen was shy almost to the point of being flustered by sitting down as a peer with an honored elder.

But both of them are graced with humor and humility, high ambitions and quiet self-assurance; both are in essence creative and by preference busy. In September 1993, when at *Down Beat's* behest Ms. Allen met with Mr. Jones in midtown Manhattan's Steinway Hall, she'd lately returned from touring Europe with vocalist Betty Carter, Dave Holland, and Jack DeJohnette, had just released *Maroons* (Blue Note) featuring original small-group pieces, and composed a suite "Sister Leola, an American Portrait," commissioned by Jazz at Lincoln Center. Hank Jones was recording a series of albums produced by French Verve (most recently issued: *Handful of Keys: The Music of Fats Waller*) and starring at the choicest New York venues, releasing duets he'd recorded with jazz master Benny Carter (*Legends,* MusicMasters), and seeing his '40s-'50s work for Savoy Records widely reissued on CD for the first time.

As Allen and Jones sat together for a chat and photo shoot in one of several closed side rooms, beyond the doors but well within hearing a piano tuner worked steadily to tune up the showpieces in the main hall.

HM Was there any time during which you were both in Michigan?
HJ Oh, no. I joined Jazz at the Philharmonic on tour in '47, and I'd been in New York a couple of years by then. I'd left Pontiac in the early '40s and went on to Flint, Saginaw, Ann Arbor, Bay City, places like that, with what at the time were called territory bands, like Benny Carew's Orchestra.

Benny was a good drummer whose orchestra never left that Michigan-Ohio-Indiana area. Lucky Thompson, Wardell Gray, and other Detroit musicians worked in that band, playing arrangements similar to those of Basie, Ellington, and Jimmie Lunceford but in sort of a nondescript style. It was a little dance band, six or seven pieces, two tenor saxophones and a trumpet, or a tenor and trumpet, that kind of thing. You couldn't get too elaborate, but it was workable.

HM Geri, what in your background is comparable?
GA I came up learning under an organization called the Jazz Development Workshop, an organization that some Detroit musicians, including Marcus Belgrave, Bernard McKinney, and

Roy Brooks, put together. [Alto saxophonist] Kenny Garrett and [Wynton Marsalis-associated bassist] Bob Hurst came up in that band too. We learned transposing there, got to hear Thad Jones's music and Ellington's—for me, for the first time as a player. At that time I was just crawling and trying to learn.

It was community-based and workshop-oriented. Marcus put bands together based on whatever was needed for our performances; we played in clubs and concerts, sometimes large concerts that would include a tap dancer or someone like that. So we experienced aspects of the tradition which I'm sure I wouldn't have had the opportunity to otherwise. But I don't think the scene at that point was as vibrant as when Mr. Jones was there. We weren't working all the time.

HJ Hank, please.

GA *(blushing)* Okay...

HJ Or Mr. Hank. *(Geri laughs)*

HM Hank, you performed at a New York City-sponsored Charlie Parker tribute last summer [1993]. Did Bird's music interest you on first hearing, in the late '40s?

HJ It certainly did. When I first came to New York I had never even heard of this kind of music. I was playing in a style reminiscent of Teddy Wilson's or Fats Waller's, a modified kind of stride. But when I got to New York the first thing I did was to go down to Fifty-second Street to see what was happening, and Charlie Parker and Dizzy Gillespie were down there with a group consisting of Max Roach, either Bud Powell or Al Haig on piano, and Curly Russell or Gene Ramey on bass. Dizzy and Charlie were playing all these unison lines—"Allen's Alley," "Moose the Mooche," "Hot House," all those things. The solo work was incredible, very, *very* fast, and without great facility, *dexterity* on your instrument, you couldn't play it properly—because they used every chord possible to play in any given line of chords, at way *way* up tempos. It was exciting, and I couldn't get enough of it. It definitely affected my style.

I couldn't do it immediately; it hadn't sunk in enough for me to think in that vein. I don't think anybody can pick it up quickly, but over the years I guess I absorbed some of it. A lot of the musicians I met in New York at the time didn't like the Parker-Gillespie style and rejected it out of hand, and some of them were pretty fair musicians. I don't know what their reasons were, I wouldn't ascribe any. But the ones who accepted it accepted it in good faith, and went ahead and tried to play the style.

Now there's no question about the validity of this style. You know that the style had validity, because it's still around and has withstood the test of time.

HM Did you adjust your piano technique to the style?

HJ You play less of a stride when you play bebop, although it's possible to play stride [a left-hand pattern] and bebop with the right hand. When George Shearing came to this country he was unique, using a stride left hand, bop right hand. Erroll Garner used 4/4 repeated chords in the left hand with his right-hand style, which is like bebop in some ways, but really impossible to describe.

But when you play bop, you almost 100 per cent abandon the left-hand stride approach. You can use it, though, for harmonic emphasis and for a balanced approach with a group. If you're playing solo—and Geri might want to comment on this; may I call you Geri?—

GA Oh, yes, *please.*

HJ —you might use a modified stride left hand to accompany a bop right hand. But from my perspective, it's better to use a very modified bebop style or no bebop style at all.

Of course, what you think and what you play may be two different things, but I think I take more of an Art Tatum approach, which is really not a bop approach, although I believe bop players incorporated some of the harmonic devices Art Tatum played. That would be my *attempted* approach, though by no means do I think my playing is on the level of Tatum's! Heaven forbid! Art Tatum would spin in his grave!

HM When Hank came to bebop, his heroes Tatum, Teddy Wilson, and Earl Hines were still active. Geri, when you arrived, were your predecessors so accessible? Or should I ask: Which pianists did you have under your fingers?

GA Mr. Jones—

HJ Hank—

GA Yes, sir. Mr. Hank Jones, for instance. Tommy Flanagan. Of course, I'd listened to Bud Powell, the bebop pianists, and Thelonious Monk. Regarding this, I have a question for Mr. Jones—

HJ Hank.

GA —Hank Jones, regarding his relationship with Mr. Monk and

Nat Cole. Where would you place yourself as their musical peer?

HJ I would *not* consider myself their peer. I consider myself a student of those players, who were, and are, some of the experts. I say "are" because I think a pianist's style never dies. I always think of Tatum as being present because his *style* lives. If you've created a style like that, it has a life of its own.

I've admired all the pianists you've mentioned, and I hear a lot of Nat Cole in quite a few pianists: Oscar Peterson, in particular, was influenced by him. I think at some point *most* pianists are. Maybe you don't even realize it, because it's such a natural style. But I think every pianist is influenced by whatever he's heard or has been exposed to. Learning is a process of absorption and sometimes rejection—a process of editing. You hear, you edit, you assimilate.

GA I never got to see the great pianists Mr. Jones is mentioning. Everything I continue to learn from Bud Powell or Art Tatum is from recordings and small portions of videotape. Fortunately, some documents allow you to see how they played, their techniques.

HM Are you, then, at a disadvantage?

GA I'm of a different generation, and I think the best I can do is study the tradition and the great pianists, try to live in the present tense in terms of my own environment and what I experienced growing up, and be honest about that. Because you can never duplicate someone else's greatness; you have to find your own way. I do believe that's part of what the tradition is about: finding your own way.

HM I'm struck by how different the New York scenes were when you each arrived. What was the term you used?

GA Vibrant, perhaps. I didn't have the good fortune to be there, but I know from others' stories that the club scene was strong. I wasn't living here until 1979, but I'd come to frequent the clubs. I remember McCoy Tyner, Cecil Taylor, and John Hicks. I saw them often then. And when I actually moved here, I heard a lot of musicians from Chicago, the Art Ensemble, AACM people in the clubs. You don't see them as much now; there's been a turnaround in what the clubs are doing. Some of my peers, my generation, who when we were growing up were trying so hard to find opportunities in the clubs—well, more of us are there, now. Guys like Kenny Garrett, Bob Hurst, and [her husband, trumpeter] Wallace Roney.

HM Hank arrived and found the new thing here. Geri *brought* a new thing here. Is that fair to say?

GA Oh, I don't know. I always *wanted* to bring in something new, but...

When I was at Howard University, Wallace was there and we spent a lot of time practicing together. He was very advanced at a very young age—at fifteen playing Clifford Brown solos. I was hanging around him a lot, and we spent a lot of time in the practice room. Also, from the time I spent with Marcus Belgrave and the musicians of the Detroit area, I was trying to learn bebop language, and Wallace at the same time, somewhere else, was doing the same thing. That was really my foundation in playing the piano. I always was trying to compose, that's another side of it; the composition part sort of moving parallel to studying the tradition. But I wouldn't say that before the past three or four years I'd found a way to make my composing and studying become one cohesive thing.

HM Did you try to adapt yourself to the AACM concepts?

GA Those musicians were the ones who were most open to giving me opportunities to play. I worked with Oliver Lake first, then Lester Bowie and different Chicagoans. Later, on a record with [drummer] Ralph Peterson, my love for the bebop tradition was more exposed, and I began to get calls to do *that*. But I was fortunate to have opportunities to work when I first came; that doesn't always happen.

I learned a lot being around the people who were supportive of me, including their concepts on composition and such. At this point—and from now on—I'm trying to bring together all of that with my background from Detroit, a very strong bebop city. Perhaps what I'm doing now is more well rounded, encompassing my respect for the whole spectrum of the music. It's coming together more because I can embrace the whole spectrum through composition, and touch on all these different areas that I love.

HJ When I came to New York and heard an entirely different concept than those I'd been exposed to, I tried to do something similar to what Geri has done. I tried to amalgamate my style with the bebop style. I didn't completely abandon my previous style because it was a style that required a two-handed approach to piano, which I always thought was the correct approach.

Bebop almost compels you to abandon that—not harmonically, certainly, but with regard to the speed and linear requirements of the right hand. So I tried to build something new.

To develop an original approach is the goal—sometimes conscious, sometimes not—of most pianists, most musicians, I think, but it's a very difficult and elusive goal. One probably comes closer to succeeding if you use Geri's approach, combining your particular creativity through composition with your concept of the bebop thing.

HM Geri, when you accompany an Oliver Lake, a Lester Bowie, a Dewey Redman—musicians who don't even share a repertoire among themselves—what do you consciously carry from one to the next that's your own? What do you adapt?

GA I recently have had the honor to work with Betty Carter in a duo setting—

HJ Oh, my, my!

GA —and she has once again brought me back to my roots, to the standard repertoire. My approach to those standards had a lot to do with what would make her comfortable, but at the same time I've been bringing that other experience of playing open forms. We play the structure; it's very important that the forms remain exact when you're playing across bar lines and placing ones [first beats of a measure] in unusual places. They're always there, even if the downbeat's not explicit.

The bebop tradition already did all this. I'm shifting the emphasis, but everything comes from that tradition. My experience from playing open forms comes into that, so I can try to allow the time to float, keeping the pulse going at the same time. I've tried to translate ideas I've gotten playing with Oliver and Lester and others into the context of bebop while respecting it—not stretching it to the point of disrespect to the tradition.

You walk a tightrope, though, because when you're working with other musicians you want to project your ideas while a collective thing is happening. It's like sharing a room, or being married for a few minutes: You have to move in order for the other person to move, and they need to move, too. I've sometimes been very strong-headed about projecting my ideas, and maybe I've offended people I was playing with. But I've learned. As you live, you find ways to make everything balance out, hopefully minute to minute, in your musical relationships.

HM   Hank spoke about his left hand, and the change in the left hand, lightening up and modifying stride; Geri's talked about the pulse and letting song forms open up—

GA   Not changing the structure, but adopting that attitude. And, like, the different approaches I might take with my left hand change based on who I'm playing with. As Mr. Jones said—Hank Jones—in a solo context—Hank, okay, I'm sorry—in a solo context I try to use a more two-fisted approach, as well. A lot of my ideas come from stride and from McCoy Tyner's use of the left hand, but I may use rhythms from the Caribbean or Africa, and/or mixed meters.

    My left hand is always functioning independently, in a rhythm-section way—but with different rhythmic emphasis because we're using different rhythms. Then, in solos specifically, my right hand improvises in a tradition similar to the bebop tradition. Depending on who the bass player and the drummer are, I might really have to change to facilitate the music: Some people play in a dense way, and I'd play less, but if they play less, I might play more. But it certainly comes from Bud Powell. He's the point of departure.

HJ   I think, Geri, you've brought up a very important point, among many, when you suggest that whatever is played contemporaneously must have *of necessity* built on what happened at some prior time. That's the way things go: You build on what has more or less been established, or what's been, let's say, *laid out* in terms of procedural directions. Then you go from there. You build on what's *there*. I think that's important, something a lot of young musicians don't quite realize, although I must say that people like the Marsalises, people who think like they do and who think like *you* do, have realized this. It's quite important. Nothing exists in a vacuum, let's say. That explains the whole thing, I think.

HM   Cannot a musician project deep respect for tradition and draw on it for much farther extensions, beginning at a place that's farther than usual from those traditions, beyond trying to play them in one's own way?

HJ   Maybe Geri has an opinion about this, and Howard, you might be knowledgeable about this, too: Is there some point, indeed, where the departure from the basis occurs, where there *is* no relation to the basis anymore? Can you just get to a point where you're suspended in midair? Is that point ever reached?

GA   I can't speak for anyone but myself. But given the context of our tradition—part of it being that we draw from our roots—I think everybody in it pretty much feels that way.

HM I'm not trying to suggest people can drop it and start on another plane. In your commission from Lincoln Center, Geri, did you feel you had to prove your connection to the tradition by playing the music of James P. Johnson or Erroll Garner or any of the greats?

GA All those musicians have affected me in a very great way. I think through compositional aspects, different personalities of all of them that I love so much come out at different times. In that composition, specifically, I drew from a lot of different places in the tradition.

Maybe not *literally:* I tried to stand in my own shoes at the same time. But the blues and the rhythms and all that—it's about swing, it's about coming from an established place. Our textures may reflect our personalities—they *will,* I hope. But the roots and the base of the music—the stomach, the place of the center, the center of gravity of it—really comes from everything that's been established before us.

That's the reason I'm so interested in Mary Lou Williams's music and Herbie Nichols's music: They're vehicles for me to learn, in which I hope to find *myself.* That's the end result I'm reaching for, to make something original from all of this study of the music!

HJ There are always, inevitably, musical links to previous periods. The great classical composers regularly incorporated folk dances and songs into their music as integral parts of their composition. That was the thing to do; nobody thought there was anything wrong with it, it was an accepted way to go. It's important to realize there will *always* be musical links, because it reestablishes the fact that something else *did* happen, which is yet compatible with whatever else is going on in any given time and place musically.

I think music should be that way. It should be a mosaic. If it were one thing exclusively, it would be pretty stale, and not rate much interest. Music has to include various elements. And as time progresses, over time, more of the individual composer's own musical viewpoint has to be there. It's sure to come to the fore, like cream always rises to the top. There's nothing wrong with that.

GA But right now, it seems, there are different camps in the music pulling at each other. One side, maybe the more visible side, suggests you have to do things in certain ways that conform to their ideas. To me, that's not what the tradition suggests, which is to study your forebears with respect, but to also try to find your own voice. Mr. Jones—Hank—it seems today there's a criterion that exists in terms of what's been established as the highest of the high level. You've reached that point, which we people who are coming up and learning are trying to get to, a point of integrity—

HJ Integrity, I'll go along with.

GA —in which we can search for our own voices. But in the music community there's a strong far-right-wing attitude about that, too; that if you don't do it *this* way, if you don't do it under *these* particular rules—that don't *necessarily* have, though they *assume* that they have, roots in the tradition but are also very confining, which is unlike the tradition—you're doing it wrong!

HJ I understand what you're saying. Here's what I believe: If you try to evaluate a performance, whether you're a critic or a listener or a musician, I think it should be based on how well or efficiently the performer does what he's attempting to do. To me, that's the only way to properly evaluate a performance or a composition.

What is the object? What was he aiming for? How close did he get to that goal? There are certain fundamentals, the basic rules of harmony as we know them. You can stretch and bend the rules of harmony in all sorts of ways. I think music ought to conform to the basic rules, let's say it should be *within* the parameters, yet at the outer limits of the rules—because what are rules? Sometimes you don't strictly stick with the rules, they're meant to be broken, anyway. As to whether you should conform to preconceived notions of what should or should not happen, conform to the style of the period, that depends on the period you're trying to express. If you're playing some period music—James P. Johnson, say—is your performance within appropriate parameters? But if you're playing some different kind of music, exploratory music or new music or a new composition, how well does your playing fit the background?

Does it fit? Maybe *that's* the key word. Does it fit what you're trying to express?

GA You mentioned there were musicians in the bebop era, predecessors of it, who rejected it, who didn't want the music to change, who maybe even fought against it. But musicians with your kind of spirit took on the battle, even if they were rejected by some of the elders. You were embracing a tradition, but at the same time saying, "Yeah, this is beautiful, but I've got to go *my* way." Great musicians like you seem to be open to that process—

HJ I don't know about the greatness. But I think you have to be open to ideas. I try to be. As you say: Who can say who's right? Only the test of time will determine it. And we can't wait around for that. You have to go in the direction you believe in today. That's the direction you have to go in.

HM Mustn't business realities come into account? Hank, you worked for CBS for twenty years. Didn't you have constraints on your work there?

HJ Even before that, when I worked with Hot Lips Page! After I'd come to New York and heard Charlie Parker and Dizzy Gillespie, I was hot to dive in and get involved in their music, but there was a fight going on mentally in my mind, and making a living took precedence, so I went on the road with Hot Lips Page for three or four months, doing one-nighters in the Deep South. South of Dearborn, Michigan.

There are times when you make concessions, but it need not change your mental direction, your overall objective. You have to keep that in perspective. This is the point you want to reach, so you aim for that, *regardless*.

The CBS thing was an example of that. Most of the time during those fifteen or so years I wasn't playing the kind of music I'd prefer to play. Musicians used to say to me, "What are you working on this staff for? You could be out making a lot more money"—I didn't know about that, but—"out doing something that you could probably enjoy a lot more."

I answered them, "It's providing me an economic base for trying to build something." I didn't lose my objective. It may have slowed me down a bit. I would have been a lot further on the road to where I want to be musically had I not worked at CBS. It had an inhibiting influence; you couldn't do the things you wanted to do. So I did a lot of recording in those days. Perhaps not enough, I'm afraid, to offset CBS's negative effects.

But the bottom line is this: You set yourself a goal and work for it. Music is like any other field of endeavor: You set yourself an objective, you work toward it, you don't let anything deter you, whether your peers agree with you or not. Maybe they're wrong, and maybe *you're* right.

GA There's enough room for everybody, hopefully.

HJ That's right. There should be a willingness to explore new ideas and let musicians perform who have a different musical approach than what you yourself are used to. You shouldn't be afraid to expose people to different ideas, and to open yourself. I don't get asked about these matters by the powers that be, though, generally.

GA Which is a travesty. People like Mr. Jones *should* be consulted, their ideas respected and presented. It would be a great shot in the arm for the musical community to experience the whole of our music, because it's broad and that's what programs like Lincoln Center's should represent: an opportunity to learn from the masters who are still in the trenches. When they present these masters, I'm sure in the front row. May I ask Mr. Jones a question? Do you consider there to be a Detroit piano school?

HJ I've heard that question asked many times. To tell you the truth, I can't see it. I don't think there's any such. Perhaps due to the fact that pianists congregated there at one time—Lonnie Scott, Art Tatum, Morgan Garreau, who might have been Tatum, recording under another name—pianists in Detroit may have been especially inspired. But the short answer is: No. I don't know a Detroit school.

GA Perhaps you're the father of it, if I may suggest so. A lot of people have patterned themselves after you. If you're not aware of it, I'm here to tell you.

HJ If that's the case, even more people will be impressed by your stylings and your energy at the piano. I'm sure you've inspired many students already, and this will happen more as your music circulates further. And *I* will be in the front row.

8
M-Base and the Black Rock Coalition

Music is best when it's conceived with conviction and realized for fun, out of love, pride, and triumph, for solace or some other inner fulfillment. Making music for money mucks it up. That's part of the Black Rock Coalition spirit, when it's happening.

Not that the BRC's members took vows of modesty and poverty, but when founded in 1985 by writer-guitarist Greg Tate, guitarist Vernon Reid, and Konda Mason, then manager of all-female black rock band Isis, they conceived "not a booking agency, management company, or demo-tape shopping vehicle, but rather a nonprofit networking and support organization for like-minded musicians and artists." The Black Rock Coalition Orchestra staged tributes to Jimi Hendrix and Curtis Mayfield, Bo Diddley, Ethel Waters, and such other "glorious ancestors" as Otis Blackwell, overlooked composer of several Elvis Presley hits. Yet the BRC, according to Tate's liner notes on its Rykodisc compilation *The History of Our Future* was "not a cover band but a vehicle for developing fresh interpretations of classic material."

It would be nice to write that despite a pose of commercial diffidence, all BRC members got rich and famous, or anyway, live highly satisfying lives—and that may yet happen. A fair number of the prominent BRC artists have recorded, including guitarist Michael Hill, vocalist D. K. Dyson, Melvin Gibbs, Jean-Paul Bourelly, Marque and David Gilmore, among others. When the BRC made its club debut on a bright-lit, steamy night at the downtown club S.O.B.'s in the mid-'80s, they were twenty-eight strong, the event more a party than a paying gig. It's pretty hard to turn a profit on a New York club one-nighter with a mob that large.

The coalition had readied themselves by performing for free the week before at the Prospect Park bandshell in Brooklyn. Here they were, amassed onstage, promising, "We're gonna have a funky good time," then delivering that very best of goods in a couple of sets that weren't about selling albums, impressing magnates, securing an audience, or punching up the public images of participating singers, rappers, writers, composers, and instrumentalists who variously announced they played in honor of Chuck Berry, Sly Stone, Funkadelic, and LaBelle. The BRC's jazz affiliations may not have been given their verbal due, but were evident in every act.

Cookie Watkins stepped out from a line of finger-snapping, hip- and shoulder-pumping vocalists. Vernon Reid, with an ear-to-ear grin, Masai-Mohawk razor-cut, and flashy suit, chopped out guitar chords in the deadly sweet rhythm of a man wielding an ax, and fellow guitarists Jerome Harris, Wayne Nesbit, and Kevin Harris hove to. Trumpeters Graham Haynes, Flip Barnes, and Mark Ledford, alto saxist Greg Osby, and trombonist Robin Eubanks held back some on the volume, knowing rock ought to be *loud* but not always the *same* loud. Geri Allen and a second synth player stirred up an electronic orchestral backdrop, light and rich as chocolate mousse. The drumming—by Will Calhoun, mostly, though others sat in—was firm to fiercely martial. Never sluggish, but not exactly based on *ching-a-ling, ching-a-ling,* either: more groove than swing.

"Rock 'n' roll is black music, and we are its heirs," the BRC boasted, all the while sneaking in such jazz heritage treasures as Dizzy Gillespie's "Night in Tunisia" (the Batson Brothers did it as an electric keyboard duet) and John Coltrane's "Naima" (sung true to his original rendition by Otha Hunter). The coalition had a rightful claim to America's pop music of the past fifty years; its blurring of genre distinctions in black music was equally valid. Since recording began, ragtime, race music, blues, R&B, doo-wop, disco, house, rap— whatever's come from the ghettos of New Orleans, Memphis, Chicago, Detroit, Philly, Newark, New York, the Southwest, and/or Florida—has been polished, powdered, and processed, cleaned up and covered by white artists, exported from the United States and reimported in Asian and European editions. Insisting on credit due, the BRC acted essentially as a plugged-in younger sibling of the AACM.

Their concert had the enthusiasm, variety, and sheer drive of Hal

Roach's Little Rascals crossed with the Johnny Otis Show. But with sardonic warnings about South Africa, cries of compassion for "The Homeless Men," a deadpan forecast of "Military Takeover," and a memorial to the young black artist Michael Stewart, who'd died, allegedly of brutality, while in New York police custody, the BRC infused community consciousness into its revue. The message stuff wasn't preachy or weepy, just as directly felt and delivered as the hot love songs and Bevis Griffin's paean to "Noisy Music."

That was a fun night, and encouraged speculation about how the BRC should best spread its gospel. How 'bout a television special, live from Harlem's Apollo Theater, or a weekly series?! Everyone involved would have welcomed whatever fame and good fortune might follow. Money? "Got to have it," in the words of more than one great American poet. But please, please, *please*. First things first.

Steve Coleman and M-Base

In the mid-'70s a serious, locally popular but otherwise little-known young Chicago saxophonist hitchhiked, with $150 in his pocket, to New York City. He checked into a midtown YMCA and started blowing his horns in the street. In ten years Steve Coleman had established himself as an ambitious and provocative player-composer-leader with several acclaimed albums, dozens of sideman credits and an armful of press clips calling attention to a posse of "M-Base structured improvisers" he'd gathered round. Coleman led a band called Five Elements, typified by funky but tight and often complex rhythms; he beamed forth a laser tone from his alto saxophone that led the groove like a thread through a needle's eye.

By the mid-'90s Coleman had much further advanced himself and the loose-knit movement, club, circle, or clique he'd dubbed the M-Base Collective. He'd led bands under that rubric, or called Five Elements, Metrics, and Strata Institute, comprising such of his peers as singer Cassandra Wilson; trumpeters Ralph Alessi, Roy Hargrove, Graham Haynes, and Mark Ledford; trombonist Robin Eubanks; saxophonists Ravi Coltrane, Craig Handy, Greg Osby, and Joshua Redman; clarinetist Don Byron; guitarists Kelvyn Bell, Jean-Paul Bourelly, Kevin Eubanks, and David Gilmore; keyboardists Geri Allen, Vijay Iyer, Andy Milne, Renee Rosnes, Michele Rosewoman, James Weidman, and Rod Williams; bassists Lonnie Plaxico and Reggie Washington; drummers Terri Lyne Carrington, Gene Lake, and Marvin "Smitty" Smith. In addition, Coleman had earned mainstream credits, working extensively with veterans including jazz diva Abbey Lincoln, acoustic bassist Dave Holland, pianist Tommy Flanagan, and Chicago *paterfamilias* Von Freeman. And he'd tried to sink roots widely, setting up several-week residencies for his groups as far from his Brooklyn home as the San Francisco Bay Area and Cuba.

For a time Steve Coleman also had the role (created by tenor saxophonist Branford Marsalis) of improvising foil in the touring band of soft-rock heartthrob Sting. Sting's short-lived Pangaea label issued Coleman's first album actually produced in the United States, emblazoned simply with his name—and the saxophonist had been picked up by RCA/Novus, a division of multinational BMG. He survived contact with Mammon, integrity intact, but for a while had been worried.

"There's a danger I see in making a whole lot of money," Coleman said once in the mid-'80s, during a lunch break from a rehearsal with Sting's band (the star himself wasn't scheduled in that day) in a New York studio. "Cats change. I see a lot of cats who are making money, and they haven't done a creative thing since. I don't want to get like that." Consequently, he'd been going out of his way to make time for unusual but low-paying encounters, such as an improv sax quartet with Osby and reed players Ned Rothenberg and John Zorn at the then-new Knitting Factory.

Trace Coleman's determination back to his upbringing. "I was born in Chicago," he continued, "and grew up on the South Side, which was good, musically, because within walking distance Von Freeman and a lot of other people were playing. I thought I was going to be a comic book artist when I came out of eighth grade; I got into music by accident my freshman year in high school, but I liked it and kept going.

"My band teacher was Alvin Lawson, who came up through Captain Walter Dyett's teaching technique; he was a stickler on scales and stuff, which was good for hardheaded kids like us. When I landed in orchestra, instead of general music, where you played a plastic recorder, the cat put a violin in my hands and said, 'This is your instrument.' I thought, 'What a drag,' but started playing it, and found it was easy. I didn't know I had a talent for it, but a lot of people were having trouble, and I wasn't.

"Then there was a girl in advanced band who played alto sax, and I figured I could get her to notice me if I asked her to teach me to play it. That's how I started. After a while I forgot about her, but kept playing. I was into practicing [John Philip] Sousa, and stuff like that. My father is a big Charlie Parker nut and nudged me in that direction, but I didn't want to hear it. My first influence was another Parker—Maceo, who played with James Brown. I played in that kind of band and wasn't serious about improvising until I went to college.

"At Illinois Wesleyan, my freshman year, I was the only black person signed up for jazz band. The white band director asked me 'Can you solo?' I said, 'No.' He said, 'You can't be in the jazz band unless you can solo.' I found out later I was the only cat he said that to. So I went back to my room, looked through my records, and my father had slipped one of those bootleg Charlie Parker records in with my stuff. I read the back, which said Charlie Parker was a genius of improvisation. I thought, 'If they write he's a genius, at least he must be *good*.' I figured I'd learn from him—so I listened, started reading about his life, heard about him from musicians. And that's when I got serious.

"One thing led to another. I read books about Kansas City, the Pendergast days, all these cats jamming, and I wanted to do *that*. Fortunately in Chicago that kind of thing was happening, and I got into it. I was eighteen or nineteen then. I tried to *be* Charlie Parker, with the exception of the drugs. He's still one of my biggest influences, musically speaking. I don't try to copy him, but I try to model a lot after him, because I feel cats of that period had the perfect balance between feeling, intellect, and trying to find themselves.

"At first, I rejected anything that didn't sound like Bird. The closer you came to Bird, the better I liked you—so one person I really liked was Sonny Stitt, who was living in Chicago. I saw him a lot. I'd go over to his hotel, wake him up in the morning. One time I banged on his door; he was all groggy, but I knew him, so I went in. I had my horn and he grabbed it, started blowing on it. What amazed me was the cat was just *soloing,* not following the melody of a tune, but I knew what tune he was playing. And it sounded like a drum. My father used to say some cats have drums in their horns—their rhythm's so strong, you can hear a whole rhythm section. Stitt had that, Bird had that, and I wanted that really *bad* then.

"I was learning from the older people, Von and Bunky Green, learning by checking them out. I had my own group that I'd write music for and play Bird tunes with. By the time I was leaving Chicago I had one of the better gigs, five nights a week at the New Apartment Lounge. Everybody got twenty-five dollars a night, which was great when you were living with your mother. I'd go buy records with the money.

"I was trying to stretch the chords and forms: I wanted to be creative, but within structure. Most of the cats were either staunch traditionalists, or they were *out* and couldn't deal with many traditional elements—or *chose* not to and, as a result, couldn't. Very few were in between. I'd see cats come through—Max Roach with Billy Harper and Cecil Bridgewater, Art Blakey, Woody Shaw. I'd say, 'They're coming from someplace, and they're into this whole other progressive thing.' I found out most of them were coming from New York. I knew I was leaving Chicago.

"A lot of cats come here with gigs or they know somebody, but I had to do the YMCA scene. It was three months before I got a gig with Thad Jones and Mel Lewis. I came to New York to play with small groups, and for the first years I played mostly with big bands. I did a couple of tours with Sam Rivers's big band, and a record— *Colours* (Black Saint), I think. Played in the Collective Black Artists band, run by Slide Hampton at the time. Another one run by Charles Sullivan. Cecil Taylor's big band, Paul Jeffrey's, and even lesser-known big bands.

"The $400 a week from Thad and Mel's orchestra was the most I'd ever made in my life, even though I had to pay hotels out of it, so it was really $250. And there'd be a tour, then four or five months off. I soon realized that wasn't enough for New York, so I had to go on playing the street for two or three years, and that's how I formed Five Elements. It was a street band we had.

"Me, Mark Johnson on drums, his brother Billy Johnson on bass, and Graham Haynes on trumpet—we had a really tight unit. Tunes: hard bop, a couple of standards, Bird heads, we played 'em really fast. We played at Fiftieth and Broadway, Forty-second Street between Fifth and Sixth Avenues, Columbus Circle—those were some of the good spots. At the time, Pignose [small, portable, power-source-included] amps had just come out. Maybe you'd hear single musicians on the street, but not a whole lot of groups; there wasn't much competition. After a couple of years, though, it got ridiculous: The police started cracking down, taking cats' instruments. By that time I'd hooked up with Doug Hammond.

"Doug lives in Germany, but he was hanging around New York then. It was interesting when we got gigs, because we played this creative music in traditional blues club-like atmospheres, all black places where almost no white people would come at all. It was a weird group: Muneer Abdul Fatah on five-string cello, Doug's drums, and my saxophone. We played in Harlem or in Brooklyn, places like

Lickety Split, the Red Rooster, the Blue Book, Dig's Den, Pumpkins. And people dug it. But then they moved to Europe. They wanted me to move to Europe, and I said, 'Cancel.' New York has its problems, but cats go over to Europe and they lose it, and they don't even *realize* they lose it. It's easier over there, but I felt if you make it here, you've made it everywhere. You go over there to hang in the expatriate scene or to settle, and you may be forgotten.

"I'd already started Five Elements, and was gigging here and there. I remember doing a benefit with Sam Rivers's band for Dave Holland, when he'd just come back from his heart attack. Then Dave contacted me. I was quite surprised; I had no idea he'd noticed me, and I asked him, 'Why me?' He was looking for the same kind of thing I was: a freedom-within-structure combination. He wanted to hook me up with [trumpeter] Kenny Wheeler, whom I'd never heard of, and later he brought in [trombonist] Julian Priester.

"Basically, Dave was doing things similar to [his well-regarded ECM recording] *Conference of the Birds*. New stuff came from what I had done with Doug Hammond, and things Smitty Smith was doing. I'd got into studying rhythms right before I joined Doug Hammond, to correct the bad time I'd had for so long. The people I liked were always rhythmic, so that helped, and I listened to a lot of African stuff—but not by putting on beads, burning incense, and changing my name. I listened to a lot of Bulgarian stuff, stuff from around the world too.

"Where a note is placed can be the whole story. So I don't look at my time as odd meters; I tend not to divide up time. I look at it in an African sense, where you have *this* rhythm and this *other* rhythm and they're related in a certain way. When writing for horns, I realize they're like drums in that they make sounds; they just happen to be tonal sounds. My primary consideration is how they fit together in terms of rhythms."

Coleman responded to a specific question with diffidence. "I have different kinds of systems, and if you want me to speak specifically about them, I can. But I have the same view that Béla Bartók had about talking technical, which is: I don't think it interests most people. There's a group of musicians who want to cop, but I'd rather talk about what I'm trying to do on a broad basis than the means I use to do it."

Pressed, he explained: "Most of the means come from living. The technical part comes from studying, but the ideas comes from living. I call my music M-Base because I figure I should have the right to

name it. I don't like calling it jazz, because you run into regular people on the street and they say, 'What do you play?' and you say, 'Jazz,'
and they have an immediate image—whether it's Grover Washington
or King Oliver or Duke Ellington or Herbie Hancock. And none of
those images sound anything alike. I don't want somebody thinking,
'Wow, he plays like Wynton Marsalis,' because it's not true.

"M-Base is just a name that means something to us, a whole
group of us. Base, because what we're trying to do is form a common language. M stands for 'macro,' which just mean big base. But
'base' is also another word, for 'basic array of structured extempora-
tions,' which is what most of us are doing. We're all involved with
improvisation, and it's usually structured. We hope M-Base won't be
such a rigid term that everybody expects us to do only that for the
rest of our lives. Anyway, it's not going to be as rigid a term as jazz,
or funk or jazz-funk or fusion, which are all terms I hate.

"I mean, I'm influenced by music; I'm very influenced by a lot
of classical musicians. Are you going to call my music jazz-funk-clas-
sical because I'm influenced by all those things? Okay, it's primarily
Afro-American music because that's my life, it comes out that way.
But I'm into Japanese culture too. And Eastern European, around the
Balkans. Are you going to call it 'jazz with other influences'? That
doesn't explain anything. Fusion? What I'm involved in doesn't
sound anything like Mahavishnu. You say 'modern,' but they've said
'modern' since Louis Armstrong.

"I'd rather avoid the question altogether. Somebody asks me
what I play, I say 'Music.' They say, 'Can you qualify that?' I say, 'I play
M-Base. Which is influenced by some of the stuff you named, but it
is *not* that.'"

For some audiences, Coleman's righteous tone, swaggering lines,
driving polyphony—his whole vibrant sound package, often including vocalists—functions as dance music. Others audiences dig the
instrumentals on *Motherland Pulse, On the Edge of Tomorrow,* and *World
Expansion* (all JMT), and think of Coleman's music as reflective, sardonic, incisive, and ethereal—grist for study, after careful listening.

Coleman said, "I'd like to have all those elements in the music:
something for people who want to dance, something for people
who are intellectual and want to find some abstract meaning, and for
people who just want to forget their troubles. But I'm not trying to
play beautiful music. Sting made a comment that he's trying to play
beautiful music. I'm not. I'm trying to play *life*.

"What I mean by that is: See a mountain, play the *mountain*—

the *essence* of what that mountain is. The shape, but not a line that has the contour of the mountain. There's the *inside* of that mountain, the mountain *itself*. Not a shadow, not an outline.

"I know that's a lifetime of work I've set for myself. But the people who are really the great musicians seem to me to have achieved that. I hear *life* when I listen to Charlie Parker, not just music. I hear everything that I experience and see, and I feel that I understand him as a result of listening to his music, as well as I can, not being there."

Coleman credits the Eastern bent of his philosophy to his teenage enthusiasm for kung fu movies, but he's developed his theories maturely, shunning dogmas and obsessions. Considering his determination, self-possession, breadth of taste, articulate intelligence, technical expertise, and pro tools, one would guess Coleman could handle creative satisfactions *and* financial rewards.

He wouldn't say what he was going after, but Coleman had no doubts what he was about. He said he was doing "the same thing I was doing in Chicago. Trying to play my music and hook up with other people who are moving in their own directions.

"We're making a conscious effort to develop something, trying to be ourselves," Steve insisted. "*Ourselves,* rather than original, because to me there's a difference. When you're really yourself, you *are* original." He might sound *close* to other musicians—twining as a strand of DNA with Osby, for instance—but Steve Coleman sounds *like* no one else.

Cassandra, Future Teller

In 1988 Cassandra Wilson released *Blue Skies*, an album produced for the small independent German label JMT of standards from Tin Pan Alley and Broadway, backed by a classic, understated piano trio. Without radical revision, she refreshed lyrics that had a past of square associations for her audience of aging baby boomers. *Blue Skies* was a turning point in Wilson's career, which had until then lingered at the edge of several possibilities. It lit a path she'd come to follow, though she resisted it for several albums more.

"The idea just came to me," drawled the vocalist, born in Mississippi in 1956, who was associated with Henry Threadgill and M-Base when she first came to New York. Wilson had jammed at the Brooklyn Academy of Music's Next Wave Festival with alto saxophonists Steve Coleman and Greg Osby, tenorist Gary Thomas, pianist Geri Allen, guitarist Vernon Reid, and drummer Marvin

"Smitty" Smith shortly before she spoke about *Blue Skies* in the fall of '88.

"Doing standards seemed like a good idea because I have two records out that show a certain direction I've been *going*, and this project shows where I've come *from*. Also, a lot of people asked me for it; maybe they thought I couldn't do it. I wanted to set those people at ease, their tongues at rest."

By giving them what they wanted Wilson actually set their tongues wagging. The glowing critical and audience reception of Wilson's versions of "Shall We Dance," "I Didn't Know What Time It Was," "I'm Old Fashioned," and "My One and Only Love" seemed to refute the directions of out jazz, black rock, and popular rap, to herald the return of an earlier idiom of twentieth-century American romantic song, a continued taste for subtly sophisticated love lyrics. The singer advanced from irregular bookings as a featured side player in New York jazz clubs to frequent appearances at the chic nightclub Nell's, where patrons chose between a semiplush living room-like lounge (ground level) and aggressive dance mixes (basement). Wilson sang in the cushy faux-living room setting, helping young urban professionals idealize their childhoods.

"I loved watching musicals on television when I was a kid," she remembered. "Like other kids, I guess, I'd memorize the words to the tunes. Yul Brynner singing 'Shall We Dance' in his inimitable way with Deborah Kerr in *The King and I*—I loved that scene. So I just delivered these songs from whatever place they existed in my own experience.

"'Sweet Lorraine' I associate with Louis Armstrong, 'Blue Skies' with Dinah Washington, 'Polka Dots and Moonbeams' with Sarah Vaughan. I heard Ernestine Anderson sing 'I Didn't Know What Time It Was,' but I'd already been singing it in different arrangements for six years by the time I did. I forget where I heard it first.

"'I've Grown Accustomed to His Face' is a song I've loved since I saw *My Fair Lady*. I heard Frank Sinatra do it, but he didn't have much influence on me. Ol' Blue Eyes is cool, but I think he borrowed a lot from Billie Holiday, phrasing-wise."

In Cassandra Wilson's phrasing, her measured forays into wordless scat, her tonal dips, rhythmic hesitations, attention to diction, alternation of subdued intimacy with liberated belting, and the enveloping depths of her warm, husky voice, there are reminders of jazz singing's queen Betty Carter (who died in September 1998).

"That's the problem with doing standards: you're going to

remind somebody of somebody you studied," Wilson acknowledged. "There was a time I listened to nothing but Betty Carter. My favorite album of hers was *The Audience With...* (BetCar/Verve reissue) because it has 'The Trolley Song,' which I really like."

Betty Carter dramatized that tune, which Judy Garland introduced in the film *Meet Me in St. Louis*, rather literally; by contrast, Wilson said, "I have a very simple approach to that kind of music. I don't think it's necessary to do something drastically different to dramatize the melodic and harmonic content of these songs. I'd rather do out stuff with my own material."

As she demonstrated on her JMT albums *Point of View* and *Days Aweigh*, her own songs like "Square Roots," "I Am Waiting," and "Never" are highly personal and sometimes off-kilter; they stick in one's mind upon second or third hearings. She's as comfortable with the odd meters and oblique lines provided by altoist Coleman and guitarist Jean-Paul Bourelly as with the proprieties observed in *Blue Skies* by pianist Mulgrew Miller, bassist Lonnie Plaxico, and drummer Terri Lyne Carrington.

And regarding influences, Cassandra said she's wide open. She has considered an album of songs identified with Aretha Franklin or by Stevie Wonder, but thinks they'd take serious efforts to arrange. "Nobody's done it"—she shrugged— "except Muzak."

She even likes what she hears on the radio. "I'm a fan of Public Enemy, and in general I'm interested in rap," she explained. "It really swings when it's done well; it does what a lot of jazz musicians say jazz does to be jazz. It's modern music, '90s music, and it also indicates how polarized our society has become. It's difficult for white people to understand the subtle nuances of the language if they aren't connected to black people.

"Yes, rap is a barrage, an assault. It represents feelings these young black kids have about society right now, and how they're waging war with culture, using the only means they have. That's why it's important for all of us to listen. Some black people might be cosmetically removed from the so-called underclass, but we're really all members of it. So that music is vital."

Will Cassandra rap?

"Oh, I don't know." She thought that droll.

Produce a second volume of standards?

"Volume two may come in thirty years, when I have a whole different perspective. Right now I'm more concerned with my new original material. I'm negotiating with several new record company people, and want to go into the studio. I'm going to chill out my traveling"—she toured Japan for the first time in '88, and was looking forward to starting '89 at a festival in Cologne—"to have a baby, due in mid-March.

"Music is far more political right now than it was in the '30s and '40s," Wilson said, "so I don't know what the American songbook is going to become. Maybe a hundred years from now my original songs will be in that songbook. I couldn't say.

"But there's a lot of humor in what I do, even in singing some of those corny but funny and romantic lyrics on *Blue Skies*. If you see me do it, maybe the irony would be more obvious."

After that interview, Wilson issued two of her most personal projects, *Jumpworld* and *She Who Weeps*. In 1991 she put out a concert album, *Live,* interpreting the challenging jazz standards "'Round Midnight" and "Body and Soul." Then she recorded *Dance to the Drums Again*, with only one familiar tune, "Amazing Grace," for Japanese Disk Union. Finally in '93, her commercial breakthrough: *Blue Light 'Til Dawn* (on Blue Note), sparely arranged so that distinctive, acoustic solos by handpicked instrumentalists—Brandon Ross (of several Threadgill projects) playing steel string guitar; Natchez, Mississippian cornetist Olu Dara; and clarinetist Don Byron, among others—wafted about her up-close effusions on history-steeped songs including "You Don't Know What Love Is," the blues "Come On in My Kitchen," and Van Morrison's "Tupelo Honey." A distillation of what she'd started in *Blue Skies, Blue Light* was an instant classic.

In '95 Wilson and her producer Craig Street followed up with the similarly affecting *New Moon Daughter* (Blue Note), in which she addressed Billie Holiday's stark "Strange Fruit," Hoagy Carmichael's "Skylark," Neil Young's "Harvest Moon," and "Last Train to Clarksville," a '60s hit for the Monkees. Singing slowly, deliberately, in a fairly narrow tonal range, couched in empathetic obbligati from Graham Haynes and Butch Morris, supportive rhythms from Brazilian percussionist Cyro Baptista (also returned from *Blue Light*) and downtown drummer Dougie Bowne, Cassandra Wilson secured her position as the era's crossover female jazz singer.

Celebrating multi-kulti trends, simultaneously appropriating pure pop with an individuality surpassing most postmodern gloss, she brought the efforts of Son House and Hank Williams together with hits by Irish rockers U2. She posted her own songs of faith in the face of adversity and the solace of sensual love—essentially, blues truths—in a manner unassuming yet sultry, offhand but seductive. Arrangements credited to Wilson and producer Street demonstrated how less is more, silence equals suspense, and resonant ambiance emphazes inherent drama.

Wilson's style owes more to Billie Holiday's and Carmen McRae's than to Ella Fitzgerald's or Sarah Vaughan's. Every drop of her malted milk alto bears the weight of coherent storytelling before it indulges any glories of vocal display. Wilson *can* exploit her range; when she releases a rare higher register phrase, or quicker-than-usual string of syllables, her prior restraint has let her sidle up to intimate striking distance. Her tempos are generally moderate, and she puts over a natural swing. She always seems aware of and responsive to the instrumental gestures around her.

In 1995 Wynton Marsalis cast Cassandra Wilson as a lead in his jazz oratorio *Blood on the Fields*, which won the 1997 Pulitzer Prize for musical composition; with startling baritone Miles Griffith and impish Jon Hendricks, she held the center of the three-CD set issued by Columbia Records. Still, she would not be constrained. Cassandra Wilson also sang entire programs of originals in English to Turkish listeners in Istanbul, and attempted vocalizations of repertoire identified with Miles Davis, from "'Round Midnight" to "Tutu," in her own concert at Lincoln Center. Without much apparent effort, she'd positioned herself to be *the* woman's voice of '90s jazz for aficionados and know-littles alike.

Vernon Reid, Then and Now

Vernon Reid is as straight about his ambitions as can be. He wanted to play his own music, be widely heard, and make a living. "What Count Basie was playing in his heyday—wasn't that commercial music? It was *dance* music," asserted the then-twenty-four-year-old guitarist with a glimmer of scorn for anyone who neeeds convincing that cutting a groove is a valid activity.

"Give me a break. Ellington, Cab Calloway—it was *all* dance music. And nobody claimed *they* were selling art."

Smart, smirking, but yet a little guarded, Reid was relatively new to interviews back in 1982. Yet he had won a bit of attention after three years in the jet stream with Ronald Shannon Jackson's Decoding Society. Raising the issue of musical commercialism, he was defending himself against a charge that hadn't been leveled: that his playing, like that of other electric guitarists, was simply designed for head-bangers. He wanted to be considered, as he considered himself, an *eclectic,* drawing inspiration from many genres, working with many bands, seriously exploring a raft of electric stringed instruments, promising concentration and freshness to his music.

He thought it clear that kids won't anymore pick up a sax like Bird or Trane, or a trumpet in sway of Dizzy and Miles. No, an electric guitar is more often the instrument of choice and availability to youngsters today. He'd like to be known as a real musician, a decoder of the utmost cosmic contrapuntal harmolodics, brave enough to face off with gamesman/reedsman John Zorn, duel with far-stretching guitarist Bill Frisell, float along with New Age autoharpist Laraaji.

"I was born in England; my parents are from the West Indies, one of the smaller Leeward Islands: Montserrat, dominated by the British. I've heard records of choral singing, hymns, and folk tunes from there which are beautiful, very clear. But I've never been there.

"We moved to Brooklyn when I was two, and I was raised here, in public and Catholic schools, till I bailed out after junior high. I was in Brooklyn Tech as an art student, studying illustration and industrial art, as well as cubism, always finding a mixture of music and cultures around me.

"I was a serious AM radio listener back then too; my favorite song was Dionne Warwick's 'Do You Know the Way to San Jose.'" He quoted words of Hal David, music of Burt Bacharach: " 'All the stars/That never were/Parking cars/And pumping gas.' Heavy lyrics. And the Temptations, Aretha Franklin, Ray Charles. My folks were into Johnny Mathis, West Indian singers like the Mighty Sparrow and Lord Melody. They had Xavier Cugat's 'Flying Down to Rio,' that single, and some of James Brown's best hits with the Fabulous Flames.

"I started playing guitar in my sophomore year of high school. There was a barber shop on the corner where the barber was really into blues, and he used to show me things on his guitar. Then my uncle—he was playing in calypso bands—he'd show me chords and things. I had wanted to play flute, but a cousin gave me an old Gibson acoustic guitar that he didn't play anymore. It had these really thick strings and high action, and it was painful for me to learn on it. I stopped for a while, then said to myself, 'I'm going to sit down and try to learn how to do this stuff.'

"Well, I kept at it. When I figured out about changing the

strings, I realized that that guitar's intonation was a mess, so I took it to the guitar store and the repair man laughed at me…

"Finally, I got my first instruction from a guy in a neighborhood music school who looked like Woody Allen and was really into the Beatles. I had to beg him to show me stuff by Kool and the Gang, Ohio Players, bands like that. But the common theme I was hearing from all these people—barber, uncle, cousin, Beatles teacher—was, 'If you stick with music, it will take you places.' I thought, 'Okay.'"

Reid's first gig was with a high school jazz workshop, playing "Afro Blue," Mongo Santamaria's song that Coltrane made famous, and charts of pop hits by Earth, Wind & Fire. "I was so nervous," Vernon remembered, "my mind was a total jumble. I had to turn to my friends to ask what tune we were doing, and when I turned back the curtain was open and there was my entire junior class, a thousand of my peers. But I did it."

From there, he played dance parties with pickup cover bands around Brooklyn and Queens. There was often someone in the band who aspired to work originals into sets of Top 40 hits. "Ha-ha," Reid said. "Guess what? The originals never happen."

He tried writing pop hooks and stayed tight with Raymond Jones, a musical partner who went on to play keyboards with Chic, tour with Talking Heads, work with Nona Hendrix's Propaganda, and who ran his own projects with Vernon on guitar. Unlike fabled predecessors—the guys who were underage but snuck into bars to hear black music—Vernon, a self-described "college-bound, middle-class black kid," just turned on the radio for advanced education.

"In 1973, '74," he said, "New York City FM radio was *out*. I was hearing Pharaoh Sanders and various people.… I didn't understand a lot of it, but I was getting into it. I was caught between two worlds.

"I mean, like Santana—whose *Caravanserai* was, to me, his best, one of my favorites. And John McLaughlin in the context of Miles Davis, all that on *Live/Evil*—that was great. Chick Corea's first Return to Forever album with guitarist Bill Connors. I had friends into rock 'n' roll, who played me a record called *Roadwork* by Johnny Winter with Rick Derringer—it had a lot of playing.

"Then Jimi Hendrix's *Band of Gypsies* album, that's timeless. But I don't want to talk about Hendrix too much, because he's like—"

Inescapable. If there's a ghost hovering above young black rock 'n' jazz guitarists, and many other musicians crying out with wildly bluesy sounds, it's Jimi (though some listeners, call 'em conservative, don't hear his feedback and distortion as anything but noise).

"The really good player is like a magnet," Reid stipulated. "Benson, Pat Martino, Wes Montgomery, Johnny Winter, McLaughlin—it's so easy to get caught up in what they're doing." He shook his head. "'They sound so good, man. I want to play like that!' It's a danger, especially for a young guitar player—and I was very aware of the danger at that time. I think one of the heaviest weights for young black guitar players who choose the idiom of rock is living up to that Hendrix image. It's hard, too, because of how people hear things and they're not really listening; they associate you with what they *want* to associate you with. It's an easy cop-out for a reviewer to say, 'Oh, yes, the pyrotechnics of Hendrix,' even when you don't sound anything like him."

"Some people mean it as a compliment, but others just mean to dismiss you. After one date I played with the Decoding Society, a guy walked up to me and sneered, "Didja ever hear of Jimi *Hendrix*???" Vernon grimaced sweetly. "I felt like smashing him.

"For a long time I wouldn't play the Stratocaster [solid-body guitar associated with Hendrix]. I wouldn't even wear a headband onstage. Now I'm not worried about that.

"But you talk about the bridge between free jazz and rock, you have to listen carefully to 'Machine Gun.' Listen to the end, where Jimi has the feedback and he's playing a really fragile line on top of it, and he's controlling the tremolo arm. The song is about Vietnam, and you can actually hear, like, the voices of men, women, and children, suffering, being slaughtered, during the war, even while he was playing that concert." Reid was awed.

"Above a certain volume, the electric guitar takes on totally different characteristics. The guitar is malleable; when it's hot, when it's really high, it becomes even more sensitive. That's what people either fail to grasp or don't *want* to grasp, but Hendrix did, and 'Machine Gun' is just orchestral. Guitarists like Pete Cosey [the AACM member who worked briefly with Miles Davis in the early '70s] had that understanding, too."

In the front line of the Decoding Society, mobile within some parameters defined by stands of guitars and a steel guitar (thick strings, typically barred with a steel slide, on a fretboard like a table with legs), Reid functioned as a member of a band. It was awfully hard to steal thunder from drummer Ronald Shannon Jackson in *any* case, but his Decoding Society wasn't arranged around soloists so much as for a group sound. Vernon played spectacularly over the band's first albums *Eye on You* (About Time), *Nasty* (Moers), and *Man*

Dance (Antilles), opening the latter's title track with a trebly, twanging descent while the twin electric basses of Melvin Gibbs and the Reverend Bruce Johnson lifted a fanfare of horns—trumpet and tenor sax—over Jackson's brisk cantor. RSJ's detailed, multileveled compositions often obscured each individual's contributions, but attentive listening reveals Reid's attentiveness starting with his selection of just the right tone from his array of instruments.

He buys lots of gear. As a conscientious pro, he wants to be ready for any call, and as a member of experimental ensembles he might be called for anything, so he considers instruments good investments. When other musicians indulge in baser instincts, clean-living Reid sinks his bucks into hardware.

"I practice only on acoustic guitar," he claimed when we first spoke. "My Washburn electro-acoustic is real nice for recording too. Onstage, I use a Les Paul gold top. I have a six-string banjo, an Italian Echo, inexpensive but good. I don't really approach it like a claw hammer banjo: more like a Chinese lute. I've thought about getting a tenor banjo and also a guitar with scalloped frets, so I could bend the strings by pushing down into the neck. And a Fender steel, like a lap steel with legs."

"I'd been with Defunkt for a while," he related; he's on the Defunkt record *Thermonuclear Sweat* (Hannibal). "I was on one of the first Defunkt gigs, working with James White. He had a great band: John Purcell playing baritone sax, Joe Bowie trombone, Ted Daniels trumpet, and sometimes Henry Threadgill or Luther Thomas on saxes. White called them his Flaming Demonics. But one night, in the middle of a set, he ran off, and Bowie started calling out 'Defunkt! Defunkt!' We began to play 'Thermonuclear Sweat.' From then on Defunkt had gigs of its own."

No wave, they called it. It wasn't Reid's only preparation: He'd taken lessons from veteran guitarist Ted Dunbar (in the mid-'70s, a member of Tony Williams Lifetime) through Jazz Interactions, a nonprofit, community-based organization. "I got a sense from him of how much was involved in jazz; here's a man who understands what this music is all about," said Reid and also from guitarists Bruce Johnson and Rodney Jones, who taught him "certain concepts concerning timing and rhythm, the idea of internal time, especially in contexts that are so-called free—so you always know where you want to go. That was further emphasized when I started working with Ronald, since rhythm and time are so important to him, along with melody and harmony. Rhythm in today's music is like this: you can't get away from it, and why should you?" Reid wanted to know.

"When I first encountered Ronald Shannon Jackson, his concept went right over my head. The second time I thought, 'I really like the way this guy plays drums, and I'd like to work with him.' A good drummer, whatever he's doin', is *happening*. I was out of college when Melvin Gibbs—whom I've known since high school, so no one can tell you better than me what a great musician he is—called to tell me to audition for Ron's band. It was Gifts then; Bern Nix [also in Ornette Coleman's Prime Time] was in it, too. Bern's great, like Howlin' Wolf cum laude, a deep mix of real blues and real intellect.

"Now, without Bern in the Decoding Society, my role has expanded; I have to do more, so you don't notice that something's missing.

"Ron's music has changed, too. He's been a big factor in my growth, from the standpoint of endurance and being able to hear different keys at once, parts, that go totally against other parts, yet make it all work. His music takes getting used to; it demands a lot of listening, and a lot of the listener, since so many things are occurring at the same time.

"A lot of people don't understand it; what I'm concerned about is that they give it a chance. Much of what I've come to love when I heard it the first time I thought, 'Oh, come *on*.' When I listened to AM radio, I wanted everything to end on a major chord. From there to this! People should give the Decoding Society's music a chance. It won't hurt you.

"Jazz has always been a people's music. I don't like the elitist trip, whether it's a jazz giant laying it down or some chick or dude on the corner. I like dressing up as well as the next person, putting on the Ritz, but the aura of 'Let's get sophisticated'—which extends into a bebop attitude—I don't dig it. [Cornetist] Olu Dara put it best; he says the bebop and classical cats have one thing in common: They both say, 'We're the ones playing the *real* thing, so give *us* the money.'

"Older guitar players who hear Hendrix and say, 'I know all the young kids like this loud stuff, but *I* don't'—the fact is that the ability to control the forces Hendrix was dealing with is difficult. Controlling that kind of guitar is difficult, just as difficult as running sixteenth notes over bebop changes. The snobbism is not about that. It's that people who can't dance *always* hate dance music, and you just can't expect everyone to like you or what you do. But sound is sound. Attitude is attitude. And when you mix sound and attitude, music is what you get. At least, so you hope.

"Good music is about integrity. Ronald Shannon Jackson's father used to sell juke boxes, so Ron's always heard that pop stuff, and he's brought a backbeat to all the people he's worked with [including Albert Ayler and Cecil Taylor, of the first generation of jazz avant-garde]. That's where it's at for him. For me, I do what I like. I'll enjoy Grandmaster Flash, then I'll want to hear Thelonious Monk at the Five Spot. And why shouldn't I? It's all coming from the same thing, the same integrity. I could listen to Stockhausen, Edgar Varese's 'Ionization,' then [bluesman] Albert Collins's *Frozen Live!*—all great music."

Thirteen years later, leading his new band, Masque, at the opening night Irving Plaza dance party of the Knitting Factory's What Is Jazz? Fest '96, Vernon Reid came on as a rock-star supreme. His thick dreadlocks flopped in his face as he stumbled across the stage with a self-conscious awkwardness reminiscent of the immortal reggae artist Bob Marley. But Reid didn't claim to be a shaman or messiah. He appeared instead as a self-satirizing showman and skeptical New Yorker.

He was making his first big local appearance since the demise of his long-running hard-rock quartet, Living Color. That group, featuring singer Corey Glover, and all original songs written by Reid, drummer Will Calhoun, and bassists Muzz Skillings and Doug Wimbish, toured internationally and recorded half a dozen CDs for Epic Records; its success was in large part due to Reid's guitar pyrotechnics. The band played the lucrative pop ballroom, arena, and stadium circuit; opened to the masses during one Rolling Stone tour; and was featured in *Rolling Stone* magazine—credited with establishing Black Rock as a thing-in-itself. Reid made his public mark with music that had as much jazz in it as does, say, Led Zeppelin. And as much wildman macho vocalizing (Corey) over brutal chords and big rhythms, around which Vernon strung all manner of off-the-wall, over-the-top guitar playing.

Here, without any singers at all, he was sputtering thirty-second notes like so many metal filings against a grinding wheel of stiff riddim. Curtis Watts looked cool behind his double bass drums, but had twice as many skins as he could actually use, and took some time to agree with bassist Hank Schroy on just where was the pocket. Reid also laid out themes big and dumb enough to satisfy whatever metal types might have been (but probably weren't) in the audience. Leonard Gruenbaum's apparently homemade science-fiction keyboards (on Masque's *Mistaken Identity* (Epic), his over-the-shoulders-cigarette-tray setup is called "samchillian tip tip tip cheeepeee") emitted timbral clouds that meshed with DJ Logic's turntable scratchings as a new dimension, far expanding the band's wedge.

Don Byron was the designated jazz player, cutting through all the noise with squealing clarinet, energy-cresting baritone saxophone, and rumblings of bass clarinet in the guttural register Bennie Maupin trawled on Miles's *Bitches Brew*—like *Mistaken Identity*, an album coproduced by Teo Macero. Another Miles reference: The tune "Call Waiting to Exhale" is based on a lick from Miles's underrated *Decoy* album. And another: Cornetist Graham Haynes stepped from the wings a couple times to blow simple but penetrating riffs.

The thing is, this chaos was totally arranged. Reid was only *mock* awkward and wide-eyed, a pose diametrically opposite to Miles's patented badness or the verbal cynicism of, say, Frank Zappa, but serving the same purpose: cover for sneaking some tough music into the act. True, he dove into the crowd in front of the stage during "Saint Cobain," to be caught by several fans (were they plants?) and hoisted back to his proper station. Yet Reid was not a man possessed—rather one entirely cogent and knowing, whatever his limitations.

You could see by his borrowings: He bear-hugged his mike in Blood Ulmer style, built to humongous volumes of Black Rock Coalition splendor, and encouraged the menace of the backbeat, its slugging relentlessness. He also let his solos dribble to an end or dry up, rather than come to a firm conclusion—that is, actually resolve.

Reid wouldn't have done that coming up in Joseph Bowie's Defunkt and Ronald Shannon Jackson's Decoding Society in the '80s. The leaders would pass him a juicy solo spot, then yank the rug out from under, cueing in dissonant horns or some sharply contrasting meter. Compositional shifts throughout *Mistaken Identity* are never quite so surprising or complex; the tracks are deftly sequenced for variety. Live the songs themselves seemed somewhat patchy.

Through the miracle of sampling Reid interspersed some funny bits of found sound. But it was when he cut loose—a smart, tough, dark, fast guitarist—that he proved there's more to Masque than meets the eye. Is it urban alternative black rock? New York acid jazz? Neo-punk funk? Whatever. Lo some thirty years, such jazz-rock-funk-fusions would not be denied.

9 Downtowners Go for Broke

In downtown Manhattan toward the end of the century musicians practiced radical collective improvisation and other fast, adaptive techniques to survive, or else created elaborate, often technologically advanced solo projects, as if self-reliance would help to clarify and distinguish their art. One example of the latter strategy was cellist Arthur Russell's *World of Echo* (Upside/Rough Trade Records). Although Russell worked in collaborative theater music projects, on pop-rock (no jazz) recordings, and flat-out disco dance hits for New York night clubs during the giddy heights of the economically flush mid-'80s, *World of Echo* and its sequel *Another Thought* are his longer-lasting contributions. All alone, playing cello (both arco and pizzicato), singing softly to himself with just the merest hand percussion but audible reverberation adjusted almost measure by measure to suggest different sonic ambiences as though one were wandering through interior chambers of a mind, Russell created a meditative music with a haunting edge.

The music of the first album, particularly, has an earthy and repetitive bluesiness, primitive and high-tech elements, wistful lyrics muttered shyly, somehow comforting. Every nuance is worked out, its provocation intentional. The varied resonances bring us closer to and farther from the performer at different angles, as if Russell's interior monologue was projected in 3-D, like a hologram. The music aspires to, and overall accomplishes, an unusual time-and-spacelessness.

It received some critical attention upon its release, but that was that. Characteristic of the reception of most truly new music in New York City, the rest of the United States, and the world, just a fraction of what risks being either mildly or radically different gets played, heard, documented, and remembered. Such musical projects must be protected by their progenitors, nurtured and determinedly kept alive. *World of Echo* was orphaned when Russell, its composer, died in 1992 of AIDs. *Another Thought,* issued by composer Philip Glass's Point Records imprint from Verve/Polygram, was compiled by Russell's friends Mikel Rouse and Don Christensen from some eight hundred hours of tapes he'd left behind.

Not the Way to Carnegie Hall

Few musical communities or shared states of mind proved so independent, quirky, distinct, and prolific from the mid-'80s through the mid-'90s as the geographically abstract Lower East Side of New York. There, experimentalists on the far shores of jazz, raw pop/rock, renegade classicism, and free improvisation without obvious commercial potential tended to produce their own albums, which were often licensed for European manufacture, distribution, and reimportation into the United States, rather than hailed at home and marketed widely. Limited-access albums could, however, serve as calling cards for artists pursuing bigger record deals, and sometimes thus were taken as raw material suitable for elaborate post-production and revised release.

For example: Keyboardist-composer Wayne Horvitz edited *Dinner at Eight* and *The President,* two albums he'd issued through West Berlin's Dossier label, into *This New Generation* for U.S. Elektra/Musician. The original LPs depicted, through archly poignant melodies and going-nowhere rhythms, urban life of little substance or change, in which a radiator knocks out a beat, tires squeal in the street, sax figures quiver hardly more than wallpaper designs. With wryly mannered assistance—from Elliott Sharp (guitars, bass), Doug Wieselman (clarinet, tenor sax), Joey Peters (electronic drums), and Chris Brown (gazamba, wing) on *Dinner,* as well as guitarist Bill Frisell, percussionist Bobby Previte, and bassist Dave Hoftstra on the rockier *President*—Horvitz (playing Yamaha DX 7, electronic keyboard choice of the era, and RX 11 drum machine) crafted casual all-instrumental songs full of nostalgia and foreboding. Not "jazz" in the sense of solos swinging over changes, Horvitz's pieces nonetheless had jazz roots—what else *could* they be?—and transformed conventions with beguiling strangness.

Sharp and Hard

Similarly, composer/producer/multi-instrumentalist/bandleader Elliott Sharp developed an imposing body of work that found outlet through scattered independent labels, including his own Zoar. *Carbon*, his first album featuring his band of the same name (with Leslie Dalaba, trumpet, on two cuts; David Linton, electric talking drums, metal percussion; Mark Miller, snare, toms, conga; Charles K. Noyes, bass drums, bowed cymbal and snare; and Sharp on guitars, bass, reeds, basstubinet, and 'bone) was a soundtrack of heavy industry run amok, with booming blocks of textures, not riffs or phrases in any usual sense, as the music's components. Carbon repeatedly pounded slam-bang rhythms for their juice; tempo changes indicated a winding-down or shifting of gears. There were winds harsh as those blown on ancient double reeds by the master musicians of Joujouka, Morocco, in the mix, too.

Sharp's music is characteristically unrelenting. With Carbon on *Six Songs/Marco Polo's Argali* he worked with a standard guitar-bass-drums trio *and* a sextet that featured two trombones. Wordless muttering and ultraheavy guitar lines seep through a wall of rigorously processed percussion on some of the tracks. The tunings as well as the rhythms of "Argali," which takes up the entire second side of the long-playing record, are based on the Fibonacci number series, an equation evident in such natural structures as the chambers of seashells. The ensembles Sharp convenes are usually quite adept with such thorny material.

Like many artists enduring the daily grind of Gotham, Sharp searched the clash of cultures, the snarl of schedules, the din of demolition, irrepressible nature, and urban decay for evidence of order and beauty. In recordings such as those compiled on his "best of" CD *Monster Curve* (SST), he transformed his discoveries through post-modern processes into a kind of techno-tribal hard core.

"I've always used extended techniques to make new instruments out of old ones," said Sharp, whose shaved head and Easter Island profile grace the cover of *Monster Curve* as a shadow on a sidewalk. "I use found stuff and I build things to create what I hear and can't otherwise get. That's how I use sampling too. Slowing sampled sounds down, for instance, can reveal new voices and melodic contours."

Sharp's inventions include the slab, "a horizontal base for four strings, with a movable bridge in the center and pickups on either side so you have *eight* playable string lengths," and the pantar, "the top of a sweeping-compound can constructed with a ridge that's a great natural bridge, so with four strings, tuning pegs, a contact mike, a cymbal in the center, and amplification it sounds like someone banging a Dumpster or like a bass or a *mbira* [West African 'thumb piano']." Composing and improvising, performing solo computer music or collaborating with East Village all-stars in ensembles such as Wayne Horvitz's President, Sharp's activities by the late '90s bespoke thirty years of experimentation and far-ranging study.

Born in Cleveland and raised through high school in suburban White Plains, Sharp got a grant to be a scientist's assistant at Pittsburgh's Carnegie Mellon University during the summer of 1968. "I worked on building better fuzz boxes, designing a crude but effective ring modulator, and altering my consciousness—I had some friends in the chemistry department." His thick lips twisted in fond recollection. "It was a good summer for that."

He'd had the standard piano and clarinet lessons as a youngster, "but never played a note of music. It wasn't until I got a guitar that I began learning how to *hear*. The library in White Plains had an especially good collection of records, including Harry Partch and Stockhausen. And I really liked John Cage's writings. So when I got a guitar I stuck paper clips on it, and, much to the chagrin of my parents, sat in my room playing long feedback compositions." Soon Sharp met like-minded rock 'n' rollers.

"First as Colonel Bleep, then as St. Elmo's Fire, our music was influenced by Captain Beefheart, Miles Davis, Ornette Coleman, and the Grateful Dead. We lived in Ithaca, where I went to Cornell in anthropology but dropped out. I went to Bard College in 1972, studied world music and improvisation, Ellington and Monk with trombonist Roswell Rudd; in 1974, I went to Buffalo to pursue a graduate course in composition. My pieces at that time always operated between improvisation and composition."

Enthralled by John McLaughlin's Mahavishnu Orchestra, the Art Ensemble of Chicago, and systematic AACM reedsman Anthony Braxton, playing bluesy rock for money and fun, and studying with ethnomusicologist Charles Keil, Sharp decided he had something of his own to offer.

"When I moved to New York in October of 1979," he

explained, "I wanted to document the profound effect of being immersed in New York life, so I recorded *Rhythm and Blues*, solo pieces each outlining a different aspect of my instrumental technique. I put it out on my own label, Zoar. The next thing I worked on was the *ISM* record with Bill Laswell and Olu Dara, among others. Then my outside producing activities developed."

The ragged but vital No Wave scene was cohering in New York's late-night, low-rent clubs as the '80s arrived, and Sharp introduced bands including the Hi Sheriffs of Blue, Mofungo and the Ordinaires on his Zoar anthology *Peripheral Vision*. "As a producer, you have to tread the line between your personal esthetics and what the band itself wants to be," Sharp understood. "You end up working with bands you hang out with, people you see every day."

At least you do if you're Elliott Sharp. He and his colleagues are heard on about two dozen Zoar productions, the German label Dossier (for which he was an ad hoc A&R man), the Chicago imprint Atavistic, and the California independent SST, which besides *Monster Curve* issued Sharp's satirical song cycle *In the Land of the Yahoos*. Where might that be?

"The New York ethos is about novelty," said Sharp. "Everybody's trying to find the latest gadget before anyone else has it, make their mark with a certain gimmick they get or the latest fad."

He'd made his mark by investing fads with substance, and expanding his musical consciousness. After a weekend trip to Chicago in the early '90s he'd come home to contrive a distinctly Lower East Side blues band. Nor did he stop *there*. Sharp's gone on to compose for string quartets (including Kronos) and orchestras (in the U. S. and abroad), for computers (predating late '90s electronica), and for cross-culturalists from Pakistan, Korea, Italy, Erewhon.

Improviser Unlimited

If Sharp was far-out, he usually took off, like science fiction, from familiar territory. In the '80s his neighbor John Zorn was busy composing musical works with precedents suggested by Karlheinz Stockhausen, Mauricio Kagel, Earle Brown, rules of sports, and complex board games like those produced in the '60s by the firm Avalon Hill. Zorn's "Cobra," which by the late '90s was probably the modern American composition performed more than any other since Terry Riley's "In C," was an ingenious, stimulating, and engrossing way to channel interactive improvisation.

A recording released by the Swiss label hatArt of both a live concert and a studio session caught a particularly stellar Zorn crew—accordionist Guy Klucevsek, vocalist and deliberately *un*studied guitarist Arto Lindsay, turntable specialist Christian Marclay, harpists Carol Emanuel and Zeena Parkins, keyboardist Anthony Coleman, synthesist David Weinstein, tape player Bob James, trombonists Jim Staley and J. A. Deane, Elliott Sharp, Wayne Horvitz, Bill Frisell, and drummer Bobby Previte—cued in to be as free as they'd like, with no dictated notes, through fast juxtapositions of solo, group, and sub-group exchanges. Such a "Cobra" was like intellectual Ping-Pong-in-the-round. To play it—as members of the Jazz Journalists Association did at the Knitting Factory once during the three years in which diverse volunteer groups took up its challenge, monthly—required quick reflexes and improvisational chops, instrumental abilities, a grasp of multi-tiered rules, decent short-term memory, and finely honed degrees of competitiveness and cooperation.

"The way I work is linear. I work in blocks," Zorn explained in a 1986 interview originally published in *Ear* magazine. "That's something I learned from Stravinsky and from cartoon music. Cartoon music and Stravinsky's early music—really *all* of his music—exist in block form. One thing happens, then it stops, and something else happens, then *it* stops, and something *else* happens. This happens in different degrees in everybody's music. Some people are more interested in slow development, and the blocks become very similar to one another; some people are more interested in sharp changing, contrasting things, where the development is more oblique.

"I try to put my music on the furthest extreme of that side, where things don't add up *at all*. The development seems *not* to be happening. One thing follows another in such a crazy and illogical fashion that people at first can't make sense of it. But of course in time.... It's just a matter of what you're used to hearing. Now I think people can hear my music and the way it changes from thing to thing, and they don't say, 'Oh, it's so crazy, it doesn't make sense,' they just follow it and say, 'Well, it's like reading a book or following a travelogue.' They make some kind of comparison they can deal with. And in another ten, twenty, fifty years I think that sort of development will be seen as a narrative form in itself, and will make sense to people; it won't be so outrageous. But even for me, at first it was pretty crazy.

"You see, the music that I loved from maybe age fifteen on, after I was introduced to it, was the music of the maverick composers like

Varese and Ives and Cage and Partch, Kagel and Stockhausen; these composers were all on the cutting edge of what they were doing, and it was *that* tradition that attracted me. So from the beginning I was interested in exploring different sounds. Improvising was there, but in different degrees, as I went on.

"When I went to St. Louis [for college], I was introduced to jazz music, which is a heavy improvising tradition, and at that time Anthony Braxton, the AACM, the St. Louis–based Black Artists Group were all doing a lot of new work, exciting things, trying to incorporate some of the structural ideas of the composers that I mentioned with a black improvising tradition, and I thought some of the results were really great, *inspiring*. I liked the energy and the intensity that they brought to the music. That was in some way lacking in a lot of the so-called serious contemporary music being made at the time. With very few exceptions, it was a dry academic scene of lifeless old farts.

"A lot of the composers of my generation were introduced to many, *many* different kinds of music as they were growing up, because so much music is available on disc," said Zorn, whose personal CD and record collection is fantastically broad. "This is different from a hundred years ago. Now anything that's been performed is basically available to be heard, in some form or another, and a composer is usually *voracious* about hearing things. A lot of the people of my generation who grew up in the '60s, introduced to ethnic musics from India and from Africa, enjoyed mixing these different things together and got involved in improvisation in one form or another. Many of us share an interest in these varied musics.

"I have a musical vision based on that way of breaking things down into blocks, having them very contrasting from one to the next, having them pose a kind of problem, like a code or a mathematical formula. What I try to do when I'm improvising really *freely* with other people is use different tactics and strategies and timings to get them to change in some way. If I do a loud sound at just the right moment, they might be surprised and stop and change what they're doing. Or if I come in and match their sound in some way, then slowly bring it somewhere else, and then stop—sometimes if I follow them, they start following me, and if *I* change I can get *them* to change, too, to make something different happen. I have lots of little tricks like that to try to get my sounds happening.

"When I started working to structure pieces with improvisers, my first thought was: 'Here is a series of individuals, each has his own personal music. All worked on their instruments, on their own, to develop a highly personal language, that's often not notatable. It's often a kind of music that Pierre Boulez would say 'can't be written down on a staff.' So my problem was: How can I involve these musicians in a composition that's valid and stands on its own without being *performed*, and yet inspires these musicians to play their best, and at the same time realizes the musical vision that I have in *my* head?

"My first decision, which I think was the most important, was never to talk about language or sound at all. I left that completely up to the performers. What I was left with was *structure*. I can talk about *when* things happen and when they *stop*, but not *what* they are. I can talk about *who* and in what *combinations*, but I can't say what goes on. I can say, 'A change will happen *here*,' but I can't say what *kind* of change it will be.

"I began creating very simple structures—combinations, for example, of all the possible duets in a twelve-piece group, all the possible trios. Then I'd work them all out, order them, and the players would go through this ordering, along with another set of rules that made it a little more complicated than just going through one after another—first *these* two people, then *these* two people.

"Then I began devising different game rules that the improvisers would play that would make it a little more fun, a little more exciting and challenging than just reading something off a page. That's no challenge at all for an improviser. What I came up with is a series of rules, like a trading system—one person plays, then the next person plays, then the next person plays—and event systems, where people independently perform events. Everybody can perform one event each, for example, but nobody can time it at the same time with anybody else. There might be a series of downbeats where at a downbeat a change will happen—if you're playing, maybe you must stop; if you're not playing, you may come in. That's just one example.

"With each new piece, I made up new sets of rules, sometimes incorporating similar ideas and systems from old pieces into new pieces but changing the sequences, or the overall way it was put together. I would perhaps get a series of fifteen systems, each one able to spark a different set of relationships among players, then figure out a way that these different systems could be used by them. What orders can they be performed in? Can several be performed at the same time? Can some be called by certain players and others *not*?

Are there certain powers that certain players can have that other players can't have? The pieces got more and more complicated. 'Cobra' and 'Xu Feng' and 'Hu Die,' my newest pieces, are the most complicated in terms of structure and game that I've come to yet."

The kaleidoscope quality of Zorn's resulting music is impressive, and transporting. If, to the uninitiated, it seems that no stunning discovery of the improvisation is long sustained or developed, that without tapes and samples few motifs are repeated, or that during performances inspired bits of music are often interrupted and seldom reestablished, that doesn't faze Zorn at all.

"I think I have done a very different thing than what my heroes were all about," he said. "Partch, Varese, Ives—the idea of those composers locking themselves up in a closet, composing their music, never or seldom having it performed—that's different than being on a scene, meeting people, exchanging ideas. I'm a performer as well as a composer. I'm right there down on the stage, and that's a very different situation.

"Improvising with other people is a source book for ideas for me, a workshop where I learn new ideas for composing pieces. I see things that *can't* happen in improvisation that I want to *have* happen, so I go and write a piece around it. Players' languages attract me, whether they have a highly personal language of a very wide vocabulary or very narrow vocabularies; it's what they *do* with their vocabularies that makes them interesting. Perhaps they're able to find new contexts to use their sounds in through my pieces, and create situations where what they do sounds different than it usually does.

"I believe my music can be played by musicians from any background, from anywhere in the world," he continued without false modesty. "It's truly a universal language. And my idea is to get that happening, to mix people from different backgrounds together in the same kind of melting pot, and have it come out as one unified music. I think this comes back from being brought up in New York. You can't get a more mixed city than this. The different languages, that kind of a mix, comes through in my music.

"Because I was working in a game structure and wasn't talking about sounds, I became familiar with everybody *else's* sounds, and they've become a part of my musical vision, so it's almost like I've come to represent the scene in a certain way. But still, it's the manipulation of the musical material that in the long run is the real contribution, and I think the game structures have moved me so that I can return to written music and come up with something completely different, something that has not happened before, except maybe in cartoon music, which is the only tradition I really feel a sonic affinity toward."

If "Cobra" is not Zorn's greatest lasting achievement, it is wondrously original work. Through it, and by constantly touring Europe and establishing himself in Japan, Zorn came to represent Lower East Siders' audacity, and their utter resistance to the imposition of musical limits. By the mid-'90s Zorn had won a following among hardcore fans of international punk-rock via Naked City, a composition workshop with Bill Frisell, Wayne Horvitz, Fred Frith on bass, drummer Joey Baron, and vocalist Yamatsaka Eye; among elevated circles of serious improvisers like the austere English guitarist Derek Bailey; and as a breakthrough composer receiving orchestra commissions from the Brooklyn Philharmonic, for one. Zorn also helped instigate a wave of confrontational music in Japan, and raised some hackles appropriating graphic images of tortured Asians for two of his CD booklets. Did the jazz tradition continue to interest him?

"It absolutely presents challenges to me as a saxophone player," he said in '86. "Jazz is the language of the alto saxophone, which is what I play. To play that instrument, you've got to listen to Charlie Parker, to Ornette Coleman—those are just *musts*. So I study that music, and I enjoy performing it, but I don't fool myself—it's just fun for me, but that's not my tradition, not what I want to listen to of *mine*."

But in the mid-'90s Zorn was blowing as ardently as any jazz saxophonist ever has, with a quartet (featuring trumpeter Dave Douglas, bassist Greg Cohen, and drummer Joey Baron) he named Masada, after the hill in Judea where Jewish resistance fighters committed mass suicide rather that fall to Roman seige. Zorn's improvising was brilliant, based on an enormous book of tunes he wrote that expanded on Sephardic modes and the Ornette Coleman/Don Cherry late '50s free melody style. Masada was documented in ten lovingly self-produced CDs, released by Japan's daring Disk Union label, available in the United States largely as hard-to-get imports.

Masada spearheaded Zorn's outright campaign for "a New Cultural Renaissance—one in which all Jews everywhere could find pride and meaning"—through music. In the mid- to late '90s, Zorn's imprint Tzadik issued a couple of dozen albums of Lower East Side conceptualists exploring a surprisingly radical and ornate Jewish jazz, which reimagined its mythic Easter European heritage, recalled the American baby-boom generation's assimilation, and groped toward new accommodations with black and Latin Americans, Asians, and Arab Middle-Easterners. *The Revenge of the Stuttering Child,* a 1997 Tzadik release with readings of Palestinian Ronny Sonneck's poetry in English and Arabic offset by Elliott Sharp's moody arrangements for his guitars, electric mandocello, mandolin, bass clarinet, saxes, and computer processing as well as harp, accordion, cello, piano, and the drum *dumbek,* mined themes of historic proportions and immediate feeling. In the same season Tzadik released compilation albums of downtown artists hailing two entertainers who'd previously been considered pure mainstream as "great Jewish musicians": France's singer-songwriter Serge Gainsbourg and America's own Burt Bacharach.

Zorn had concluded our interview saying, "There are a lot of us being bagged together as the downtown improvising scene, the Lower East Side improvising scene, but what does this really mean? It's a little deceptive. True, we all work with improvisation, we're attracted to it and draw inspiration from it. But each of us uses it to a different degree, and in a different way. It's really important to stress the individuality of each person."

So, yes, Zorn, Sharp, and Horvitz (who relocated to Seattle, as did Bill Frisell) were among the post-jazz-plus scenemakers and happenings-producers, largely responsible for establishing the musical tilt of the the Knitting Factory, which from the mid-'80s on served as base camp for an international "downtown" avant-garde. But scores of musicians participated in the Lower East Siders' events and charted directions of their own, often documenting themselves on recordings that were, until 1989, most readily available from a loft on lower Broadway that housed the New Music Distribution Service.

Founded by pianist-composer-arranger Carla Bley and trumpeter Michael Mantler, principals of the late-'60s Jazz Composers Orchestra Association that produced concerts and recordings, NMDS was the hub of a widely dispersed, low-profile network of artist-producers, record stores, and performance venues. For years, self-styled composer-auteur Kip Hanrahan was resident publicist; later aficionado-producer Yale Evelev annotated the annual NMDS catalogue. For most of the tiny companies it dealt with NMDS was the only game in town. Its eventual business collapse put the very notion of artist labels in jeopardy.

Subsequently, each artist label had to search for distribution separately, through less-connected and barely motivated regional dealers. All was not lost: NMDS set the stage for the surge of independent rock labels of the late '90s. By then, many of the Zorn-Sharp-Horvitz cohort had won themselves some space. It may have been gritty, scruffy, and crowded but it was also lively, unpredictable, and artistically serious—whether or not it was on the Lower East Side.

The Microscopic Septet

What was special about the Microscopic Septet was not their look but their sound. True, the players donned red Shriner fezzes to perform "Lobsters on Parade," but their costumes, leaning to vintage '40s-'50s men's wear, reflected a mélange of skewed melodies, ersatz Latinisms, polished sax section harmonies, jazz history-ranging rhythms, and earnestly expressive solos, demonstrated through half a dozen small-label releases.

"Basic to this band is a curiosity about the weird edge," explained pianist Joel Forrester, coleader with soprano and alto saxophonist Phillip Johnston of the Micros. "In just about every number, we try to push toward the point that's *out there*. That's what we're all gunning for."

At first exposure, Micro's music usually sounded funny *ha-ha,* not funny *weird*—maybe the result of Forrester and Johnston's grasp of styles familiar to kids of all ages as soundtracks for animated cartoons. John Zorn and clarinetist Don Byron also celebrated this genre, with their specific tributes to the late Warner Bros. composer Carl W. Stolling and composer-bandleaders Raymond Scott and John Kirby.

But upon further listening, Micros' music revealed twists of lyricism and irony that distinguished it from retrovision. The Micros' mood was almost always upbeat, its melodies catchy, its precision impressive though not prissy. Laughter was an acceptable reaction when the Micros played, although "some people aren't comfortable with the fact that there's a lot of humor in our music," Johnston reported, sitting on the roof of the building on the Bowery in which Forrester had built himself an artist's loft. We enjoyed a 360-degree view of lower Manhattan.

"We'd better undress that point," Forrester added. "People either are laughing along with us or just don't get it at all."

"I see our music as good-natured, but there's a certain strangeness about life that pop music tries to deny, to convince you that 'really, everything's alright,'" Johnston continued. "Once you realize everything's *not* alright, and it's never going to *be* alright, a certain humor comes with that. And *that's* alright.

"But our music, if it's nothing else, is definitely jazz," he insisted. Johnston disliked "style" bands that play music *about* jazz, rather than jazz *itself*. "Jazz is something that's always changing, so of course our music is different than the way it was in the '50s. It incorporates all the things *we've* experienced."

What they had experienced (the vagaries of careers as instrumentalists scuffling in the clubs and international gig marts available from New York for some twenty years) and how they'd endured it (with eyes on the long haul, tongues-in-cheeks curled around grains of salt) came through every Micros' show. When we spoke in July 1988, they'd recently played a series Mondays at Sweet Basil while Gil Evans's big band toured the world, a free Summerstage show in Central Park, and the internationally renowned Montreal Jazz Festival. They'd long seemed due for wider recognition.

Johnston and Forrester had met on the Lower East Side in the early '70s, formed the Microscopic Septet in 1980, and maintained remarkable personnel consistency—with alto saxophonist Don Davis, bari saxist Dave Sewelson, bass and tuba player Dave Hofstra, and drummer Richard Dworkin on their albums *Offbeat Glory, Take the Z Train, Let's Flip,* and *Beauty Based on Science.* (Tenor saxist Paul Shapiro replaced John Hagan in 1984.) Revering jazz giants Charles Mingus and Thelonious Monk (the Micros' sole cover was a lovingly detailed version of Monk's "Crepuscule with Nellie"), the band's leaders could accept the postmodernist tag "as long as it's recognized we're part of a musical process that started a long time ago and will be going on after we're just a record," Forrester stipulated.

"Always before in modern times, the latest thing was the *only* thing possible, and you had to completely dump on everything that already went down," explained the pianist, who had, for a while, used the stage name Dr. Real. "It used to be that there was a definite avant-garde. I have the feeling that now the whole human race is the avant-garde. So you're completely free to take from all the elements, all the modern forms brought forward. The Micros can throw one thing right next to another, and as long as it swings, it's okay."

"It's gotta swing," Johnston concurred, "whether it's Latin, or r&b or straight-ahead blowing. Orchestration is really important in our music too—using the instruments as effectively as possible. And people say we sound like more than seven instruments. In fact, that's one of the ideas behind our name: that our arrangements and orchestrations are reductions of a big band for a small group. But swing, that's the foundation of what we do."

Other jazz artists built careers on the same foundation; the Micros weren't so odd as all that. They broke up in 1992, though, after a particularly savage review in the *New York Times* of their Knitting Factory-JVC New York Jazz Festival performance negated some interest they'd gained at a major label.

In fact, the Micros got even smaller. They hadn't recorded for any very well established—or even surviving—label, though they were great fun live, and generally well received when they performed.

They'd earned a decent reputation, a fair following, and their signature sound gave musical identity to "Fresh Air," a long-running National Public Radio interview show. Yet strangely, neither the Microscopic Septet, Joel Forrester, nor Phillip Johnston were noted in the standard jazz references books available prior to 1998. That year Johnston reacquired master tapes and rights to the Micros' albums and persuaded a fairly stable independent firm, Koch Jazz, to reissue the first of them, *Take the Z Train*, so that his old gang would finally be represented on CD.

Woman of a Hundred Voices

Shelley Hirsch slipped through a roomful of roles, affecting and discarding accents as fast as a practiced shopper tries on blue jeans— with members of the Microscopic Septet at the Bitter End; with John Zorn at Brooklyn Academy of Music; with David Weinstein's advanced electronics at Dance Theater Workshop, the Kitchen, Roulette and Experimental Intermedia; with Loisaida (Lower East Sider) improvisers at one of those odd gigs that could occur anywhere, anytime. For a long while she didn't have a record of her own, only a cassette, "Power Muzak," in which she whispered, groaned, meowed, and offered up fragments of oratorios in pseudo-foreign languages like a Berlitz-blitzed soul singer

"I'm a vocalist-improviser-composer-performer-person," Hirsch said. "An actress, also. I am a New Yorker, from Brooklyn. I have a very complex personality. Lot of dynamics. I've been living downtown for twelve years [as of 1986], and working in the downtown area for that long, also doing a little bit of uptown work. I just started doing more improvisation in the last five years, I would say.

"Well, actually no—I *always* was an improviser. I'm talking ten years old: I used to put on performances and make up songs and dances and everything else. In fact, I was on a television show when I was in sixth grade. We were having class elections and they asked us to write speeches. I was the person who was made to go on television and make an impromptu speech. Even though I'd written what I thought was a fabulous speech for someone's presidential career in the sixth grade, they thought I was a better improviser. So I went on the show and made up a speech. That's my actual first professional experience, improvising.

"I do a lot of movement also. I'm using the whole body as an instrument. Words play into that. I find their rhythmic connections. Movement, extended along with the voice, creates musical ideas."

"Maybe you'd like to do this interview in dialect?" I suggested.

"OK," she said, turning cockney. "I'll switch into a coupla different things because I find sometimes I can't get my feelings out unless I find a rhythmic slot for it. So I adapt the movement and the sound, and then let the ideas start flowing." From the herky-jerky moves and up-tilted, side-long glance of an Eliza Doolittle, she morphed into flowing gestures, pursed lips, fluttering eyelashes, and mock Italian. "Like, if I want to talk in a slower way, something totally different will come out when I talk like that or I sing like that."

Does she take on a different persona?

"I do, but I feel it really is me, and I find a nuance expressed better when I change the enunciation and the space in speech syntax. Sometimes I'm just talking normally, and I say to people, 'OK, *nalati tes*...' [a made-up dialect]. It's just normal. There's no distance any more between my performance and my real life. I often just have to find some other way of expressing things, aside from just speaking in this normal tone."

So improvisation as used in music spilled over into her everyday life?

"Definitely. It goes back and forth because I use what happens in daily life all the time. Like the 'Sinbad the Sailor' thing I did at Experimental Intermedia." Her Sinbad, shipwrecked on an island, fell into a gulch littered with jewels, and was eventually saved by a giant bird attracted by the sparkling gems. Hirsch sang braggadocio, despair, wonder, suspense, and delight all in Sinbad's Arabic brogue and made scene transitions with wordless melisma, imitating the ship flailing, the flapping of the enormous bird, everything complete as in a radio play. "If I spot a diamond on Canal Street, it brings up Sinbad again.

"When I was seventeen I had my first solo apartment in New York on Ludlow Street, a fantastic ethnic area. And people heard what I did. They said, 'This is like Balinese jazz, or something.' So I had the idea to go to study...*something*. I went to California to study Kabuki, which was one thing I knew of that combined voice, movement, and theater. That didn't work out, but I *did* join a theater group. And then I moved to Holland.

"I traveled around Europe. I was nineteen by that time. And I tried to join a theater group there, but I ended up singing with a swing band. And then I was going to go to India to study, because I lived with somebody who had lived there for a long time, but that didn't happen. I came back to the States, and kept on absorbing all this information. I didn't return to Europe for another ten years. Then I went to Italy, and the next year started touring central Europe a lot, going to Morocco, also, with side trips to Portugal and Spain."

Was it unusual for a woman to break into international free improvisation?

"Being a vocalist sets you apart in a way," Hirsch responded. "It's kind of a privileged position. A lot of people [improvisers] don't like the idea of traditional vocalists, and are worried about being upstaged, because when you're using words people tend to listen to that more. So there might be problems playing with other musicians who want to keep things very equal, but I've been lucky finding great people to play with. I think the vocalist issue becomes more of an issue than the woman issue, although I wish that I had more women to play with. I'm playing with men all the time."

Did she think women have a different sensitivity to or sensibility about improvisation? Was her product different because of her gender?

"Hmmm," she considered. "I would say your own personal history has some effect on what you're doing, and in *that* there's a difference. But not just because of *being* a woman. A woman who's been in society living this way, being affected by things the way she is, plays a certain way. I don't think it's necessarily a biological thing. When I'm improvising well, getting very loose with it, I find women have an incredible response to what I do. In Europe, especially, the women go crazy and tell me they really can relate to what I'm doing. I find that very interesting. I use words, though, a lot, and the way that things come out, the combinations of feelings and very abstract things...

"After my performances, women have come up and offered me things, cried—things like that. What these people say they feel is that I'm very open and expressing feelings that ordinarily people try to keep back. Now obviously, when you listen to my 'Power Muzak' or, say, 'Sinbad,' you're not thinking, 'This is very emotional.' I don't think it comes through in *everything,* but I think that there is *something* very revealing in what I'm doing. Something exposed. That might be more of a woman's thing than a man's. I think what women often respond to in me, and that maybe some men would be more afraid of, is the kind of way I can be very exposed. Some men appreciate that also. But I think women have a particular connection to it."

How is the voice a special instrument?

"For one thing, I'm not carrying things around with me all the time. It's something that I can use every moment of the day, and always do. It's always right there, very immediate. And for improvisation, especially, it's there. It always comes out, finds new outlets, new places. You respond to the acoustics of every different room you're in in a different way. My voice is always available, always accessible. That's one thing I miss in a lot of improvisation. I think people go along with a lot of these ideas of what improvisation is, but I'm looking to be more spontaneous with it, through it.

"I'm working with a lot of what I'd call 'found footage,' listening to a lot of different kinds of music, just being open to sounds that I'm hearing around. And I don't think there's any limitation on the voice. I've studied classical voice technique, and I've had teachers say, 'Oh, don't do *that,* because if you do that, you're going to have a hard time producing *this* Western sound.' But I'm not interested in those limitations. So I work on refining the material that I take in, and expanding my techniques.

"I've always loved working with percussion instruments, and I love a lot of ethnic string instruments. Chinese zithers and Western harps, dumbeks and log drums, things with a variety of sounds. That's what I'm after, I guess: finding different sounds and seeing the ways they mix together. That's what's particular to the music that I make: I'm interested in combining all these different elements, stringing them together into something different than the individual elements.

"I was opposed to using electronics for a long time, but I started multitracking myself, and that enabled me to really expand what I was doing. And then David Weinstein, who's a codirector of Roulette and a musician and composer, said, 'You've got to try my delay. You've got to try this. It's perfect for you. You can layer all these things and it's like live, rather than sitting in a studio and doing it over again. This thing keeps it repeating, and you can punch in the new sound right away.'

"So I tried it, and was hooked. Preparing for a concert, I've had days where I've sat for six or eight hours, it keeps going and going and going, and feeds me like another musician because it's always sustaining…. I don't use it to create a lot of electronic effects. I'm interested in using it as a live compositional device. So I can add new information into it, and sustain that while I add *newer* information."

Were there traditional jazz singers, or classical opera singers, for that matter, she'd been influenced by?

"Oh, I feel influenced by *everything,*" Hirsch maintained, "but I *love* Billie Holiday, I love Victoria De Los Angelos too, who sings opera, but not only opera. And I was very influenced by *Carmen* when I was growing up. My parents listened to Frank Sinatra and Johnny Mathis, [cocktail piano duo] Ferrante and Teicher, and Tony Bennett. I grew up with that kind of material, in a tenement building which was very busy; you'd walk past a door and hear different strange sounds coming out. I heard a lot of Frank Sinatra, but in my neighborhood, East New York, Brooklyn, I listened mostly to Motown music. I love Aretha and Otis Redding, in particular. Someone lived in that building who loved Yma Sumac, the Peruvian singer. I didn't know who she was till years later, but I'd been listening to her, and she sort of crept into me, too.

"Irony plays a very important role in what I do, I find. I like to take different perspectives, shift fast, moment to moment. Maybe I'm trying to cover all the bases, but I like to step outside of things, and make a comment, interject a sense of humor. Being totally inside, and being something else that's outside, and commenting on it— that's what I do."

Sound Producer as Visionary

"My projects happen mostly by accident," claimed Hal Willner, soundtrack producer of Robert Altman's films including *Short Cuts,* based on short stories by the late American "dirty realist" writer

Raymond Carver, and *Kansas City,* a paean to jazz during that town's Depression-era apotheosis. Incidents in Carver's fiction, Altman's films, and Willner's total-concept soundtrack design might seem to share only temporal connection, yet nothing in any of them occurs out of nowhere. Considering Willner's unusual accomplishments—he's longtime music director of the television staple *Saturday Night Live,* the man who chose the musical guests introduced by smooth-jazz sax star David Sanborn on the short-lived but fondly remembered TV program *Night Music,* and producer of albums in which rock 'n' roll, jazz, and new-music notables have emerged from obscurity, made career comebacks, or stretched their talents in unpredictable directions—"mostly" is no explanation.

Willner had prepared, perhaps unconsciously, to realize music in narrative terms—and vice versa—since his youthful fascination with old-time radio shows in which stories were told through sound. As a teenager in the late '60s and early '70s, he appreciated "concept albums with beginnings, middles and ends that somehow transcended the music and became almost visual."

"And you know the producer Joel Dorn, right? I had an internship with him in Philadelphia, and he used to make records like this with jazz artists. Remember the spin-through-the-radio-dial on Yusef Lateef's *Part of the Search,* and the story behind Rahsaan Roland Kirk's *Case of the 3-Sided Stereo Dream*? I think it's a real loss nobody makes albums like that anymore."

These albums, reissued in the late '90s on Dorn's 32 Jazz label, foreshadowed Willner's creation of a genre-defying genre in which reinterpretations of a noted composer's work by widely diverse musicians reveal unexpected implications. His discography as a concept-album producer includes tributes to Federico Fellini's favorite soundtrack composer (*Amacord Nino Rota,* Hannibal), composer-pianist Thelonious Monk *(That's the Way I Feel Now,* on A&M), Kurt Weill *(Lost in the Stars),* songs from vintage Disney films (*Stay Awake),* and the brooding bassist Charles Mingus *(Weird Nightmare,* on Columbia). Willner also produced successful career comebacks for '60s-rock singer Marianne Faithfull, albums of readings by poet Allen Ginsberg and satirist William Burroughs set to downtown-esque music, works by admired if lesser-known jazz musicians (the Beaver Harris–Don Pullen 360 Degree Music Experience *Well Kept Secret*), and a restoration of long-lost tapes by comic social critic Lenny Bruce (for fantasy). The list is the wish fulfillment of a man with broad tastes, an encyclopedic memory for jazz and pop, a sense of larger structures (naturally, he's listened to classical European chamber and symphonic music), and very good connections. Willner's unplanned way began in high school.

"I was into radio programs like *Inner Sanctum* and the Orson Welles productions, then I got interested in records like the Beatles' 'White Album,' the first Blood Sweat & Tears, Coltrane's *A Love Supreme,* and Miles's *Sketches of Spain.* They took me somewhere, they were like journeys through dreams. In fact, I was going to call the Monk album *Monk's Nightmare* until Steve Lacy suggested the title we used."

Anyway, "Weird Nightmare" was the title of a Charles Mingus composition, and perfectly fit Willner's 1992 Mingus production.

"Mingus is a logical choice for me to make—his music works with this kind of approach. I try not to think of too many possible subjects, and I've never done anyone who's *not* dead, because then you have a complete career to work with. I'd like to do an Ellington project; it would be a great excuse to immerse myself in his music, study it and become more expert." That's why he did Kurt Weill.

"I originally intended just to examine the music of Nino Rota with one artist," Willner says of his first cast-of-hundreds album production. "But I got a vision in the night to do it with Carla Bley, Jaki Byard, and Muhal Richard Abrams. Then Chris Stein and Deborah Harry [of the band Blondie] wanted to be involved, and when the record came out, it got all this attention. I thought, 'This is going to be my record production high-water mark. It won't get better than this.'

"Then after Monk died I was sitting in Carnegie Hall at some jazz fest memorial to Monk, getting freaked that Terry Adams from NRBQ and Donald Fagen from Steely Dan and all these other people who really had a love of Monk weren't performing, and that the jazz people who were playing Monk's music were making it boring. Monk's music was *never* boring. When Oscar Peterson came on, that was *it*—he had even put Monk down. So there was my Monk idea. And after that, the question was 'Who else?'"

Willner had by the mid-'90s called on stylists as disparate as New Orleans' falsetto extraordinaire Aaron Neville and downtown cut up John Zorn to participate on his albums, which come off as less eclectic than visionary. He's mixed such outsiders as the self-styled "Peruvian songbird" Yma Sumac with such insiders as Beatles drummer Ringo Starr. He's effected obvious but never before attempted pairings, such as soprano saxophonist Steve Lacy with drummer Elvin Jones, and surprisingly powerful meetings, such as

Sonny Rollins with Leonard Cohen, or Betty Carter and Branford Marsalis with blues bassman Willie Dixon. He's provided invaluable A&R suggestions to bands with their own distinctive sounds—for instance, Los Angeles barrio homeboys Los Lobos, and on the other edge of the world, East Village new jazz vaudevillians the Jazz Passengers.

Many of Willner's mixes and matches immediately announce themselves as inspired: Sting sings Weill's "Mac the Knife"; the Marsalis brothers play a medley of melodies from early Fellini; Sun Ra's Arkestra swings "Pink Elephants on Parade" from *Dumbo*. On the Mingus tribute, arrangements by black-rock guitar star Vernon Reid, saxman Henry Threadgill, and pianist Geri Allen, among others, use the justly intoned musical instruments of the late composer Harry Partch, some under portions of Mingus's exaggerated autobiography read by Robbie Robertson (formerly of the Band), novelist Hubert *(Last Exit to Brooklyn)* Selby Jr., and Chuck D, a gangsta rapper. Willner said his ideas are always at the service of undervalued or misapprehended twentieth-century classics.

"I look for music that has influenced or *can* influence different types of musicians, and music that can break down so it flows from Todd Rundgren to solo Randy Weston to Zorn with Arto Lindsay and Wayne Horvitz to Terry Adams to Eugene Chadbourne's Shockabilly to [New Orleans' populist guitarist] Mark Bingham with John Scofield and Steve Swallow, without seeming like a novelty," he explained. "That's one of my favorite sequences on the Monk album—check it out."

Sheer pleasure in making the never-before happen seems to motivate Willner, who for most of the '80s and '90s lived modestly next door to Charlie Parker's final home in Manhattan's East Village. His personal style is unpretentious, and he brings a fan's respect to his productions' subjects. That's generally won him kudos from critical purists, though some pop musicians feel a need to defend their versions of beloved jazz against possible complaint.

"I like Hal's records; whether or not serious-minded people approve of them is irrelevant," said Elvis Costello, who sang the challenging title track of Willner's Mingus tribute *Weird Nightmare*. "There's a place for different interpretations of great music; having different musicians keep the music alive by playing it cannot diminish any version which to some ears is truer or closer to the original. Whatever comes out of my work on the Mingus record will be because of my love of his music—not to promote myself."

Same with Willner, though he doesn't *completely* abjure the spotlight. On Monk's "Misterioso," after tenor saxist Johnny Griffin blows a fervent solo over Carla Bley's swirling orchestral chart, Willner himself is the Voice of Death.

And the Walls Came Tumblin' Down

The place: the Knitting Factory. The event: a gala "Second Seder," semipublic party celebrating the Jewish spring festival of Passover. The players: that extended community of downtown improvisers, composers, and musical individualists who often fall through the cracks because they're beyond classification or category. Of course, most of them, in their youth, embraced some basic tenets of jazz—high standards of performance, spontaneity and depth of expression, love of rhythmic propulsion, creative freedom with due respect for formal structures—and besides any inherited religion, have kept something of that faith through their subsequent studies, enthusiasms, experiments, and adventures.

Here was Shelley Hirsch offering the age-old blessing over the ritual dinner's first cup of wine, with splatter/squeak/wail obbligato from clarinetist David Krakauer; the chameleon chanteuse had just released her mostly richly inhabited sound piece, *O Little Town of East New York,* on John Zorn's Tzadik label. Behind banquet tables jammed to overflowing on the Knit's balcony, trombonist Art Baron (leader of the Duke's Men Ellington repertory combo and regular in the Lincoln Center Jazz Orchestra) played tuba in a standup trio with soprano saxophonist Steve Elson of the Borneo Horns and accordionist Ann DeMarinis to accompany the traditional dipping of vegetables in salt water, recalling tears shed during the exodus from Egypt but also the bounty of spring's renewal.

Roy Nathanson, frontman of the Jazz Passengers, conferred with Hal Willner, producer of high-concept projects, about where to hide the *afikomen,* a piece of matzoh whose whereabouts is supposed to distract kids through the evening-long reading of the Passover Haggadah. Nathanson sniggled "The Pink Panther" theme on his alto. The Klezmatics' trumpeter Frank London spun out rampant klezmer licks while a video of Brooklyn Hassids baking the holiday's unleavened bread was screened. Elegant, blond Nora York sang "Go Down Moses," and the hall stilled for a grainy videotape of Dr. Martin Luther King Jr. delivering his "I have a dream" speech, like

Moses envisioning the Chosen advancing past him into the Promised Land.

Bassist Mark Dresser and his daughter introduced the Four Questions. She was the Wise Child, asking, "Why is this night different from all other nights?" followed by Laurie Anderson, speaking, she explained, less as the Simple than the *Immature* Child who didn't even *try* to comprehend the story. Then Steven Bernstein with a pocket trumpet and his toddler Rex Louis came on as the Child Who Doesn't Even Know How to Ask. Finally John Zorn, drummer Joey Baron smiling broadly behind him, unleashed an ear-piercing alto sax howl as the Rude or Rebellious Child, who demands, pointedly, "What does this service mean to *you*?"

Zorn's sonic violence shredding the mellow air was actually essential to this avant-garde—No? Call it hip, then, if middle-class—gathering. No ritual that apprehends the spiritual needs of Jews (or artists, or virtually any select sect) in New York now (or probably anywhere, anytime) would be complete without a bolt of rude reality. Sting though it might, Zorn's solo addressed a haunting conundrum before the congregants, one that's nagged ever more insistently at certain American baby boomers attaining uneasy middle age. Do we—whoever we are—have interests and values distinct from the multitude's? Where does individuality originate? What responsibilities come with it?

An increasing number of Jews, jazzers, and unconditional music fans have found balm for these inquiries in the revival of klezmer. Originally the Jewish greenhorns' wedding music that adapted melodic themes, rhythms, and song forms from Eastern Europe in the spirit of New York's Roaring '20s, klezmer was founded by clarinetists Naftule Brandwein and Dave Tarras (Ben Webster and Coleman Hawkins types, respectively, each with collections of their decades-old hits available in the late '90s on CD). Through World War II and its aftermath, klezmer was commercialized, decimated, demoralized, outdated, and eclipsed—then miraculously reborn in the '70s when bluegrass mandolinist Andy Statman discovered Tarras humbly at work in the Catskills, helped him reemerge, procure federal arts grants, and reenergize the field. Since the birth of the New Klezmer Orchestra by students of Boston's New England Conservatory, the ranks of klezmer ensembles have swelled, and in the mid-'90s the music won national mainstream attention via violinist Itzhak Perlman's presentations of it on nationwide tour and

PBS TV specials, as well as through sober reconstruction by probing intellects such as jazz clarinetist Don Byron (*Plays the Music of Mickey Katz*, Elektra/Nonesuch).

Contemporary klezmer has its own progressive wing: Religiously observant Statman, renowned for clarinet as well as mandolin now, brings the specific gravity of Coltrane, a kind of Afro-Izro modalism, and pulsating rhythmic suspensions to his album *Klezmer Music: A Marriage of Heaven and Earth* (Ellipsis Arts), while bands such as the Klezmatics deal knowledgeably with klez sources and repertoire, striving to play the certifiable idiom in the moment, with feeling.

Beyond klez, music that partakes of both the Jewish past and present is ever more prevalent, emerging from unlikely reaches of the Diaspora. There's Israeli-Palestinian jazz by the combo Esta, Sephardic guitar productions as lush and scrumptious as smooth jazz by Luis Delgado, fusion versions of ancient prayers featuring a studio minion including saxophonists Lee Konitz, Dave Liebman, Bob Berg and Bob Mintzer, guitarist Steve Khan, keyboardist-accordionist Gil Goldstein, drummer Dannie Gottlieb, and singer-songwriter Carole King on Ben Sidran's *Life's a Lesson* (Go Jazz). And there's the radical branch that's thrived in radical New York.

Zorn might be regarded as big *macher* of that town, but he's been burdened with many roles since the mid-'70s: nerdy performance artist, ruthless deconstructivist, East Village poster boy, comprover par excellence, games-maker and genre-cracker, Japanese punk-pop star, Knit Fac core consultant, raging saxophonist—as well as producer of rare, gemlike records on Tzadik (Yiddish for a righteous man, perhaps even a saint, who performs good works in anonymity). Among the Tzadik catalogue's two hundred CDs is a series wrapped in metallic-inked covers adorned with Judaic graphic symbols and literary references. They represent a music that seems to have sprung from Zorn's importation of a tribe of radical Jewish musician-warriors for an evening-length presentation in a weeklong international festival of first-rank innovators (Ornette Coleman rated an evening for a project, too) in Munich, Germany, in 1992.

"Zorn just invited a lot of New York Jews and encouraged us all to play and ask questions," remembers Nathanson. "Everybody was there: me and Anthony Coleman, Shelley, Krakauer, Marc Ribot, Tim Berne, Frank London and the Klezmatics, Mark Feldman, Laurie Anderson, Richard Teitelbaum, John Lurie [of the Lounge Lizards], who's half-Jewish…"

Nathanson pauses with a bit of unease. "I don't know if it's right to point out the differences between people," he explains. "The Jewish ideal is not to be proud or ashamed of distinctions, but just to accept them, like 'That's how it is.' But I know I play in a cantorial, keening, querulous way that, hard as I try, isn't *black.*" This from a guy who came up with organist Charles Earland's funky combo and the suave Lounge Lizards, then cofounded the Dolphy-meets-Spike Jones Jazz Passengers with a fully integrated, multi-kulti crew.

Nothing new in that: American Jews, like descendants of Italians, Hispanics, and the Irish, have joined African-Americans in jazz since its recorded beginnings. Clarinetist Mezz Mezzrow was Louis Armstrong's main man, and had a direct connection with Gene Krupa, Bix Beiderbecke, and the Eddie Condon gang. Benny Goodman didn't deny his heritage, making Depression-era hits from features like Ziggy Elman's "And the Angels Sing." Al Cohn, Stan Getz, Lee Konitz, Dick Hyman, and other *landsmen* (co-religionists) of postwar generations did nothing to deny their heritage.

But they didn't get together, either, to study and recast the music of their grandparents and the old country, then blast their audiences in raw assault. "Knitting Factory music" is sometimes a synonym for harsh, dissonant, challenging sounds. Zorn's New York Jews stormed into Munich flush with attitude, impelled by deep personal matters of identity, claiming their group prerogatives—akin to Max Roach and Archie Shepp exploring African-American nationalism in the '60s, or Wynton Marsalis proposing New Orleans nativism today. Not that Zorn's posse was particularly conclusive, or boasted any group accord. No more so than the Latin jazzers, or Asian-American improv troupes.

"My band Rootless Cosmopolitans was named after the euphemism Stalin used against Jews and Trotskyites," states Marc Ribot unapologetically. The guitarist backed up Lou Reed in Munich and also led some Cosmopolitans who were about to be drafted into his even rockier band, Shrek. "Russians called 'rootless cosmopolitans' were sent to Siberia or executed, and when I was getting together repertoire from so many different sources, I thought, 'Maybe Stalin had something there; we *are* 'rootless cosmopolitans.' With Shrek, I'd recorded kind of a punk-rock song called 'Yo, I Killed Your God.' Under the circumstances in Munich, playing that seemed pretty bold, and we also did 'Commit a Crime' by Howlin' Wolf, which I felt, in the context, referred to the same thing."

Attitude-plus: The Munich concert climaxed with the premiere of Zorn's "Krystallnacht," a composition named after the Nazi hooligan rampage that initiated open warfare on Jews in Germany. Zorn had the black box concert hall's lights turned off and its doors locked so the audience couldn't escape.

The rhetoric behind such confrontational expression begs investigation. It is truly radical or Jewish? Zorn says it's not. Other musicians identified with the movement squirm at the terms.

"When I was at New England Conservatory, late '70s to early '80s, I was studying jazz and great black music," says Frank London, brazen trumpeter of the Klezmatics (their most recent release as we spoke in '96 was *Possessed,* Xenophile) and leader in his own right (having recently issued Hasidic *New Wave/Jews and the Abstract Truth*, Knitting Factory Works). "I was involved with processes of improvisation from the Art Ensemble of Chicago through John Cage, playing salsa, starting Les Miserables Brass Band—'Any music, as long as it's brass!'—working in a Haitian band, taking African, classical, and jazz gigs. And klezmer, as just another one of those things.

"It's funny: Matt Darriau, reeds player in Les Miserables and the Klezmatics, is not Jewish but his father loved Jewish culture, so he grew up hearing Jewish music. Me, Jewish, had no Jewish music in my house. Never heard black music except for soul. I grew up with rock 'n' roll. But you can study. I attended a Creative Music Studio seminar Roscoe Mitchell taught, and he said, 'Music is a form. Anyone can study and learn to play a form of music.' This does not contradict the fact that klezmer is Jewish music or that jazz is African-American music. There are white jazz players, non-Jewish klezmer players, and not every black musician can play jazz, nor can every Jew can play klezmer.

"Of all the different influences in the Klezmatics, jazz is probably the smallest. We never play anything with a swing beat. We do very little creating of harmonic chord structures to build improvisations on, because, of our players, the rhythm section—our bass and accordion player—are furthest from that tradition. What we take from jazz is more from the American musical tradition—American like Ives, Cage, and Thoreau. We're talking about doing whatever we want! Not iconoclasm—individualism and openness! Making twentieth-century music!"

"What's radical these days?" scoffs Roy Nathanson. "Nearly nothing. They got TV ads about a revolution…in gym shoes! Is it radical to ask questions? To elaborate on musical ideas a certain way? Radical because it's not in the mainstream? Woody Allen, the Marx

Brothers, and S. J. Perelman are part of a radical Jewish lineage, which also connects to Sun Ra! But calling it 'radical' is saying it's less than what it was, which was *inspired*.

"Radical gives me a headache," he mock complains, "but Zorn's an incredible salesman." Admiringly. Nathanson's no slouch himself, proud of his new Joel Dorn–produced Passengers album with singer Deborah Harry, prouder still of *I Could Have Been a Drum* (Tzadik), his third collaboration with Anthony Coleman, and, for the first time since the guitarist left the Passengers, Ribot, too.

"What it has to do with being Jewish is it's three Jewish men getting together to meditate on being middle-aged. It has this cantorial quality, it's repetitive in a special way, it seems to have something to do with language. It's not that we're playing an Eastern scale, but something about timbre, about how I approach and play any one note. The songs are sort of prayers that aren't about swing *or jazz.*" Nathanson says, "I don't know what it is. But the ability to live with an unresolved position is an essential attitude of Talmudic thinking."

"I was interested in the radical-Jewish-expression idea in the beginning because I believed there was an area of transgression to be addressed," asserts Ribot. It was transgression, in the minds of some of the thoroughly assimilated American Jewish musicians, just to identify oneself by that religious affiliation while playing in Germany. "The first radical Jewish music fests were interesting and kind of exciting because we, the players, didn't have any rules.

"Then we learned to act properly, 'like Jews.' We learned to play klezmer scales most of us hadn't heard before and probably couldn't tell from related Turkish scales. A lot of people were presenting 'Jewish music' in a hybrid context, playing klezmer scales and punk noise/avant-jazz aspects in quick succession. It was always clear which represented Jewishness.

"On the European fest circuit, it got so being 'really' Jewish came to mean playing klezmer scales and being angry at Germans, who in my experience were mostly *philo*-Semitic. To me that seemed like 'acting Jewish,' which I'm not interested in, as opposed to enacting Jewish principles. I mean, nobody tells me what attitudes to assume. So I quit. I'm not a radical Jew anymore. I'm a cowboy, a spaceman, an Eskimo."

"I don't call myself a Jewish musician," says Shelley Hirsch. "I don't just think of myself as Jewish, though I am. My upbringing was not observant; in fact, I wanted to be more Jewish than my parents because I loved the cantorial singing, and I wanted something of the spiritual side, especially later in my life when we were all looking at Eastern religions.

"Now in a *O Little Town of East New York,* I take as one role a very much more Jewish woman, Aida Vidzer. *O Little Town* is all me, singing, in a lot of voices—part jazz, and many parts new music—with David Weinstein using five synthesizers. And there was one piece I did in '80, 'I Am a Jew,' set in an odd meter, where I sang 'Hatikva' on one track, and on another track recorded a woman with a Yiddish accent singing over and over, 'The killing, the killing, haven't we learned?' But when it came out on an album I had to wonder, 'What is my record doing in a bin labeled Israeli Singers?'

"The basic thing is, I explore my identity in my work, and that includes all my own contradictions. I used to hate the way Jewish women sounded, that stereotypical Long Island Jewish accent, but now I have a friend who has that nasal thing in her voice but who's so warm, loving, and open that I've come to associate it with beauty and warmth. 'You don't *look* Jewish'—I used to take that as a compliment, but I don't anymore. And I've got to admit, when I was growing up in the neighborhood—well, I always wanted to be with the *Italian* boys."

"I don't think klezmer has anything to do with my identity as a musician, a Jew, or anything else," announces Anthony Coleman, who's tackled, abstractly but directly, subtle issues concerning Judaism with his unique, mysteriously compelling *Self-Haters* album (its nearest precedent may be Roscoe Mitchell's *Sound,* the first released AACM album, from 1966) and his relatively more conventional piano trio *The Sephardic Tinge* (both on Tzadik). "But I have an ambiguous relationship to Judaism," he allows, "and to jazz too, having studied with Jaki Byard when I was very young and having idolized Ellington, then gone off from that to study composition at Yale, and everything since.

"Well, better ambiguous than ambivalent. Ambiguous is interesting, and I'm very interested in questions of what constitutes identity, very against the concept of *trying* to be something you're not.

"I'm fine with the identity I have, though it's totally contradictory," Coleman maintains. "I was raised an American, celebrating Christmas. The history of Jewish music in the twentieth century didn't touch me, though it was part of my background, and my grandparents went on about carrying on Jewish tradition because of people lost in the Holocaust. I considered myself more from the keyboardist-composer tradition.

"But in Munich in 1992, it came up: Is Judaism a *thing*? What's Jewish about me? I started trying to look at my affections to see if there's any reason to them or was my music just me in my room, isolated. One results was *Self-Haters*, of which there are two kinds, you know: those who are called that like Philip Roth, who expose something the greater Jewish community doesn't want exposed, and those who have their noses done and change their names and reject the suburbs they came from and actually want to *accept*.

"*Self-Haters* reacts to Theodore Adorno too; I quote him on the liner notes to the effect that the blue notes of jazz, like the falling 'pitiful intervals' associated with Jewish music, represent the little voice struggling against the big power and so are doomed to failure because they're expressions of weakness.

"I thought about that. 'What if whining is a *good* thing?' I tried to get into that, with Doug Wieselman on E-flat clarinet; me singing, playing keyboards and trombone often at the same time; Jim Pugliese on trumpet and drums; Fred Lonberg-Holm on cello, and Michael Attias on bari sax and other reeds. Is it jazz? We've got no real rhythm section, no concept of solos, but we play [the standard] 'You Don't Know What Love Is' and it sounds right in the context. I'm happy if people find it sounds cantorial. We play Ellington's 'The Mooch' too, which was an easy choice.

"I came up with *The Sephardic Tinge* after asking myself: What really *were* my musical roots? Me and David Krakauer, growing up in New York, always loved Latin music. It was always there, like a folk music: you don't have to ask about it, it just accompanied the rituals in your life. I first heard klezmer at age twenty-four, and it had nothing to do with my rituals. So I looked at the connections between Latin and Jewish music, Ladinos and Sephardic people, looked at the uses Monk and Ellington made of the Latin tinge, thought about the mambos and cha-chas Jewish people danced to at weddings and bar mitzvahs. I didn't intend to make a statement so much as to ask some questions.

"There might be people who adopt this marketing label and then try to be the Big Jew, saying if you want to play Jewish music, it's got to be *this*—klezmer or kosher or whatever—and *that*. That's just silly. I think I'm dealing with the religion—not like the klezmer people do, but as a court jester, a gadfly. After all, I'm interested in the trope of Jewish alienation. *That's* something about Judaism, too."

Indeed it is, and something music of any people works to alleviate. Why is so much radical Jewish jazz, at least the kind created by

Manhattan's downtown crowd, what Knitting Factory boss Michael Dorf calls "hard-to-listen-to music"? Because with the bitter comes the sweet? Because superficial satisfactions don't soothe historic insecurities? Because restless cosmopolitans never stop in their quest for the sounds of surprise?

Some questions are posed for eternity. In radical Jewish music, in the improvisatory investigations and high concepts of the so-called downtown, perhaps in any expression leading to future jazz, there is no end in answers.

10 Wynton Marsalis: Conclusions, Part 3

What limits pertain to jazz? Said Wynton Marsalis in 1984, "No limits. Any kind of ensemble can be jazz if all the instruments are creating, improvising in the tradition of jazz music. It has to be spontaneous creation in a mobile environment with respect for the history of each instrument. Not two people playing funk, and one person playing a bebop solo on top of an E-minor chord. That's not jazz.

"People all want American music to go backward. They still want us in the fields singing spirituals and chants. They try to tell you Duke Ellington was doing that; Duke Ellington refined that into art. We don't have to go back to that. Then they say that's an indication of soulfulness. Soul is one of the most misunderstood concepts in jazz. Soul is something everybody has, just some people are more in touch with it than others. Louis Armstrong was soulful, but the feeling he gets, Duke gets another feeling, Clifford [Brown] gets another—and would you say Clifford was less soulful than Louis? Or just that they're soulful in different ways? They were both soulful because they could play trumpet the way they played it, and grew up and realized what they were growing up like.

"See, what people do is they take what they know, and what they think is good, and use that for their point of reference. Like the cats in my band— I love my band, Kenny Kirkland and Jeff Watts are the greatest young musicians on the scene, and they get no credit. People say Kenny can't do this, and Jeff can't do this, but they don't hear what they *are* doing, because they're too busy hearing what they've *already* heard. Then they say it sounds derivative.

"What you have to do is not look at part of something and make that into the whole. When you hear my records, I want you to listen to the sound of each piece, the flow of it, just like you would with any music. I listen to the sound of music, then the textural changes. Then I think, what are they trying to say in this? And I figure out what's going on, not theoretically, but musically.

"When I study, I listen to certain things, specifically, for a reason. What's on this record? What chord is this? How does he get to this chord? What's the development section to this? What's the drummer doing here? What chord does this effect? How do these two people hear this? How can you achieve this effect?

"The most important thing in jazz is swing. Rhythm. If it don't swing, I don't want to hear it, it's not important to hear. Whatever it is, if it's not swinging, it's not jazz. There are different feelings of swing, but if it's swinging, you know it. And if you ain't swinging, you ain't doing nothing.

"The whole band must swing. You can't have weak links in your thing. Every musician in your band has to be as good as the others—has to hear just as well, understand the concept as well, think on his feet just as well. See, our music is really for the moment; that's what makes it so exciting. That's why it can either be sad or great.

"We're just trying to come up with an improvisation on the spot. *Bam!* D over E flat. What is that? You know, immediately, what the chord is. You're going to five, you know what the rhythm is, you just have to respond. But it has to be correct; it's not just playing any kind of thing. You don't just hit a chord 'cause you feel like hitting it; you got to understand the logic of the progressions of harmonies. The logic of sound, the logic of drums, the logic of how bass parts should go. Contrary motion. That's what my brother and Kenny Kirkland understand real well. [Kirkland died in 1998.] On those records, I didn't write out any music for 'Bell Ringer' and those long tunes. I just said, 'Branford, play a contrary motion there. Kenny, what do you hear on top of that, man? Jeff, what rhythm do you think would fit there?' Good ears, man. *Musicians.*"

I asked him, "Do you yourself hear music your small ensemble isn't capable of, just because of instrumentation?"

"No," he replied, "I don't hear any. I only play for, and think about, that band. But we play only 30 to 40 per cent of what we're capable of, definitely. We'll come off a gig all depressed because the stuff sounds so sad, and we'll say to ourselves, 'Hey, we're gonna get this.' We know what we have to do; it's just a question of doing it.

And we're going to do it, because we want to, we want it bad. We practice and we play; we don't just wait for the ability to play to descend on us; we're going to *learn* how to play. It's a matter of time. Five, six, eight, ten years, fifteen, who knows? We'll get to it.

"And this is what we need: younger musicians. Cats like Charnett Moffett, the Netman, sixteen years old, coming over to my house every day to learn about harmony on his bass, to learn about music. To the young people who read this: We need young musicians trying to really learn how to play the music and researching and learning how to play their instruments. Not all these little sort of pop-type cult figures, talking all the time; heroes who have these spur-of-the-moment, out-of-their-minds, left-bank, off-the-wall theories about music, which make no sense at all to anybody who knows anything about music. We shouldn't get rid of them: they're important because we know through them what bullshit is. But musical terms are very precise. These terms have histories to them. Just because these cats wear wigs, they figure that's going to make them able to come up with theories on music!"

"Has jazz *had* its golden age, or is the music still growing, changing?" I asked.

"Everything is growing and changing," he said. "Jazz is in the present tense, the creation of it; the audience hears that. That's innovation, a balm on twentieth-century music. The evolution's not over. It's just that nobody's doing nothing to it right now."

"Do you feel a lot of pressure, as a guy who looks good, plays sharp, and studies, to represent the young musicians coming up now?"

"No, there's no pressure on me"—he declined the suggestion—"'cause that's how I am. When I was going to high school, I never owned one suit. I didn't know what it was to spend money. I went to school with the same pair of jeans on every day, a T-shirt and shirt from Sears on top of that. Alright? Now, when I come on, I do what I want to. I like to be clean, because I used to look at album covers of cats with suits on, and I'd say, 'Damn, look at that suit, boy, let me get one, I wish I had a suit.' I like suits; I like to be clean when I go to work, playing music that I think is important in front of people.

"Now, the underlying thing is, I love the music. See, I'm not out here trying to garner publicity. I've got publicity, right? I don't call people asking them to interview me. I didn't call CBS and ask them for a record contract. Just for some reason, I started playing with Art Blakey, then the next thing I know I got a record contract, everybody's writing reviews on my stuff, I'm playing wth Herbie Hancock and Ron Carter and Tony Williams—it happened just like that.

"I was still trying to learn how to play the music. I didn't come to New York to be a jazz musician. I didn't even know people were still playing jazz. I grew up in the '70s; there wasn't any jazz in the '70s. Now I'm being like I want to be. I like suits, so I put a suit on. I got the money to buy a suit because I do gigs. People think when I went on the road I was making long money; I wasn't making *any* money. I had to pay for all the planes, all the band, pay for all the booking agents. People were telling me how dumb it is to be playing jazz, nobody don't play jazz no more, why are you playing jazz? See, people don't understand the behind-the-scenes.

"I'm playing jazz because I want to play the music. I love this music, man. I love the music. I stay up all night playing music. I love music. Now, you can say what you want to say; I've got such strong opinions because I love the music, and I hate to see bullshit put up as the real thing. That's the only reason, not because I want people to think I'm *it*. I know I'm not Louis Armstrong; I'm not fooling myself. When I hear jazz, *great* jazz, there's no other feeling like that for me. No other feeling. None. And I really love the music. Beyond all the other stuff, the publicity and the hype will be gone eventually, but the music will still be there, and I'm going to still be playing it if I'm still alive—or trying to *learn* how to play it—because I realize how great the music is, and that's what's most important.

"Musicians are losing sight of this; they want to be stars. People ask me, 'How do you get over?' I never in my life thought about getting over. I never thought about doing records. All I ever did was wonder: How can I play this mother-lovin' trumpet and get better? How can I learn to play the music? Art Blakey loves the music—he's not still out here with his band because of the money he makes, or because he can stand up in front of people and give the speech that he gives. He just loves to play music, and that's what I do, man.

"I hate to go on the road, go to Europe or Japan, and deal with all that. I'd rather be in New Orleans with my partners on the corner, talking, doing whatever we're doing, going out to the lakefront like we used to do. But I love music, man; that's why I came to New York. I was by myself, scared; I didn't know what was happening. I'm from New Orleans, man, I didn't know.... But as much as I love the masters, I can turn around right in the same breath, and say that what's going down now is nowhere. It's not complex. Schoenberg is complex, but that level is not what's happening here. What the critics call complex is not complex music.

"Can you see where the music is going?"

"Yeah, I can see. I know what it's going to do. Maybe I won't be the one to do it, but somebody might come up, I'll hear them, I'll know it if they're going to be the one. And the *people* will know.

"People do not want to hear what's being played now; they know bad shit when they hear it. I can listen to Schoenberg and analyze those pieces, I've read *Structural Functions of Harmony* and I know what's in that book—I'm not guessing—I *know* what he's saying. I sat down for hours until I knew what was being said. So the theories now hurt me more than anything, because these people are not sincere, and they don't want to pay the dues it takes to learn how to play this music. They don't swing at different tempos. What you must learn to play our music is *not* being learned—and cats are getting over.

"It's a drag I have to say this. In Bird's time, if a mother couldn't play and he got on the bandstand, Bird and them would say, 'Hey, man, get off the bandstand.' Jo Jones threw a cymbal at Bird. Then the vibe was that way. Now, everything's cool. Whatever you say is cool. But it ain't.

"Okay, now ask me some questions and I'll give you short, hot answers so people will think I'm crazy. We don't want this to be tame."

Okay…

HM Are you going to make any music videos?

WM I'll try that, I guess, but it will have to have a plot, and not be just some reason to show women with their asses hanging out.

HM Are you going to have any women in your band soon?

WM If they can play like Bird, yeah. You know, I don't discriminate. If you can play, you can play, regardless of whoever you are.

HM Was winning two Grammys this year your biggest honor yet?

WM No. The biggest honor I ever had is for me to play with the musicians I've played with. To stand onstage with Ron and Herbie and Tony, Sonny Rollins, Dizzy Gillespie, to have the opportunity to talk with them and have them teach me stuff.

HM How do you get on with your dad now?

WM *(with a big smile)* Me and my daddy are tighter than…My daddy, man, he showed me so much stuff. That's my dad. Last night, when we were in New Orleans, at one o'clock in the morning he stayed up and waited for me so we could rap, and then he even took this tune off the record with me, together. I mean, me and him, all those hours I hung with him—I used to idolize my dad, man. Go hang out with him on all the gigs and try to be hip. Now, ask me about the avant-garde.

HM What do you think of the avant-garde?

WM Avant-garde means "to be in front of," right? That's what the words mean. But to be in front of, you got to have something behind you.

HM And that applies to both people making up theories that are nowhere as well as people with conservatory backgrounds? It's like there are two avant-gardes now.

WM That stuff is so funny, it doesn't even deserve commenting on.

HM So what is mainstream now? Are you in the mainstream?

WM I don't know. I hope so. I don't know where I am.

HM Herbie and Ron and Tony—is that the mainstream, the tradition as it moves along?

WM Not just them—Herbie, Ron, Tony, Chick, Jack DeJohnette...

HM Lester Bowie?

WM No, but don't say, I can't...

HM Billy Bang?

WM Billy Bang is cool. My brother likes him...

HM David Murray? Arthur Blythe?

WM Arthur Blythe, yeah. I don't shrug on David, man, I love David. I can't say nothing about David, man, that's my partner.

HM Well, that's fine.

I turned the tape off. Wynton said something like, "See, the problem with them cats is they don't know enough about music. Like this one you mentioned, he's got to learn how to *rest* when he's playing."

11 Hothouse Culture: Jazz Clubs in the '90s

They are the fans, the curious, the walk-bys, the drop-ins. They are couples on dates who barely know each other, and lovers who want to be together without having to talk, eat, or follow a movie's plot. They are the restless and the lonely who cannot imagine, ask for, or find a better place to go. They are the listeners, the heart and soul of the jazz audience. Since the '20s Jazz Age and for the rest of the twentieth century, they—you and me—have flocked to the jazz clubs.

Today we seem to be an endangered species. Like other such creatures, our ranks have been thinned, our way of life put on the line by new patterns of business and leisure, communications and habitation. Entertainment is now a commercial enterprise dominated more than ever before by international corporations, and the tidal wave of global electronic media has all but swept away the cozy local joints where jazz traditionally took root, grew, and bloomed.

"You used to be able to work all the way across the country," recalls jazz laureate Jon Hendricks, celebrating his seventy-fifth birthday in September 1996, the week we spoke at the New York City club Iridium. He was successively touring in Europe, performing at the Monterey Jazz Festival, and hosting a galaxy of guest artists in a season-opening Jazz at Lincoln Center concert in twenty-seven-hundred-seat Avery Fisher Hall. "Lambert, Hendricks, and Ross"—the premiere vocal group of the pre-Beatles era—"in the early '60s we did lots of concerts, but played clubs in every city, too: Minneapolis, Chicago, Dayton, Ohio, Cleveland, Buffalo, Rochester, all the way down South.

"It's not that way anymore. Rock changed that, and our dwindling economy. The transportation, the lodging costs—it's hard to sustain jazz clubs under this economy. In Europe it's possible; there are lots of clubs. In the United States, they're virtually nonexistent. And the expense of the ones that survive! It used to cost maybe $50, $60, for an evening. Now if you have a baby sitter and include cover charges, dining, drinks, and parking, an evening in a club can cost $150, $200. You have to save up for it. It's simply not viable to be in clubs."

"I do more concerts and festivals than club work," admits Joshua Redman, the tenor saxophonist. He maintains his quintet-with-road-manager/soundman on a weekly payroll, and so tries to keep busy always. "I love playing clubs, but the percentage of jazz-jazz clubs as opposed to even a House of Blues or Bottom Line—mixed-music clubs—is very small in my total activity.

"It's not that the audience isn't coming out," he hastens to add, "we get great attendance wherever we go. But if I played only clubs, there would be only a handful of places in the United States I could go. And I want to play everywhere."

There are, apparently, audiences for Redman everywhere, and, just as ubiquitous, people who would gladly attend jazz clubs.

"Oh, no, we're here because we have to be," jests Cho, longtime bartender at New York's Sweet Basil. "We're working," says Oliva, his alternate, sipping a beer, sitting on a barstool, on what's supposed to be his night off. He's kidding, too; these guys are jazz club loyalists. "You're writing about people who go to jazz clubs?" Oliva goes further. "It ought to be autobiographical."

He's got a point. Though on many Friday or Saturday nights the lines out front of the dedicated jazz-jazz Manhattan clubs (besides Basil, the Blue Note, Iridium, and the Village Vanguard are in the late '90s the most prominent featuring nationally touring acts) suggest that jazz audiences are diverse and legion, for later sets and on weekdays one encounters much sparser crowds, usually comprising jazz students, critics, record-company types, and music-business professionals. Joshua Redman, James Carter, or Branford Marsalis may indeed draw crowds. Other worthies—Dewey Redman, say, or Lester Bowie or Ellis Marsalis—can find themselves playing to hardly anyone or a busload of foreigners.

"We get tour groups on a package deal maybe once or twice a week," Oliva mentions. "A lot of them are Japanese, and there used to be more. It's okay—they come in to experience the club, they eat and listen to whoever's here. The name 'Sweet Basil' means something to them, and they go away happy."

Which may be more than can confidently be said about the New York club regular who, in pursuit of good, true jazz, suffers the Blue Note's overcrowded tables and airline-schedule drink service, inhospitable reception at the Vanguard's door, or Iridium's food service distractions. If Basil's bookings have been erratic, it's still the friendliest of New York's first-rank-clubs, and one can enjoy quality jazz time there for less than twenty-five dollars.

Yes, the Blue Note books stellar double bills and showcases newcomers on Monday nights, its sightlines are unimpeded, and its sound is mixed by pros. There are no better room acoustics in the jazz world than at the Vanguard, oddly shaped like an ear laid flat, and its legacy of cultural history, advancing on a seventh decade, is unmatched: The ghosts of Coltrane and Dolphy, Kirk, Monk and Mingus lurk about. Iridium, a newer straight-ahead spot, smartly situated across the street from Lincoln Center, has Daliesque design notes that set a tone of chic fun. But a night at any of them, for the average jazz joe or jane, is on the order of a special event, rather than a casual neighborhood drop-in where one sees friends, nurses a beer, soothes the soul.

Maybe that's due to their top-drawer New Yorkiness. Some secondary Apple clubs—Birdland, in both its '80s Upper West Side and late-'90s Times Square locations; Visiones, which closed at the beginning of '98; the Jazz Standard, trying to establish itself just off Park Avenue South; and the all-night-long Smalls come to mind—are (or were) less pretentious and cheaper, with equally cool if underhyped music. Maybe elsewhere the club scene's thriving.

"I'm staring at a map of the United States," said Rick Saylor, of the Jazz Tree, an artists' management group, "and I can tell you where in the country the clubs that support national acts are.

"Boston has Scullers and the Regatta Bar, which are both in hotels. Washington, D.C., has Blues Alley, Seattle has Jazz Alley, Oakland has Yoshi's. In St. Louis, Barbara Rose has moved her Just Jazz series from the hotel it's been in for years to a restaurant, Jazz at the Bistro. In L.A. there's Catalina's, primarily a restaurant, and the Jazz Bakery. In Philly, Zanzibar Blue has less than one hundred seats. In Chicago, there's Joe Segal's Jazz Showcase, and in Detroit a new place called the Magic Bag.

"Fort Worth's Caravan of Dreams, Rockefeller's in Houston, and New Orleans's Tipitina's are part of what we call the 'reefer circuit,' rock bars that have survived twenty-some years. Santa Cruz has Kuumbwa Jazz Workshop, presenting national acts on Monday nights. In St. Paul there's the Dakota, a restaurant; in Toronto, Sybil Walker's Top o' the Senator, and the Montreal Bistro. That's just about it. A guy like bassist Ray Brown travels that circuit, goes to Europe and Japan, then starts the circuit over again.

"It's weird. Miami, for instance, is good-sized, has a tourist trade, lots of New Yorkers in exile and jazz performer-professors at colleges in the area. But I just read a *Miami Herald* article that said there's not enough audience to support a jazz club.

"There are at least a handful of jazz fans everywhere, even where there aren't clubs. Sometimes you have to reach them by playing concerts. We work with local promoters, jazz societies, community groups, fine arts presenters, colleges, not-for-profits, bookers of small theaters—they're all part of the network we stitch together.

"But there's a sense of community at a jazz club. It's built to be a viable entity every day, an outpost, a bastion where somebody made a career choice to promote the jazz cause. The club owners we know are mostly in their sixties or seventies now. They dug in a while back and established themselves for the long haul."

"I'm seventy now," says Joe Segal, who in March 1996 opened the Jazz Showcase at his umpteenth Chicago address in the fifty years since he first presented bebop sessions at Roosevelt College. "Bebop is still the music of the future. It will be to my dying day."

Segal is an archetypical jazz presenter who has ridden the ups and often downs of the music's finances, nurturing strong relationships with his favorite artists and holding fast to certain principles: "Matinees on Sundays at 4 P.M. for kids. No smoking, modest general admission, no minimum, and we don't push drinks. But we may have to start doing that soon, to stay open." Segal has encountered overhead fees at his present site, attached to a restaurant, which he wasn't responsible for during the fifteen years his jazz club was off the lobby of the Blackstone Hotel.

"The Blackstone took care of ASCAP and BMI licensing fees, and also the entertainment tax," Segal reports. "The Happy Medium management did that for us at Rush Street, too," he says of the space he had under a disco on Chicago's glossy nightlife strip in the '70s.

"But at our new location we're seeing people we never saw during our fifteen years at the Blackstone: older black fans who wouldn't go there and older white fans who wouldn't go to the 'South

Side,' even though it was really downtown, just a couple blocks from the Loop.

"We opened with John Scofield to draw the kids," he explains, very savvy, "then had Hank Crawford for the South Side," i.e., the black community. "We tried a local band led by [pianist] Judy Roberts and she did well, I think because Marian McPartland touted it at her own gig a few weeks before.

"Most owners of the new clubs in town are corporate types who don't care much about the music. They open beautiful rooms without sound systems and draw yuppies who don't care about the music either. Their places are about cigars and noise.

"Too bad." He shrugs. "There used to be a lot of clubs for national jazz here. I think I'm the only one left."

"It's certainly not what it was," sighs pianist Marian McPartland, an annual visitor to Segal's club who credits her profile among current audiences to her National Public Radio program *Piano Jazz* rather than to her fifty-plus years of playing. "There's a big change from when Jimmy [McPartland, cornetist, her late husband] and I first went into the Brass Rail in Chicago in the '40s. And I remember my first time in New York, walking up Broadway, turning into a club called the Aquarium where Satchmo was playing. Another down the street had Gene Krupa with Anita O'Day, and there was the Down Beat, and Jimmy Ryan's...Oh, these names make me very nostalgic.

"In New York we still have Bradley's and the Knickerbocker," she says of clubs that turned the city's cabaret laws to their advantage by becoming piano jazz rooms (but Bradley's closed in 1997). "It was sad that the Cookery went under, and Fat Tuesday's going out made me mad because the management there wasn't taking care of business, yet it's jazz that gets the bad name for not drawing.

"I think owners of jazz clubs have to be braver—like Joe Segal, who really loves the music, and Lorraine Gordon at the Vanguard, who loves it just as Max [her late husband and founder of the Vanguard] did. Jazz clubs have changed, certainly, but they haven't died. They charge more—it's not like the Hickory House, where you could nurse a beer all night—but they exist. You have to ferret them out. Ben Tucker, who was a fine bassist, has opened a club in Savannah, Georgia. I was even at a nice club in Juneau, Alaska.

"There are clubs, and people attend them. I'm not pessimistic about it. I think there will be another upswing. I feel it in my bones."

"We don't have a place right now, we're floating," conceded Marguerite Horberg, principal of Chicago's Hot House, which she called "a jazz club, loosely: an Afro-centric club programming jazz, new music, and rhythms from around the world." In 1996 she was without a house to be hot in. "We lost our home," said Horberg, whom I've known through several stages as a presenter, "because we were successful. The landlord, seeing that, kept increasing our rent. So I'm producing concerts in different places, to stay alive until we find a new place we like. It's been more than a year now. We've kept our associations with the Jazz Institute of Chicago, with the AACM—who we mercilessly exploit however and whenever possible," she drawls (every reader should know she's kidding), "and we've produced a Women in Jazz Festival. We've done well with David Murray, and a lot of other musicians who otherwise don't get to Chicago, whom our friend Joe doesn't book, like Don Byron, Abdullah Ibrahim, and Henry Threadgill.

"But we are not the new model jazz club," she emphasized. "Most new clubs are interested in bop, postbop, the Young Lions, cabaret, and torch singers. Things that are inside. We're more interested in music that grew out of the '60s, jazz that's freer, more improvised—the dashiki and noise thing most traditional jazz listeners run from. We're similar to Koncepts Kultural Gallery in Oakland, the Knitting Factory in New York, and District Curators in D.C.

"I've learned that to book so-called 'marginal' acts we need sponsorship or subsidizing. The gate won't pay for them. Without a subsidy to pay a real wage to the musicians, the sound crew, and ourselves, we'd have to charge fifty dollars and up. We want to stimulate a new audience, so we charge five dollars to twenty dollars." Horberg claimed such audience stimulation and fund-raising (her not-for-profit umbrella organization has received MacArthur Foundation grants) had been effective.

"The biggest change I've seen has been exponential growth of younger people turned on to outside music," she said. "It used to be I'd be one of ten at an AACM concert, and now 250 to 300 people will show up at for one. This generation of club-goers got multiculturalism in high school, they're used to a crossover or fusion—not the '70s commercial variety—of rock and jazz and other information. They're comfortable with all of it.

"To make money I'll book a local Latin dance band. People come and drink and jack their bodies. But I won't do that all the time," said Horberg, who had already in her mind an upcoming fall schedule.

"We'll have the twenty-one-piece Afro-Cuban Matanzas troupe and Spirit of Havana, with [Canadians] Jane Bunnett and Larry Cramer. We've got Cindy Blackman's quartet with Gary Bartz. Where, I don't know yet. Call for local listings. I'd say we're the Rave Hot House—we announce the location just hours before the event."

Welcome to the jazz club of the future. But in 1998 Horberg re-opened Hot House in the South Loop. It's spacious, nice, and funky. Should we worry that new jazz venues are not what they were? Joshua Redman did, sort of.

"What's so special about clubs is the intimacy, the audience almost onstage so I can communicate with it directly," he said. "There's no substitute for that. Especially with jazz, which changes so much based on the rapport between the musicians and the audience, it can be incredibly invigorating. Also a club has the acoustic intimacy. However good a concert hall or festival sound system is, it's bound to lose some acoustic subtlety and shading.

"I love playing concerts too, reaching so many people at once, concentrating on making one show my statement to a community. I play to three times as many people at a concert in the Bay Area as in a week at Yoshi's. But I insist we alternate concerts and clubs there, and elsewhere too.

"Because as much as I love to play concerts, I'd be distraught if there were no jazz clubs left. An intimate setting for a small audience in an acoustic setting over time is key to development for jazz artists. Jazz was born in the clubs, developed there, and needs the energy and special experience of clubs to remain vital.

"But jazz needs even more than that."

Acknowledgments

Thanks to the crowd around the Jazz Record Mart—Bob Koester, Washboard Hank, Big Joe Williams, and especially Jim de Jong—where I first listened, as a teenager. Thanks to all those musicians who've talked with me about their lives, especially those not discussed here because of space limitations. Thanks to my editors, including (but not limited to) Larry Blumenfeld and R. Dante Sawyer *(JazzIz)*; Art Lange, Ed Enright, John Ephland, Chuck Carman, and Charles Doherty *(Down Beat)*; Marc Weidenbaum and Suzanne Mikesell *(Tower Pulse!)*; Richard Cook, Mark Sinker, and Tony Herrington *(The Wire)*; Carol Tuynman and Larry Birnbaum *(Ear)*; Robert Christgau, Tom Carson, and Joe Levy *(The Village Voice)*, and to the publishers; also to Thurston Briscoe, Tom Cole, Manoli Weatheral, Caryl Wheeler, and others at National Public Radio. My great appreciation to photographers Lauren Deutsch, Marc PoKempner, the late Lona Foote, and the late D. Shigley for their perspectives; to my colleagues Kevin Whitehead and John F. Szwed; and to Susan Katz. Thanks also to this book's editor, Sheldon Meyer—indeed, all the supportive people at Oxford University Press.

Rosalis Moon Mandel has been a source of inspiration, as has my wife, Kitty Brazelton, whose own music reflects the spirit and strength of our Lower East Side. I'm also grateful that my mother, Marjorie Kahn Mandel, encouraged me to type—and rewrite, rewrite—in the fifth grade, and that my father, Robert E. Mandel, has always appreciated a good story.

Index

A&R (artists and repertoire), 7-10, 20, 169, 185

AACM (Association for the Advancement of Creative Musicians), 32, 45-46, 66, 69, 70, 131, 137-38, 146, 160, 168, 171, 206

AACM Big Band, 32, 45

Aaronson, Cynthia "Cindy" (Davis), 125-26, 130, 131-32

About Time records, 160

Abraham Lincoln Center (Chicago), 33

Abrams, Muhal Richard, xi, 30, 31-37, 44, 70-71, 184

acid jazz, 7, 164

Ackley, Bruce, 41

Adams, George, 27, 28

Adams, Terry, 184, 185

Adderley, Cannonball (Julian), xiii, 77, 93

Adorno, Theodore, 193

Afam Gallery, 33

"Africa," 44

Africa Brass, 28

African diaspora, 28

African drums, 29, 41, 44, 45, 181

African Flower, The, 110, 111

African Game, The, 9

African music, 28-29, 40, 43-44, 140, 151, 152, 171

African-Americanism, 189

African-Brazilian Connection, 28-30, 43

"Afro Blue," 159

Afro-Cuban de Matanzas, 206

AIDS, 165

Ailey, Alvin, 60

Air, 33

Air Lore, 71

Ajaramu, 33

ak Laff, Pherroan, 129

Akbank jazz festival, 64, 157

Alessi, Ralph, 147

Ali, Amin, 100

Ali, Rashied, 101

"All the Things You Are," 98

Allen, Geri, 9, 109, 133-44, 146, 147, 153, 185

Allen, Woody, 159, 190

"Allen's Alley," 135

Altman, Robert, 64, 182

Amabutho Male Chorus of Soweto, 40

Amacord Nino Rota, 183-84

"Amazing Grace," 156

America—Do You Remember the Love?, 100

American Clavé records, 54

American Dance Theater, 60

American Indian music, 26, 56

American Jazz Masters, 34

American music, 146, 154, 190, 195

American Music Theater Festival, 131

Amistad (slave ship), 125

Ammons, Gene, 70

"And the Angels Sing," 189

Anderson, Ernestine, 154

Anderson, Fred, xi, 33

Anderson, Ivie, 113

Anderson, Laurie, 187, 188
Anderson, Ray, 46, 59, 92, 129
"Angel," 103
Angel/EMI Records, 110
Angels in America: The Millennium Approaches, 125
Angels in America: Perestroika, 125
Ann Arbor, Mich., xiii, 134
Ann Arbor Blues Festival, xiii
Another Side of Abbey Road, 90
Another Thought, 165
Antilles records, 160
Apocalypse, 79
Apollo Theater, 43, 147
Aquarium, the, 205
Aquired Immune Deficiency Syndrome. *See* AIDS
Arab Middle-Easterners, 175
Are You Glad to Be in America, 100
Arista-Freedom, 42
Armstrong, Louis, ix, 6, 7, 15, 18, 19, 21, 65, 152, 189, 195, 198, 205
arrangements, 87, 155, 157, 196
Art Ensemble of Chicago, xi-xii, 8, 33, 36, 44, 122, 126, 137, 168, 190
Artists House records, 100
ASCAP, 204
Asian-American improvisation, 189
Asian-Americans, 110
Asians, 146, 175
asiko, 41, 44
Association for the Advancement of Creative Musicians. *See* AACM
"At the Cafe Centrale," 48
Atlantic Records, 27, 38, 93
Attias, Michael, 193
audience, x-xi, 3-4, 5, 11, 24, 38, 79, 81, 95 103-4, 118-19, 201, 202, 203-4, 206, 207
Audience With . . ., The, 155
Audioquest records, 110
Aura, 78
Austin, Patti, 84
Avalon Hill, 169
avant-garde, ix, xi-xii, xiii, 6, 7, 9, 11, 23-46, 47, 163, 177, 200
Avery Fisher Hall, 201
Ayler, Albert, 24, 33, 42, 50, 52, 122, 163

Bacharach, Burt, 158, 175
Backer, Steve, 12
BAG (Black Artists Group), 36-41, 44, 171
Bailey, Derek, 174
Baker, Chet, 92
Ballads (Coltrane), xii
Band of Gypsies, 159
Band, the, 185
Bang, Billy, 60, 200
Banks, Cheryl, 60
Baptista, Cyro, 156
Bard College, 168
Barker, Danny, 16, 17, 76
Barker, Thurman, 62, 63
Barnes, Flip, 146
Baron, Art, 186
Baron, Joey, 174, 187
Baroque music, 20
Barron, Kenny, 55
Bartz, Gary, 207
Basie, William "Count," xi, 65, 76, 134, 157
Bass Desires, 94
Batiste, Alvin, 17
Batson Brothers, 146
Battle, Kathleen, 113
Battle Royale, 47-48
Beatles, 90, 159, 184
Beauty Based on Science, 177
bebop, 5, 11, 6, 41, 57, 58, 95, 123, 129, 135, 136, 138, 139, 142, 195, 204, 206
Beck, Joe, 78
Beefheart, Captain (Don Van Vliet), 168
Beiderbecke, Bix, 189
Belgrave, Marcus, 134, 138
Bell, Kelvyn, 147
"Bell Ringer," 196

Belo Horizonte, 81
Bennett, Tony, 182
Benson, George, 78, 83-91, 160
Benton, Brook, 132
Berg, Bob, 188
Berkeley, Calif., 50
Berklee College of Music, 91, 120
Berlin, Irving, 19
Berne, Tim, 7, 188
Bernstein, Rex Louis, 187
Bernstein, Steven, 187
Berry, Chuck, 146
Beyond the Blue Horizon, 90
big bands, xi, xiii, 9, 11, 42, 53, 71,
    120, 121, 122, 150
Big Boss Band, 89
Big Fun, 78
Billboard, 116
Bingham, Mark, 185
Birdland, 203
Birnbaum, Larry, 35
Birth of Tragedy, The, 129
Bitches Brew, 80
Bitter End, 178
Black Artists Group. *See* BAG
"Black, Brown and Beige," 129
black music, xi, 24, 146, 154
Black Rock, 100
Black Rock Coalition, 145-47, 164
black rock music, 100, 102, 143-47,
    157-64
Black Saint records, 42, 49, 61
Blackman, Cindy, 207
Blackwell, Edward, 45, 53, 55, 119-21,
    129
Blackwell, Otis, 145
Blake, Eubie, 111
Blake, John, 9, 100
Blakey, Art, 18, 27, 117, 118, 123, 150,
    197
Blanchard, Terence, 7
Blankart, Beppie, 60
Bley, Carla, 121-22, 175, 184, 186
Blondie, 184
Blood on the Fields, 8, 157

Blood Sweat & Tears, xii, 184
Bloom, Jane Ira, 7
Blue Bird, 100
Blue Book, the, 151
Blue Light 'Til Dawn, 156
Blue Note club, 3, 9, 123, 202, 203
Blue Note Records, 8, 100, 110, 117,
    119, 134
Blue Skies, 153, 155, 156
blues, xii, 26, 67, 76, 91, 93, 96, 98,
    103, 113, 141, 146, 156, 169, 184
Blues Alley, 203
Blues for Coltrane, 54
Blues Preacher, 100, 103
Bluiett, Hamiet, 9, 27, 28, 41, 100
Blythe, Arthur, 7, 41, 43, 55, 100, 200
BMG Records, 7, 12, 148
BMI, 204
Bob Thiele Collective, 55
"Body and Soul," 156
"Body Talk," 90
Bonfa, Luis, 90
boogie woogie, 57
Borneo Horns, 186
Boston, Mass., 15, 187, 203
Bottom Line (club), 3, 202
Bourelly, Jean-Paul, 145, 147, 155
Bowden, Mwata, 45
Bowie, Joseph "Joe," 44, 45, 161, 164
Bowie, Lester, 33, 36, 37, 39, 46, 69,
    138, 139, 200, 202
Bowne, Dougie, 156
Braden, Don, 47
Bradford, Bobby, 55, 56
Bradley's (club), 3, 205
Brandwein, Naftule, 187
Brass Rail (club), 205
Braxton, Anthony, xi, 33, 34, 41, 45,
    122, 168, 171
Brazilian rhythms, 29, 30
BRC. *See* Black Rock Coalition
Brecker Brothers, 114, 123
Brecker, Michael, 113-116, 123
Brecker, Randy, 114, 123
Breezin', 84, 88

Brewer, Teresa, 55
Bridgewater, Cecil, 150
Brimfield, Billy, 33
Brooklyn, N.Y., 15, 41, 43, 45, 146,
    148, 151, 153, 158, 159, 174, 178
Brookmeyer, Bob, 121
Brooks, Avery, 64
Brooks, Roy, 135
Brown, Cameron, 28
Brown, Chris, 166
Brown, Clifford, 18, 58, 138, 195
Brown, Earle, 169
Brown, James, xii, 50, 149, 158
Brown, Marion, 129
Brown, Ray, 204
Brubeck, Dave, xi, 94
Bruce, Jack, 54
Bruce, Lenny, 183
Bryant, Ray, 117
Brynner, Yul, 154
Buckley, Tim, xii
Buffalo, N.Y., 201
Bulgarian music, 151
Bunnett, Jane, 207
Burnham, Charles, 102
Burrage, Ronnie, 8
Burrell, Dave, 54, 55
Burroughs, William, 183
Burton, Gary, xi, 92, 111
Butler, Dr. George, 7-8
Byard, Jaki, 184, 192
Byron, Don, 125, 147, 156, 164, 176,
    188, 206

cabaret, 205, 206
Cage, John, 168, 171, 190
Calhoun, Will, 9, 146,163
California, 41, 89, 109, 180
"Call Waiting to Exhale," 164
Calloway, Cab, 157
Cameo, 114
Cameroon, 29
Campbell, "Little" Milton, 69
Candido, 28
Capitol EMI records, 8, 9

Caravan of Dreams, 203
Caravanserai, 159
Carbon (band), 167
Carew, Benny, 134-35
Caribbean rhythms, 26, 28, 140
Carmen, 182
Carmichael, Hoagy, 156
Carnegie Hall, 85, 119, 184
Carnegie Mellon University, 168
Carrington, Terri Lyne, 147, 155
Carroll, Baikida, 130
Carter, Benny, 88, 134
Carter, Betty, 113, 134, 139, 154-55,
    185
Carter, James, 202
Carter, Jimmy (President), 6
Carter, John, 55
Carter, Ron, 15, 55, 198, 199, 200
cartoon music, 170
Carver, Raymond, 183
Case of the 3-Sided Stereo Dream, 183
"Caseworks," 40
Cashbox, 116
Catalina's, 203
Catskills, 187
CBS, 7-8, 15, 48, 143, 197. See also
    Columbia Records; Sony Music
CBS Studios, 143
Celebrating Sinatra, 119
Central Park Summerstage, 177
Chadbourne, Eugene, 185
Chambers, Dennis, 81, 94, 96
change, xi-xiv, 3, 6, 7, 11, 13, 24-25,
    35, 73, 81, 148, 171, 172, 197, 201-
    2, 204-5
Changes One, 27
Changes Two, 27
Charles, Ray, 91, 158
Charlie Parker jazz festival, 135
Cheatham, Doc, 8
Cherry, Don, 58, 123, 174
Chess Records, 93
Chester Springs, Pa., 29
Chic, 159
Chicago, Ill., x, 33 , 37, 66, 69, 76, 93,

125, 131, 146, 147, 148, 149, 153, 169, 201, 204, 205-7
Chicago Jazz Festival, 48, 90
Chicago South Side, x, 32, 148, 204, 205
Chicago Symphony Orchestra, 131
Chief Bey, 41, 44
Child City, 33
Chimnoy, Sri ,78
Chinese lute, 161
"Chinese music," 6
Chinese zithers, 181
Cho, 202
choral singing, 9, 56, 69, 158
Christensen, Don, 166
Christian, Charlie, 75, 88
Chuma, Yoshiko, 60
church, 16, 26, 56, 59, 67, 26, 113
Cinque, 132
Circle Campus, Univ. of Illinois, xiii
Civic Opera House (Chicago), xiii
Clapton, Eric, xii, 78
Clarinet Summit, 50, 55
Clark, Curtis, 59, 62
Clarke, Kenny, 7
classical music, 4, 15, 19, 20, 26, 67, 68, 71-72, 79, 81, 82, 94, 98, 106, 111, 126-29, 131, 152, 163, 168, 169-71, 174, 183
Cleveland, Ohio, 122, 124, 168, 201
Clinton Recording Studio, 51
clothes, 64, 146
Cobham, Billy, 79
"Cobra," 169, 173, 174
cockney, 179
Cohen, Greg, 174
Cohen, Leonard, 185
Cohn, Al, 189
Cole, Nat "King," 83, 85, 97, 137
Coleman, Anthony, 170, 188, 191, 192
Coleman, Denardo, 100
Coleman, George, 8, 47
Coleman, Ornette, ix, x, 6, 13, 24, 33, 51, 72, 99, 100, 101, 110, 121, 122, 162, 168, 174, 188

Coleman, Steve, 117, 188, 147-53
Collaboration, 86
Collective Black Artists band, 150
Collins, Albert, 163
Cologne (Germany festival), 156
Colours, 150
Coltrane, John, x, xi, xii, 6, 7, 20, 24, 28, 33, 49, 51, 54, 70, 72, 77, 78, 81, 90, 121, 122, 146, 158, 159, 184, 188, 203
Coltrane, Ravi, 147
Columbia Records, 7, 8, 48, 84, 91, 100, 157, 197. See also CBS; Sony Music
comedy, xiii, 12, 176, 183, 190
commercial music, x, 4, 5-7, 10, 20-21, 27, 33, 46, 49, 52, 81-82, 84-91, 94-99, 114, 119, 143, 148, 156, 157, 163, 201, 206
"Commit a Crime," 189
composition, 6, 20, 25-26, 29, 32-36, 40-44, 48, 53, 55, 58, 59, 60-63, 65, 66, 71-72, 76, 80, 82-83, 89-90, 92, 94, 95, 98-100, 106, 110, 111, 118-19, 121, 125-33, 138, 141, 151-53, 156, 164-67, 169, 170-74, 178-79, 181-82, 189, 190-92, 196-97
Concord Records, 118
Condon, Eddie, 189
Condon's, 51
conduction, 57-63
Conference of the Birds, 151
Conjure, 54
Connecticut Sound, the, 93
Connick, Harry Jr., 8
Connors, Bill, 159
Conservatory Royal (Liege, Belgium), 59
Cooke, Sam, 91
Cookery, the, 205
cool jazz, 6
Copland, Aaron, 20
Cora, Tom, 62
Corea, Chick, 6, 80, 96, 124, 159, 200

Cornell University, 168
Coryell, Larry, 79
Cosey, Pete, 33, 160
Costello, Elvis, 185
Cox, Billy, 76
Cox, Ida, 113
Cramer, Larry, 207
Crawford, Hank, 205
"Crayon Bondage," 60
Creative Music Studio, 190
Cream, xii
"Crepuscule with Nellie," 177
Criner, Clyde, 130
Crispell, Marilyn, 45, 130
crossover, 8, 75, 76–78, 79, 82, 84–85,
    88–91, 93, 96, 98, 156, 157–59,
    163–64
Crouch, Stanley, 49
CTI records, 84, 90
Cuando auditorium, 60
Cuber, Ronnie, 84
Cugat, Xavier, 158
Current Trends in Racism in Modern
    America, a Work in Progress, 62–63
Cyrille, Andrew, 48, 110

D., Chuck, 185
Dakar, Senegal, 28
Dakota (club), 204
Dalaba, Leslie, 167
Daley, Richard J., 33
Dance Theater Workshop, 178
Dance to the Drums Again, 156
Dances and Ballads, 43
Daniels, Ted, 161
Dara, Olu, 56, 101, 156, 162, 169
Darriau, Matt, 190
Datcher, Irene, 103
David, Hal, 158
Davis, Anthony, 8, 54, 125–33
Davis, Christopher, 126, 127, 129
Davis, Don, 177
Davis, Eddie "Lockjaw," x, 122
Davis, Miles, ix, xiii, 6, 7, 8, 15, 18, 20,
    24, 58, 77, 78, 80, 87, 88, 89, 90,

91, 92, 96, 99, 110, 122, 133, 157,
    158, 159, 164, 167, 168, 184
Davis, Richard, 54
Davis, Thulani, 126, 127, 130, 131
Dawkins, Ernest, 45
Dawkins, Jimmy, xii
Days Aweigh, 155
Dayton, Ohio, 201
De Los Angelos, Victoria, 182
de Jong, Jim, xii
de Lucia, Paco, 80
Deane, J. A., 57, 170
Dearborn, Mich., 143
DeCarava, Roy, 25
Decoding Society, 157–60
Decoy, 91, 164
DeFrancesco, Joey, 7, 11, 82
Defunkt, 161
DeJohnette, Jack, 9, 121, 124, 134,
    200
Delgado, Luis, 188
Delmark Records, xii, 34
DeMarinis, Ann, 186
Denmark, 34, 50, 55
Derringer, Rick, 159
Desire Develops an Edge, 54
Detroit, Mich., 99, 135 138, 144, 146,
    203
Detroit piano school, 144
Devotion, 76, 77
Di Meola, Al, 80, 96
"diatonic harmolodic tuning," 101
Dick, Robert, 112
Diddley, Bo, 145
Different Perspectives, 116, 119
Dig's Den (club), 151
"Diminuendo and Crescendo in
    Blue," 55
Dinner at Eight, 166
discipline, 81
Disk Union (DIW), 8, 9, 38, 48, 49,
    51, 55, 100, 156, 174
District Curators, 206
DIW. See Disc Union
Dixon, Gayle, 100

Dixon, Willie, 185
Dixon-Turré, Akua, 100
DJ Logic, 164
djembé, 29, 41, 44
DL Media, 10
"Do You Know the Way to San José,"
    158
Dogon A.D., 42
Dolphy, Eric, 28, 41, 51, 109, 121, 123,
    189, 203
Don Byron Plays the Music of Mickey
    Katz, 187
Don't Try This At Home, 114, 116
Donaldson, Lou, 57, 88
Donegan, Dorothy, 8
"Donna Lee," 72
doo-wop, 146
Doolittle, Eliza, 179
Doors, xii
Dorf, Michael, 194
Dorge, Pierre, 55
Dorn, Joel, 183, 191
Dorsey, Tommy, 116
Dossier records, 166, 169
Douglas, Dave, 174
Down Beat (club), 205
Down Beat magazine, xi, 11, 115, 48,
    134
"downtown," 165, 193
D'Rivera, Paquito, 7, 8
Dr. John (Mac Rebbennack), xii, 92
Dr. Real, 177
Dreamkeeper, The, 9
Dreams, 114
Dresser, Mark, 45, 125, 130, 187
drugs, 149, 168
Drummond, Ray, 55
Drums of Fire, 43, 44
"Duet for Big Band," 61
Duke's Men, 186
dumbek, 175
Dumbo, 185
Dunbar, Ted, 161
Dunham, Katherine, 43
"Dust My Broom," 77

Dworkin, Richard, 177
Dyett, Captain Walter, 148
Dyson, D.K., 145

Ear magazine, 35, 170
Earland, Charles, 189
Earth, Wind & Fire, 159
East New York, 82, 186
"East Side, West Side," 80
East St. Louis, Mo., 44
East Village (Lower East Side,
    N.Y.C.), 66, 168, 166, 169, 174,
    175, 176, 178, 180, 185
Eastern Europe, 81, 151, 152, 174
"Easy Living," 90
Eckstine, Billy, 85, 88
ECM records, 118
Ehrlich, Marty, 46, 131
Eight Bold Souls, 45
"80 Degrees Below," 72
'80-'81, 114
El-Shabazz, El Hajj Malik, 127, 128
electric guitar, 75, 157-58, 160
Electric Ladyland, 110
Electric Outlet, 92
Electric Wind Instrument, 114-16
Electric Theater, xii
electronica, 169
Elektra Records, 117
Elektra/Musician, 8, 166
Elektra/Nonesuch, 41, 42
Elektric Band, 96
Ellington, Edward Kennedy "Duke,"
    ix, xi, 7, 43, 50, 55, 60, 65, 71, 110,
    111, 112, 124, 127, 128, 134, 135,
    152, 157, 168, 186, 192, 193, 195
Ellipsis Arts, 188
Ellis, Herb, 75
Elman, Ziggy, 189
Elson, Steve, 186
Emanuel, Carol, 170
Epic Records, 163
Episteme, 126, 128, 130
Erewhon, 169
Erguner, Sulieman, 64

Erskine, Peter, 115
Esen, Aydin, 7
Esta, 188
Estes, Sleepy John, xiii
Ethnic Heritage Ensemble, 45
ethnic string instruments, 181
Eubanks, Kevin, 9, 147
Eubanks, Robin, 116, 117-19, 146, 147
Europe, 9, 12, 76, 81, 100, 111, 124,
    127, 130, 134, 146, 151, 166, 180,
    183, 191, 190, 201, 202
European scene, 76
Evans, Bill (pianist), 77, 81
Evans, Bill (reeds player), 80
Evans, Gil, 32, 58, 59, 177
Evelev, Yale, 175
"Every Day I Have the Blues," 89
Ewart, Douglas, 36
Experimental Band, 32, 45, 70,
Experimental Intermedia, 178
Eye, Yamatsaka, 174
Eye on You, 160

Fabulous Flames, 158
Fagen, Donald, 184
Faithfull, Marianne, 183
fans, 3, 11, 23, 80, 97, 103-104, 151,
    201, 204. See also audience
Farlow, Tal, 78
Farnon, Robert, 86
Farrell, Joe, 84
"Fast Life," 43
Fat Tuesday's, 3, 205
Fatah, Muneer Abdul, 150
Favors, Malachi Maghostut, 37
Feather, Leonard, 42
Feldman, Mark, 125, 130, 188
Fellini, Federico, 183, 185
Fender bass, 33
Fender lap steel guitar, 161
Fenley, Molissa, 130
Ferrante and Teicher, 182
Fibonacci number series, 167
Fifth Avenue (N.Y.C.), 150
Fiftieth Street (N.Y.C.), 150

Fifty-second street (N.Y.C.), 135
Firewall Festival, 64
Fitzgerald, Ella, 132, 157
Fitzgerald, F. Scott, 109
Five Elements, 147, 150, 151
Five Spot, 163
flamenco, 26, 79
Flaming Demonics, 161
Flanagan, Tommy, 136, 148
Flash, Grandmaster, 163
Flint, Mich., 134
Flock, the, xii
Florida, 66, 146
Florida State University, 66
"Flowers for Albert," 50, 53
flute, 111-13
Flute Force Four, 110
Flying Colors, 120
"Flying Down to Rio," 158
folk music, x, xii, 76, 158
"Follow Your Heart," 81
For Alto, 34
Ford, Ricky, 28
Forman, Mitchell, 80
Forrest, Jimmy, x
Forrester, Joel, 176-78
Fort Ord, Calif., 58
Fort Worth, Texas, 59, 203
44th Street Suite, 55
Forty-second Street (N.Y.C.), 59, 126,
    150
Foster, Frank, 86, 89
Fountain, Eli, 62
Four Questions, the, 186
Fourth Symphony, 81
Franco, Guilherme, 28
Franklin, Aretha, xii, 155, 158, 182
Franklin, Rodney, 7
Franks, Stanley, 48
free jazz, ix, xi, 11, 24, 32-33, 40, 50,
    99, 206
freedom, ix, 4, 5-6, 33, 63, 128, 170,
    171
"Freedom Jazz Dance," 116
Freedom Principle, The, 36

Freelancing, 100
Freeman, Chico, 9
Freeman, Sharon, 28
Freeman, Von, 148, 149
"Fresh Air," 178
"Friendly Chap," xii
Frisell, Bill, 94, 123, 158, 166, 170, 174, 175
Frith, Fred, 174
From the Soul, 119, 121
Frozen Live!, 163
funk, 91, 119, 195, 102, 152
Funk Machine, the, 115
funk music, 102, 152
Funkadelic (Parliament-Funkadelic), 17, 81, 146
fusion, 11, 70, 102, 114, 123, 152, 164, 188

G, Kenny (Gorelick), 90
Gainsbourg, Serge, 175
Gamble and Huff, 43
gamelan music, 95
games, 59, 169-74
Garcia, Jerry, 78
Garland, Judy, 155
Garland, Red, 77
Garner, Erroll, 136, 141
Garreau, Morgan, 144
Garrett, Kenny, 135, 137
Gaye, Marvin, 43
Gayle, Charles, 109
gender differences, 180
"Gentle Rain," 90
Germany, 58, 66, 129, 150, 191
Gershwins (George and Ira), 10, 126
Getz, Stan, 47, 189
Ghetto Follies, 60
Giant Steps, ix
Gibbs, Melvin, 145, 161, 162
Giddins, Gary, 34, 49, 54
Gifts (band), 162
Gillespie, John Birks "Dizzy," 6, 7, 58, 119, 122, 133, 143, 146, 158, 199
Gilmore, David, 145, 147
Gilmore, Marque, 145

Ginsberg, Allen, 183
"Give Me The Night," 90
Glass, Philip, 92, 162
Glover, Corey, 163
"Go Down Moses," 186
Go Jazz records, 188
Goa, India, 66
God, face of, 83
Goldstein, Gil, 188
Gomez, Eddie, 115
Gonsalves, Paul, 51, 55
Good Morning America, 10
Goodman, Benny, 189
Goodman, Jerry, 79
Gordon, Dexter, 52, 85
Gordon, Lorraine, 205
Gordon, Max, 205
"Goree," 28
gospel music, 26, 56, 59, 67, 103
Gottlieb, Dannie, 188
Goya, 60
Gramavision Records, 92, 126
Grammy awards, 8, 9, 199
Grand Central Station (N.Y.C.), 59
Grant's Music Studio, 58
Grateful Dead, the, 11, 168
"Gratitude," 28
Graves, Milford, 25, 54
Gray, Wardell, 134
"Great Black Music—Ancient to the Future," 37
Great Britain, 66, 80
"Greatest Love of All, The," 85
Green, Benny, 9
Green, Bunky, 149
Green, Freddy, 76
Grey, Arvella, xii
Griffith, Miles, 157
Griffin, Bevis, 147
Griffin, Johnny, 47, 93, 186
GRP Records, 117
Gruenbaum, Leonard, 164
Gueyé, Mar, 41
guitar, 50, 75-76, 80, 86-89, 96, 97, 98, 101-2, 158-61, 162, 168

Gumbo Ya Ya, 110
Gurtu, Trilok, 81

Hackenbush, Dr. (Groucho Marx), 39
Haden, Charlie, 9, 119, 121
Hagans, Tim, 121
Hagedorn, Jessica, 60
Haggadah, 186
Haig, Al, 135
Haitian music, 190
Hakim, Omar, 94
Hall, Jim, 87-88
Hammer, Jan, 79
Hammond, Doug, 150, 151
Hammond, John, 84
Hampton, Slide, 150
Hancock, Herbie, 6, 77, 83, 86, 110,
    114, 152, 198, 199, 200
Hand Jive, 94
*Handful of Keys: The Music of Fats
    Waller*, 134
Handy, Craig, 147
Hank the Crank, xii
Hannibal records, 161
Hanrahan, Kip, 27, 54, 109, 175
Happy Medium, 204
hard bop, 6, 123
Hargrove, Roy, 7, 11, 147
Harlem, 27, 43, 48, 85, 111, 112, 147,
    151
"Harlem," 112
Harlem stride pianists, 111
Harmolodic Guitar with Strings, 100
harmolodics, 99, 102, 103
Harper, Billy, 150
Harper, Heather, 113
Harris, Beaver, 28. 183
Harris, Craig, 8
Harris, Eddie, 34, 94, 116
Harris, Jerome, 146
Harris, Kevin, 146
Harris, Vandy, 33
Harrison, George, 78
Harry, Deborah, 184, 191
Hartman, Johnny, xii

Harvard University, 125, 127
"Harvest Moon," 156
*Hasidic New Wave/Jews and the Abstract
    Truth*, 190
hatArt, 170
"Hattie Wall," 43
"Have You Seen Sideman," 55
Hawk, 64
Hawkins, Coleman, 51, 187
Haynes, Francis, 28
Haynes, Graham, 146, 147, 150, 156,
    164
Haynes, Roy, 54
Hearinga Suite, The, 34
Hearst, Patty, 131
Heath, Jimmy, 129
Helias, Mark, 45, 129
Helland, Dave, 11
Hellborg, Jonas, 80
Hemingway, Gerry, 45, 125, 129, 130
"Hemispheres," 130
Hemphill, Julius, 41
Henderson, David, 60
Henderson, Fletcher, 65
Henderson, Joe, 10, 94
Hendricks, Jon 85, 157, 201
Hendrix, Jimi, xii, 11, 50, 76, 78, 110,
    145, 159-60, 162
Hendrix, Nona, 159
"Here's That Rainy Day," 90
Herman, Woody, xi, 120, 122
Hersch, Fred, 110
Hi Sheriffs of Blue, 169
Hickory House, 205
Hicks, John, 44, 54, 55, 137
Higgins, Billy, 54, 119
"High Priest," 48
Hill, Andrew, 9
Hill, Michael, 145
hillbilly music, 67
Hines, Earl "Fatha," 136
hip-hop. 7
Hirsch, Shelley, 178-82, 186, 188, 191
Hispanics, 189
History of Our Future, The, 145

Hodges, Johnny, 70
Hofstra, Dave, 166, 177
Hoggard, Jay, 9, 129
Holiday, Billie, 10, 131, 132, 154, 156,
 157, 182
Holland, Dave, 117, 118, 119, 121, 134,
 148, 151
Holocaust, 192
Home, 52, 56
"Homeless Men, The," 147
Hometown Sessions, 120
"Honky Tonk Bud," 45
Hoodoo Man Blues, xii
Hopkins, Fred, 9, 54, 55, 61, 71
Hopkins, Lightin', xiii
Horberg, Marguerite, 206-7
Horvitz, Wayne, 57, 166-67, 168, 170,
 174-76, 185
Hot House (club), 206-7
"Hot House," 135
House, Son, xiii, 156
House of Blues, 202
house music, 146
Houston, Texas, 203
"(How Much Is That) Doggie In The
 Window," xiii
Howard University, 138
"Hu Die," 173
Hubbard, Freddie, 84, 88, 90, 123
Humility in the Light of the Creator, 34
Hunter, Otha, 146
Hurst, Robert, 135, 137
Hussain, Zakir, 79
Hutcherson, Bobby, 123
Hyde Park Arts Center (Chicago), 33
Hyman, Dick, 189
hymns, 158

"I Am a Jew," 192
"I Am Waiting," 155
I Can See Your House from Here, 94
I Could Have Been a Drum, 191
"I Didn't Know What Time It Was,"
 154
"I have a dream" speech, 186

"I Heard That," 43
"I'm Old Fashioned," 154
"I've Grown Accustomed to His
 Face," 154
Ibrahim, Abdullah, 117, 206
Ichigakigiwa, Japan, festival 51
Ida Noyes Hall, 33
Illinois Wesleyan University, 149
"Impressions," 90
improvisation, x-xii, 3, 4-5, 18-19, 25,
 26, 33-35, 39-40, 42, 47-48, 51,
 53-54, 58-63, 65, 68-70, 72, 80,
 87, 98, 101-3, 106, 123, 130-32,
 165, 169, 170-75, 178-80, 196
Impulse records, 54
"In a Mist," 90
In a Silent Way, 77
"In C," 169
In the Beginning, 26
In the Land of the Yahoos, 169
In Touch. . . but Out of Reach, 64
India Navigation records, 125
Indian classical music, 79, 81, 171
Infinity, 114
Inner Sanctum, 184
Interboogiology, 56
"Into the Night," 85
"Ionization," 163
Iridium (club), 201, 203
Irving Plaza, 163
Isis (band), 145
Israeli-Palestinian jazz, 188
Istanbul, Turkey, 49, 64, 66, 157
"It's All in the Game," 90
Italian Echo banjo, 161
Italy, 42, 49, 169, 189
"Itsbynne Reel," 116
Ives, Charles, 81, 171, 173, 190
Iyer, Vijay, 147

Jack Johnson, 78
Jackson, Lawrence "Jacktown," 120
Jackson, Mahalia, 113
Jackson, Michael Gregory, 129
Jackson, Milt, 84

Jackson, Ronald Shannon, 54, 101, 157, 160–63
James, Bob, 84, 170
James, Elmore, 77
James, Skip, 78
Janus, ix, xiv
Japan, 9, 45, 48, 51, 58, 64, 81, 100, 127, 152, 156, 174, 188, 198, 202
Jarman, Joseph, xiii, 34, 36, 37, 45, 122, 126
Jarreau, Al, 85
"jazz," 59, 102, 120, 152, 166, 176, 182, 186, 191, 195, 198, 202
Jazz Advance, ixx
Jazz Age, 109, 201
Jazz Alley, 203
Jazz at Lincoln Center, 134, 141, 144
Jazz at the Bistro, 203
Jazz at the Philharmonic, 134
Jazz Bakery, 203
jazz clubs, 3, 4, 27, 32, 38, 84, 85, 92, 95, 99, 100, 113, 126, 129, 134, 137, 146, 150–51, 154, 201–6
Jazz Composers Orchestra Association, 175
Jazz Development Workshop, 134
Jazz Institute of Chicago, 206
"Jazz Is the Teacher (Funk Is the Preacher)," 103
Jazz Journalists Association, 170
Jazz Messengers (band), 27, 117
Jazz Passengers, 12, 185, 186, 191
Jazz Record Mart, xii, 34
jazz record sales, 8–10, 116
Jazz Showcase (club), 203, 204
Jazz Standard (club), 203
jazz tradition, 6, 11, 36, 94, 200
Jazz Tree (management), 203
jazz-rock, 76–79, 80–82, 91–97, 100–103, 114, 145–47, 157–64, 167–69
Jazzpar Award, 34, 50, 55
Jefferson Airplane (band), xii, 90
Jefferson, Eddie, x
Jeffrey, Paul, 150
Jenkins, Leroy, xi, 33, 45, 67

Jewish music, 174–75, 186–94
Jewish resistance fighters, 174
Jimmy Ryan's, 205
jingles, 97
JMT Records, 116, 118, 153
"John Henry," xii
"Johnny McLaughlin, Electric Guitarist," 81
Johnson, Billy, 150
Johnson, J.J., 116
Johnson, James P., 128, 141
Johnson, Lonnie, 75
Johnson, Marc, 94
Johnson, Mark, 150
Johnson, the Reverend Bruce, 161
Johnston, Phillip, 176–78
Jones, Christine Rrata, 33
Jones, Elvin, 54, 81, 184
Jones, Hank, 133–44
Jones, Jo "Papa," 199
Jones, Philly Joe, 122
Jones, Raymond, 159
Jones, Rodney, 161
Jones, Spike, x, 189
Jones, Thad, 135, 150
Joplin, Scott, 71, 127
Jordan, Clifford, 123
Jordan, Ed "Kidd," 41
Jordan, Kent, 7
Jordan, Marlon, 7
Jordan, Stanley, 9
Joujouka, Morocco, 167
joum-joum, 29, 41, 44
Juilliard School, 4, 105
juke box, 163
Jump World, 156
Jumpin' Punkins, x
Juneau, Alaska, 205
Jus' Grew Orchestra, 60
"Just Friends," 86, 98
"Just the Two of Us," 90
"Just the Way You Are," 98
JVC New York Jazz Festival, 12, 51, 55, 178

Kabuki, 180
Kagel, Mauricio, 169, 170
Kalaparashua ara Difda (Maurice
    McIntyre), xii, 33, 34
Kansas City, 64, 91, 149, 182
Kansas City, 183
Kay, Connie, 93
Kaye, Pooh, 60
Keene, Christopher, 126
Keeper of the Flames, 118
Keil, Charles, 168
Kele Mou Bana, 26
Kerr, Deborah, 154
Kessell, Barney, 75
Khan, Steve, 188
Kind of Blue, ix, xii
Kinetic Playground, xi
King, B.B., 89
King, Carole, 188
King, Dr. Martin Luther Jr., 186
King and I, The, 154
King Records, 27
Kingston, Jamaica, 95
Kirby, John, 176
Kirk, Rahsaan Roland, xi, 109, 183,
    203
Kirkland, Kenny, 16, 195, 196
Kisor, Ryan, 7, 11
Kitchen Center for Music, Video and
    Dance, 62, 178
Klezmatics, The, 186, 188, 190
klezmer, 187-90, 192
*Klezmer Music: A Marriage of Heaven
    and Earth*, 188
Klucevsek, Guy, 169
Klugh, Earl, 86
Knickerbocker (club), 205
Knitting Factory, 3, 11, 64, 100, 148,
    170, 175, 178, 186, 188, 189, 206
"Knitting Factory music," 189
Koch Jazz records, 178
Koester, Bob, xii
Koncepts Kultural Gallery, 206
Konitz, Lee, 188, 189
Kool and the Gang, 159

Kool Jazz festival, 9
Krakauer, David, 186, 188, 193
Kremer, Guidon, 81
Kronos String Quartet, 169
Krupa, Gene, 189, 205
"Krystallnacht," 190
Kudu records, 84
Kuumbwa Jazz Workshop, 204

LaBelle, Patti, 117, 146
Labeque, Katia, 80
Lacy, Steve, 125, 184
LaFaro, Scott, 122
Laird, Rick, 79
Lake, Gene, 147
Lake, Oliver, 101, 138-39
Lambert, Hendricks, and Ross, 201
Landmarks, 119
Lang, Eddie, 75
language, 5, 30-31, 61, 62, 65, 83, 87,
    112, 130, 131, 133, 138, 152, 155,
    171, 173
Laquise, Michael John, 133
Laraaji, 158
Las Brisas Lounge, 32
Lashley, Lester, 33
Last Exit to Brooklyn, 185
Last of the Hipmen, 56
"Last Train to Clarksville," 156
Laswell, Bill, 100, 109, 159
Lateef, Yusef, xi, 183
Latin America, 81
Latin Americans, 6, 175
Latin jazz, 189
Latin music, 28, 119, 177, 193, 206
Lawrence, Ron, 100
Laws, Hubert, 84
Lawson, Alvin, 148
Led Zeppelin, 117, 163
Ledford, Mark, 146, 147
Lee, Peggy, 132
Lee, Scott, 121
Lee, Spike, 127, 128
Legends, 134
Les Miserables Brass Band, 190

Les Paul guitar, 77, 80, 161
"Let Me Take You Home," 103
Let the Music Take You, 56
Let's Flip, 177
Levels and Degrees of Light, 34
Leverkusen Jazztage, 45
Levin, Pete, 92
Levine, Rhoda, 126, 127
Lewis, George, 129
Lewis, J. T., 29
Lewis, Mel, 120, 121, 150
Liberace, x
Liberation Music Orchestra, 9, 119
Lickety Split (club), 151
Liebman, Dave, 188
Liege, Belgium, 59
Life's a Lesson, 188
Lifetime (band), 77
"Lift Every Voice," 63
Likoba, Yebga, 29
Lila Wallace Reader's Digest Fund, 67
Lincoln, Abbey, 10, 148
Lincoln Center, 47, 51, 119, 126, 141, 157, 186, 203
Lincoln Center Jazz Orchestra, 119, 186
Lindberg, John, 46
Lindsay, Arto, 170, 185
Linton, David, 167
LiPuma, Tommy, 84
Little, Booker, 58
"little instruments," 34, 39
Litweiler, John, 36
Live (Cassandra Wilson), 156
Live...and Live Again (Don Pullen ABC Band), 26
Live at Sweet Basil Vol. 1 (David Murray-Butch Morris Big Band), 61
Live at the Fillmore East (Miles Davis), 110
Live In Zurich (World Saxophone Quartet), 42
Live/Evil (Miles Davis), 159
Living Color (band), 9, 163

Lloyd, Charles, 11, 57
"Lobsters on Parade," 176
Logan, Guiseppi, 25, 31
Lonberg-Holm, Fred, 193
London, Frank, 186, 188, 190
London Symphony Orchestra, 79
Long Tongues, 43
Looking Ahead, ix
Lord Melody, 158
Los Angeles, Calif., ix, 58, 203
Los Lobos, 185
Lost in the Stars, 183
Loud Jazz, 94
Lounge Lizards, 188
Lovano, Joe, 9, 94, 119-25
Lovano, Tony "Big T," 120, 124-125
Love, Devotion, and Surrender, 80
"Love X Love," 85, 90
Love Supreme, A, 184
"Lovers," 53
Lowe, Frank, 56, 62, 63
Lowe, Walter, 58
Lower East Side, N.Y.C. (East Village), 166, 169, 174, 175, 176, 178, 180, 185
Lucoff, Don, 10-11
"Lullaby," 44
Lunceford, Jimmie, 134
Lundvall, Bruce, 7, 8-10
Lurie, John, 188
Lush Life: The Music of Billy Strayhorn, 10
Lyons, Queenie, 27
Lyric Opera Company, 125

m'beum m'beum, 41, 44
M'Boom, 43
M-Base Collective, 117, 147-52
Ma, Yo-Yo, 81
Mabern, Harold, 8
MacArthur Foundation, 206
Macero, Teo, 78, 164
"Machine Gun," 160
"Mack the Knife," 185
Magic Bag (club), 203

Mahavishnu, 77
Mahavishnu Orchestra, 78-79, 81, 117, 152, 168
Maineri, Mike, 114, 115
mainstream, x, xi, 3, 8, 11, 18, 47, 55, 57, 67, 69-70, 75, 76, 84-88, 90, 91, 93, 98, 116, 122, 129, 122-44, 149, 154, 158, 200, 201, 202, 204, 205
"Mairzy Doats," xiii, 53
Mamas & Papas, 90
Mammon, 5, 148
Man Dance, 160
Mancini, Henry, xi
Manhattan, 3, 85, 100, 120, 134, 165, 202
Manhattan Plaza, 126
Manhattan School of Music, 132
Mantler, Michael, 175
Marclay, Christian, 62, 170
Marley, Bob, 163
Maroons, 134
Marr, Hank, 100, 101
Marsalis, Branford, 7, 8, 55, 148, 184, 185, 196, 202
Marsalis, Delfayo, 7
Marsalis, Ellis, 199-200, 202
Marsalis, Wynton, 5, 7-8, 10, 11, 15-21, 91, 105-8, 109, 135, 152, 157, 185, 195-200
Martino, Pat, 160
Martins, Lenny, 30
Marx Brothers, 190-91
Marx, Groucho, 12, 190. *See also* Hackenbush, Dr.
Masada, 174
masks, 38
Maslak, Keshavan, 59
Mason, Dave, 78
Mason, Konda, 145
Masque, 163-64
Mathis, Johnny, 158, 182
Matta, Nilson, 29
Maupin, Bennie, 164
Maxwell Street flea market, 67

Mayfield, Curtis, xii, 145
mbira, 45, 168
McBee, Cecil, 54
McCall, Steve, 54, 71
McDonald, Michael, 98
McDowell, Fred, xiii
McDuff, "Brother" Jack, 84, 85, 87, 90, 120
McFerrin, Bobby, 8, 9, 85, 92
McIntyre, Diane, 60
McIntyre, Maurice (Kalaparusha ara Difda), xii, 33, 34
McKinney, Bernard, 134
McLaughlin, John, 76-83, 92, 98, 159, 160, 168
McLean, Jackie, 94, 123
McPartland, Jimmy, 205
McPartland, Marian, 205
McRae, Carmen, 157
McShann, Jay, 92, 99
Mecca, 128
Mediterranean Concerto, 81
Medusa, xiii
Meet Me in St. Louis, 155
Mel Lewis Jazz Orchestra, 120, 121, 122
Melford, Myra, 45
"Memories of You," 111
Memphis, Tenn., 93, 146
Menotti, Gian Carlos, 128
Merkin Concert Hall, 35
Metamorphosis, 41, 43, 44
Metheny, Pat, 6, 94, 114
Metrics (band), 147
Metropolitan Opera, 127
Mexican music, 67
Mezzrow, Mezz, 189
Miami, Fla., 204
Miami Herald, 204
Miami Vice, 79
Michigan, 134
Microscopic Septet, 176-78
Middle East, 45
"Middle Passage," 130
MIDI studio, 114, 117

"Midtown Funk," 119
Midtown Motor Inn, 129
Midwest, 41, 69, 122, 132
Mighty Sparrow 158
Miles, Buddy, 76
Miley, Bubber, 111
"Military Takeover," 147
Miller, Glenn, 116
Miller, Marcus, 94
Miller, Mark, 167
Miller, Mulgrew, 155
Milne, Andy, 147
Ming, 52, 56
Mingus Dynasty, 112
Mingus Moves, 27
Mingus, Charles, 6, 24, 25, 27, 28, 31, 42, 92, 99, 110, 111, 119, 177, 183, 184, 203
Minneapolis, Minn., 38, 201
Mintzer, Bob, 188
Mississippi, 153
Mistaken Identity, 164
mistakes, 68–69
"Misterioso," 186
Mitchell, Joni, 6, 114
Mitchell, Roscoe, 34, 36, 39, 46, 122, 190, 192
MJT-3, 34
Mobley, Hank, 88
Modern Jazz Quartet, 38, 124
Moers Music, 160
Moers Music festival, 100
Moffett, Charles, 56, 59
Moffett, Charnett, 59, 197
Moffett, Codaryl, 59
Mofungo, 169
Money Jungle, 111
money, 147
Monk's Nightmare, 184
Monk, Thelonious Sphere, ix, 7, 9, 28, 89, 94, 111, 136, 163, 168, 177, 183, 184, 185, 186, 193, 203
Monkees, the, 156
Monster Curve, 167, 169
Monterey Jazz festival, 201

Montgomery, Wes, 75, 84, 88, 90, 160
Montreal Bistro, 204
Montreal jazz festival, 177
Montserrat, West Indies, 158
Moody, James, x, 122
Moondoc, Jemeel, 60
Moore, Oscar, 75
"Moose the Mooche," 135
Moran, Tim, 7
Morocco, 167, 180
Morris, Lawrence Douglas "Butch," 51, 53, 56–66, 156
Morris, Wilber, 57
Morrison, Van, 156
Morton, Jelly Roll, 7, 65, 76, 127
Mothers of Invention (band), xii
Motherland Pulse, 152
Motian, Paul, 119, 121, 123
Motown (Detroit), 57, 93, 117
Motown music, 182
Moyé, Famadou Don, 37–40
MTV, 45
Muhammad, Ameen, 45
Muhammad, Idris, 55
Mull, Martin, 93
multiphonics, 111
Munich, Germany, 188, 189, 192
Murray's Steps, 52, 57
Murray, David, 8, 27, 41, 42, 47–56, 60, 101, 109, 110, 121, 129, 200, 206
Murray, David Mingus, 51
Murray, Diedre, 64
Murray, Ming, 51
Murray, Sunny, 50, 54
Musawwir, Adamu Mustafa Abdul (James "Blood" Ulmer), 101
Music Revelation Ensemble, 100, 103
music videos, 199
musical theater, xiii
musician support organizations, xi–xii, 32–34, 36, 40–42, 45–46, 58, 59, 69, 70–117, 129, 134–35, 145–47, 150, 152, 175, 186, 206
MusicMasters records, 134

Musselwhite, Charlie, xii
Muzak, 155
Mwandishi (bands), 110
My Fair Lady, 154
My Goal's Beyond, 77
"My One and Only Love," 154
Myers, Amina Claudine, 33
myth, ix, xii, xiii, xiv, 4-7, 12-13, 24,
    38, 75, 129, 179, 186

"Naima," 146
Naked City, 174
"Naked Maja, The," 60
Nanton, "Tricky" Sam, 111
Nasty, 160
Nathanson, Roy, 12, 186, 188, 190, 191
National Ballet of Senegal, 44
National Endowment for the Arts,
    34, 124
National Public Radio, 6, 99, 124,
    178, 205
Native American music, 26, 56
nativism, 189
Navazio, Mickey, 46
Nell's (club), 154
neo-punk funk, 164
neotraditionalism, 49
Nesbit, Wayne, 146
"Never," 155
Neville, Aaron, 184
New Age music, 158
New Apartment Lounge (club), 149
New England Conservatory, ix, 187,
    190
New Haven, Conn., 125, 129
New Jungle Orchestra, 55
New Klezmer Orchestra, 187
New Moon Daughter, 156
New Music America festival, 43, 45
New Music Café (club), 130
New Music Distribution Service, 175
New Orleans, La., 93, 146, 184, 185,
    189, 198, 200, 203
New Orleans Southern University, 41
New Standards, 114

New World Symphony, 81
New York City, ix, 3, 47, 49, 81, 99,
    110, 120, 130, 135, 138, 145, 146
New York City Opera, 126
New York Kool Jazz festival, 62
New York Times Magazine, The, 5
New York Times, The, 12, 178
New York University, 120
New Yorker, The, 11
New Yoruba, 60
"new thing," ix, 24
Newark, N.J., 146
Newman, David "Fathead," 90
Newport Jazz festival, 85
Newsweek, 10
Newton, James, 8, 109-13, 125, 130
Next Wave festival, 153
Nichols, Herbie, 141
Nicholson, Reggie, 45
"Night in Tunisia," 146
"Night Before, The," 119
Night Music, 183
"Nightriders," 80
Nix, Bern, 162
No Wave, 100
No Wave scene, 161, 169
"Noisy Music," 147
Norman, Jessye, 113
North Park Hotel, x, xi
"Nostalgia," 80
Not Yet, 118
Notre Dame Collegiate Jazz Festival,
    11
Noyes, Charles K., 167
NRBQ, 184
Nussbaum, Adam, 91

O Little Town of East New York, 186,
    192
Oakland Youth Chorus, 9
Oakland, Calif., 9, 58, 203, 306
Ochs, Larry, 41
O'Connor, Mark, 116
O'Day, Anita, 205
Ode to Life, 26

Odyssey, 100, 102
Offbeat Glory, 177
Ohio Players, 159
Oliva, 202
Oliver, Joe "King," 19, 152
"On Broadway," 85
On the Edge of Tomorrow, 152
One Truth Band, 79
Open Minds records, 45
Orchestra of St. Luke's, 126
orchestration, 24, 27, 28, 30, 32, 34-
    34, 38-39, 41, 42, 55, 57, 58-63,
    69, 71-72, 76, 79, 80, 82, 92, 95,
    101, 106, 111-12, 113, 120, 121-22,
    127, 130-32, 134, 136, 140, 146,
    147, 150-51, 156, 160-67, 169-70,
    171-74, 175, 177, 181, 185, 190,
    193, 196
Ordinaires, the, 169
organ, 27, 48, 49, 76, 100, 189
Ory, Kid, 116
Osby, Greg, 9, 43, 146, 147, 148, 153
Othello, 64
Otis, Johnny, 57, 147
Ovation guitar, 77, 86
"Overjoyed," 119

Pacific Gas and Electric, xii
Page, Jimmy, 78
Page, Oran "Hot Lips," 143
Painted Bride, 49
Pangaea records, 148
pantar, 168
"Papa's Got a Brand New Bag," xii
Papp, Joseph, 59
Pareles, Jon, 50
Park Avenue South, 203
Parker, Charlie "Bird," "Yardbird," ix,
    18, 19, 54, 70, 72, 86, 87, 92, 94,
    95, 99, 133, 135, 143, 149, 153,
    158, 174, 185, 199
Parker, Maceo, 59, 149
Parkins, Zeena, 62, 170
Parliament-Funkadelic (Funkadelic),
    17, 81, 146

Parran, J.D., 131, 132
Part of the Search, 183
Partch, Harry, 168, 171, 173, 185
Passover, 186-87
Pendergast (Kansas City) regime, 149
"People Make the World Go
    Round," 90
Perelman, S.J., 190
Perlman, Itzhak, 191
Peters, Joey, 166
Peterson, Oscar, 137, 184
Peterson, Ralph Jr., 9, 54, 138
Petrucciani, Michel, 10, 121
Philadelphia, Pa., 15, 48, 60, 131, 146,
    203
Phillips, Esther, 84
Piano Jazz, 205
Piazza, Dominique, 81
Piazza, Tom, 5, 7
Pickett, Wilson, 92
"Pink Elephants on Parade," 185
"Pink Panther, The," 186
Pittsburgh, Pa., 84, 168
Pizzarelli, Bucky, 78
Plaxico, Lonnie, 147, 155
Plays Duke Ellington (World
    Saxophone Quartet), 43
poetry, 34, 60, 175
poets, 64
Point of View, 155
Point Records, 165
polka bands, 67
"Polkadots and Moonbeams," 154
Polygram Records, 10, 81
Pomona, Calif., 48
Pontiac, Mich., 134
Ponty, Jean-Luc, 79
pop music, x, 20, 26, 84, 93, 94, 98
"Popcorn," xii
Porgy and Bess, 10, 58, 94, 126, 128
Possessed, 190
post bop, 58
Powell, Bud, 7, 25, 94, 135, 137, 140
"Power Muzak," 181
President, The, 166

Presley, Elvis, x, 145
press, 10, 170
Previte, Bobby, 57, 125, 166, 170
Priester, Julian, 151
Prime Time (band), 162
Prince, 38
Prokofiev, Sergei, 68
Propaganda (band), 159
Prospect Park bandshell, 146
Prysock, Arthur, 27, 31
Public Broadcast Service (television), 187
Public Enemy, 155
Public Theater, 130
Puente, Tito, 132
Pugliese, Jim, 193
Pulitzer Prize, 8, 125, 157
Pullen, Don, 9, 23-32, 43, 44, 48, 56, 183
Pumpkin Room (club) 32
Pumpkins (club), 151
punk music, 102
Purcell, John, 9, 41, 43, 131, 161
Purple Rain, 38
Pynchon, Thomas, 80

Quartets: Live from the Village Vanguard, 119
Quartette Indigo, 100
Queens, N.Y., 94, 159
Quiet, 98

Ra, Sun (Herman Blount), xi, 12, 24, 32, 59, 110, 117, 185, 191
race, x, xiii, 6, 79, 146, 155, 189
race music, 146
radical Jewish jazz, 186-94
Radio and Records, 116
radio, x, 10, 49, 67, 84, 93, 97, 155, 158, 159, 178, 183
radio drama, 67, 184
"Radio-Activity," 80
Raghavan, R., 79
ragtime, 146
Ramey, Gene, 135

Random Thoughts, 26
Rangelev, Angel, 86, 89
rap, 146, 154, 155
Raskin, Jon, 41
Razor's Edge, The, 118
Reagan, Ronald, 4
Rebbennack, Mack (Dr. John), xii, 91
record sales, 12, 24, 52, 75, 81, 90, 166
Red Baron records, 48
Red Rooster, the (club), 151
Redding, Otis, 43, 182
Redman, Dewey, 123, 139, 202
Redman, Joshua, 47, 120, 147, 202, 207
Reed, Ishmael, 54
Reed, Lou, 189
"reefer circuit," 203
Reeves, Dianne, 9
Regatta Bar, 203
reggae, 95
Reid, Irene, 27
Reid, Vernon, 9, 145, 146, 153, 157-64, 185
Reinhardt, Django, 75
Return to Forever, 80, 159
Revenge of the Stuttering Child, The, 175
Rhythm and Blues (Sharp), 169
Rhythm and Blues (World Saxophone Quartet), 43
rhythm 'n' blues music, 26, 50, 57, 59, 69, 86, 93, 94, 98, 146, 177
Ribot, Marc, 188, 189, 191
Richmond, Dannie, 27, 28
Richmond, Va., 60
Riley, Terry, 169
ritual, 37, 38-39, 42, 112, 146, 186-87
Rivers, Sam, 43, 100, 150, 151
Roach, Hal, 146-47
Roach, Max, 43, 111, 122, 135, 150, 189
Roadwork, 159
Roanoke, Va., 27
Roaring '20s (Jazz Age), 109, 187, 201
Roberts, Judy, 205

Robertson, Robbie, 185
Robinson, Smokey, 90
Rochester, Cornell, 100
Rochester, N.Y., 201
rock 'n' roll, x, 26, 38, 57, 81, 94, 146,
    168, 202, 204
rockabilly, x
Rockefeller's (club), 203
Rolling Stone magazine, 163
Rolling Stones, x, 163
Rollins, Sonny, 18, 45, 51, 52, 69, 70,
    79, 91, 94, 123, 185, 199
Romance and Revolution, 110
Ronstadt, Linda, xii
Roney, Wallace, 137-38
Roosevelt College, 204
Rootless Cosmopolitans, 189
Rose, Barbara, 203
Rosewoman, Michele, 60, 147
Rosnes, Renee, 10, 147
Ross, Brandon, 62, 156
Rota, Nino, 183, 184, 185
Roth, Philip, 193
Rothenberg, Ned, 148
Roulette (performance space), 178,
    182
'Round Midnight (film), 96
"'Round Midnight," 89
Rouse, Mikel, 166
ROVA Saxophone Quartet, 41
Rozie, Lee, 129
Rozie, Rick, 129
Rubalcaba, Gonzalo, 9, 120
Rudd, Roswell, 168
Rundgren, Todd, 185
Rush Hour, 119
Russell, Arthur, 165
Russell, Curly, 135
Russell, George, 9
Russell, Leon, 84
Russian Collection, The, 110
Rykodisc records, 126, 145

S.O.B.'s (club), 3, 145
Sacred Common Ground, 26, 56

Saginaw, Mich., 134
Sain, Oliver, 41
Salish-Kootenai reservation, 26
"Salt Peanuts," 6
Sam, Magic (Sam Maghett), xiii
samchillian tip tip tip cheeepeee, 164
San Francisco Bay Area, 110, 148, 207.
    See also Oakland, Calif.
Sanborn, David, 92, 183
"Sanctuary," 90
Sanders, Pharoah, 159
Santamaria, Mongo, 159
Santana, Carlos, 78, 80, 159
Saratoga Springs Jazz Festival, 85
Saturday Night Live (television), 119,
    183
Saturday Night Live band, 119
Savannah, Ga., 205
Savoy Records, 134
Saylor, Rick, 203-4
Schroy, Hank, 163
Schuller, Gunther, 119, 133
science fiction, 129, 169
Scofield, John, 9, 27, 91-99, 119, 123,
    185, 205
Scott, Lonnie, 144
Scott, Raymond, 176
Scott, Shirley, 122
Scullers (club), 203
Seattle, Wash., 175, 203
"Second Seder," 186
Segal, Joe, 203, 204
Seidel, Richard, 10
Selby, Hubert Jr., 185
self-haters, 193
Self-Haters (band), 192
Selmer saxophone, 114
Senegal, 41, 43, 44,
Sephardic music, 174, 188
Sephardic Tinge, The, 192, 193
Serbian music, 67
Service, Robert W., 45
Sewelson, Dave, 177
Shabazz family, 126
Shadow Vignettes, 45

Shaheen, Simon, 67
Shakill's II, 56
Shakill's Warrior, 48, 56
Shakti, 79, 81
"Shall We Dance," 154
Shange, Ntozake, 54, 60, 129
Shankar, L., 79
Shankar, Ravi, 79
Sharp, Elliott, 166, 167-69, 170, 175, 176
Sharpe, Avery, 9
Sharrock, Sonny, 78
Shaw, Woody, 8, 85, 150
She Who Weeps, 156
Shearing, George, 136
Shepp, Archie, xi, 121, 189
Shipp, Matthew, 45
Shockabilly (band), 185
Short Cuts, 182
Shorter, Wayne, 6, 77, 123
Shrek (band), 189
Sidran, Ben, 188
Sills, Dwight, 7
Silver, Horace, ix, 28, 57, 93
Silverman, Leigh, 35
Silvers, Sally, 60
Simon, Paul, 114
Sinatra, Frank, x, 88, 154, 182
"Sinbad the Sailor," 179-80
singers, 9, 27, 84-91, 102-3, 113, 153-57, 157, 178-82, 206
"Sister Leola, an American Portrait," 134
Six Songs/Marco Polo's Argali, 167
Skatalites, 95
Sketches of Spain, 184
Skillings, Muzz, 163
"Skylark," 156
slab, 168
Smalls (club), 203
Smith, Larry, 86
Smith, Leo, xi, 33, 69, 129
Smith, Lonnie, 84, 120
Smith, Marvin "Smitty," 94, 118, 147, 151, 154

Smithsonian Institution Jazz Masterworks Orchestra, 119
smooth jazz, 188
So Near, So Far, 94
"So What?," 90
social music, 78, 123
Society for Ethical Culture, 35
Soft Machine, the, xii
"Softly As in a Morning Sunrise," 98
Soldier Field, xi
Something Else!!!!, ix
Song For, 34
Sonneck, Ronny, 175
Sony Music, 7, 48. *See also* CBS; Columbia Records
"Sophisticated Lady," 111
Soul Note, 110, 118
soul music, 26, 50, 57, 67, 86-88, 93, 103, 113, 187-88, 193, 195. *See also* rhythm 'n' blues
Sound, 34, 192
Sound Aspects records, 62
Sousa, John Philip, 148
South Side of Chicago (Chicago), x, 32, 148, 204, 205
Southern Illinois University, 44
Spaces, 80
Spaulding, James, 41
Spell #7, 60
Spirits of Havana, 207
spirituality, 103, 113, 195
sports, xiii, 169
"Square Roots," 155
SST records, 167, 169
St. Louis, Mo., 40, 171, 203
St. Matthews, S.C., 101
St. Paul, Minn., 204
Staley, Jim, 170
Starr, Ringo, 184
State of the Union, 60
State University of New York— Buffalo, 168
Statman, Andy, 187, 188
Stax records, 93
Stay Awake, 183

steel guitar, 160
Steely Dan, 184
Stein, Chris, 184
Steiner, Nile, 114, 115
Steinway Hall, 134
"Steppin'," 43
Steps Ahead, 114, 115
Stevens, Halsey, 20
Stewart, Bill, 94, 120
Stewart, Bob, 61
Stewart, Michael, 147
Still, William Grant, 127, 128
Sting, 148, 185
Stitt, Sonny, 87, 122, 149
Stockhausen, Karlheinz, 163, 168, 169, 171
Stolling, Carl W., 176
Stone, Sly, 146
"stoop and hit," 39
Stop the World I Want to Get Off, 129
"Straight Life," 90
"Strange Feeling," 111
"Strange Fruit," 156
Strata Institute (band), 147
Stratocaster guitar, 160
Stravinsky, Igor, 170
Strayhorn, Billy, ix, 10, 110, 111
Street, Craig, 156, 157
stride piano, 135, 136, 140
String Trio of New York, 45
Structural Functions of Harmony, 199
Stubblefield, John, 43, 69
"Suburban Blues," 93
Sugiyama, Kazunori, 51
Suite for Frida Kahlo, 110
Sullivan, Charles, 150
Sumac, Yma, 182, 184
Sunrise, Sunset, 55
Superfly, xii
Swallow, Steve, xi, 91, 121, 185
Sweet Basil (club), 3, 54, 123, 202, 203
"Sweet Lorraine," 154
"Sweet Lovely," 53
Sweetwaters (club), 85
swing, 124, 177, 191, 196

Swing Era, 5
Swing Journal, 48
Symbionese Liberation Army, 132
Symphony Space, 35
Synclavier, 80, 81
systems, 70-72, 101-2, 151, 171-73, 196, 197, 199

tabla, 79
tabula, 29
Tacuma, Jamaaladeen, 54, 100
"Taicho," 119
Taiko drummers, 64
"Take Off from a Forced Landing," 60
"Take the A Train," 60
Take the Z Train, 177
Tales of Captain Black, 100
Talking Heads, 117, 159
Tanya, 125, 130, 131, 132
Tapscott, Horace, 58
Tarras, Dave, 187
Tate, Grady, 55, 86
Tate, Greg, 145
Tatum, Art, 136, 137, 144
Tavenier, Bernard, 96
Taylor, Cecil, ix, 6, 24, 28, 33, 40, 137, 150, 163
Taylor, Creed, 84, 90
Taylor, James, 114
Teagarden, Jack, 116
technique, extended instrumental, 111
technology, 63, 97, 118, 121, 150, 165, 181
Teitelbaum, Richard, 188
television, x, xiii, 52, 81, 84, 119, 147, 179, 183, 187
Temptations, the, 158
Tenor Legacy, 120
Testaments, 66
"Thank You Very Much Mr. Monk," 28
Tharp, "Sister" Rosetta, 67
That's the Way I Feel Now, 183
"Theme Song for Peter Gunn," xi

therapy, music as, 88
Thermonuclear Sweat, 161
Thiam, Mor, 28, 41, 44
Thiele, Bob, 48, 54
Third Stream music, 6, 133
"This Masquerade," 84, 88
This New Generation, 166
Thomas, Gary, 153
Thomas, Luther, 161
Thomas, Michael Tilson, 79, 81
Thompson, Lucky, 134
Thoreau, Henry David, 190
Threadgill Sextette, 71
Threadgill, Henry, 33, 35, 45, 66-73,
    109, 110, 153, 156, 161, 185, 206
Three Compositions of New Jazz, 34
Three Guitars, 80, 83
360 Degree Experience, 28
Threepenny Opera, 129
timba, 30
Time, 10
Tin Pan Alley, 55, 98, 153
Tipitina's (club), 203
Tokyo, Japan, 66
Tone, Yasanow, 62, 63
Tonight Show band ,117
Too Much Sugar for a Dime, 67
Top o' the Senator, 204
Toronto, Canada, 204
Toussaint, Allen, 93
tradition, xiii, 5-6, 18-21, 24-29, 35-
    38, 51, 57-59, 61, 65, 67-68, 71,
    75-76, 93, 94, 99, 105-106, 110-
    12, 113, 118, 120, 121, 122-23,
    127, 134-44, 146, 154, 157, 158-
    60, 170-71, 175-77, 182, 186-94,
    195
traditional jazz, 38, 69
Tri-C Jazz festival, 124
Tricks of the Trade, 56
"Trolley Song, The," 155
trombone, 116, 117-18
trumpet plunger specialists, 111
Tucker, Ben, 205
"Tupelo Honey," 156

Turkish music, 191
"Turn Your Love Around," 90
Turré, Steve, 119
Turrentine, Stanley, 57, 84, 88
"Tutu," 157
twentieth century, 3, 185
twentieth-century music, 190
Tyner, McCoy, 9, 28, 54, 114, 117, 137,
    140
Tzadik records, 174, 186, 188, 192

Ulmer, James "Blood," 7, 54, 99-104,
    164
*UMO Plays the Music of Muhal
    Richard Abrams*, 34
Under the Double Moon, 125, 130
United Nation Jazz Orchestra, 119
United States, 6, 62, 64, 77, 81, 100,
    119, 127, 146, 148, 166, 201, 202,
    204
Universal Language, 119, 121, 122
Universal Music Group, 10
University of California—Irvine, 110
University of Chicago, xi-xii, 33, 40
University of Illinois—Circle
    Campus, xiii
Upchurch, Phil, 84
Upside/Rough Trade Records, 165
U.S. tours, 51, 201-2, 203-4
USA Today, 10
U2, 156

Vacca, Tony, 7
Van Halen, Eddie, 96
Van Vliet, Don (Captain Beefheart),
    168
Vanilla Fudge, xii
Varese, Edgar, 163, 171, 173
variety shows, xiii
Vaughan, Sarah, 113, 154, 157
Verve Records, 10, 94, 134, 166
Very Very Circus, 66
Veterans of Foreign Wars, 70
Vick, Harold, 122
Vidzer, Aida, 192

Vietnam, 58, 81, 160
Village Gate, 3
Village Vanguard, 3, 52, 119, 123, 202, 203, 205
Village Vanguard Monday Night Band, 119
Village Voice, 49
vina, 79
Vinayakaram, T.S., 79
Visiones (club), 3, 203
Visions of the Emerald Beyond, 79
Vogt, Andrew, 41
voice, 113, 131-32, 154, 157, 178-81

Wadud, Abdul, 9, 130
Walker, Amos "Junior," 59
Walker, Sybil, 204
Walker, T-Bone (Aaron), xiii
Wall Street Journal, 10
Waller, Fats, 135
Walrath, Jack, 27
Ward, Carlos, 29
Warford, Rita, 33
Warner Bros., 77, 85
Warwick, Dionne, 158
Washburn electro-acoustic guitar, 161
Washington, D.C., 64, 203, 206
Washington, Dinah, 26, 154
Washington, Grover Jr., 84, 90, 152
Washington, Reggie, 147
Waters, Ethel, 145
Waters, Muddy (McKinley Morganfield), xiii, 67
Watkins, Cookie, 146
Watrous, Bill, 116
Watson, Bobby, 9
Watts, Curtis, 163
"Wayangs, Number Four and Number Two, The," 130
WBGO-FM, 85
"We Are a Nation," 131
"We Shall Overcome," 63
Weather Report, 80, 116
Webster, Ben, 42, 51, 187
wedding music, 187

Weidman, James, 147
Weill, Kurt, 129, 183, 184, 185
Wein, George, 7, 85
Weinstein, David, 170, 178, 182, 192
Weird Nightmare, 183
"Weird Nightmare," 184
Well Kept Secret, 28, 183
Welles, Orson (Mercury Theater for the Air), 184
Wells, Junior, xii, 43
Werner, Kenny, 121
Wesleyan University (Connecticut), 129
Wess, Frank, 8
West Africa, 26, 28, 29, 43-44, 112
"West African Snap," 43
Weston, Randy, 54, 84, 185
Whalum, Kirk, 7
Wheeler, Kenny, 151
"When Blue Turns Gold," 80
When Life Is Cheap and Death Is Taken for Granite, 66, 73
"Where the Mississippi Meets the Amazon," 130
White, James, 161
"White Album," 184
White House, 6
White Plains, Ohio, 168
White Rabbit, 89
Whitney Museum of Modern Art, 59
Why Not? record company, 28
Wieselman, Doug, 166, 193
Wilberforce, 57
Wilkerson, Edward, 45
"Will You Still Be Mine?," 90
William Patterson College, 120
Williams, Big Joe, xii
Williams, Buster, 28, 86
Williams, Cootie, 112
Williams, Hank, 156
Williams, Mary Lou, 141
Williams, Rod, 147
Williams, Tony, 77
Willner, Hal, 28, 109, 182-86
Wilson, Cassandra, 109, 147, 153-57

Wilson, Philip, 44
Wilson, Teddy, 135
Wimbish, Doug, 163
Winelight, 90
Winter, Johnny, 159-60
Withers, Bill, 90
Wolf, Howlin' (Chester Burnette),
    xiii, 69, 162, 189
Women in Jazz festival, 206
Wonder, Stevie, 85, 98, 119, 155
Woods, Phil, 129
Workman, Reggie, 54
World Expansion, 118, 152
"World Is a Ghetto, The," 90
World Negro Arts Festival, 43
World of Cecil Taylor, The, ix
World of Echo, 165
World Saxophone Quartet, 40, 50,
    54
Wright, Clyde "Fats," 26
X, Malcolm, 126
X (film), 127
X (recording), 131
X—The Life and Times of Malcolm X
    (opera), 125-28, 130, 131
X-Man, 110
Xenophile records, 190
"Xu Feng," 173

Yale University, 25, 128, 129, 192
Yamaha DX 7 keyboard, 166

Yellow Springs Institute of the Arts,
    29, 30
Yiddish, 188, 192
YMCA, 147, 150
"Yo, I Killed Your God," 189
York, Nora, 186
Yorkshire, England, 76
Yoshi's (club), 203, 207
"You Don't Know What Love Is,"
    118, 156
Young, Larry, 76, 77
Young, Lester, 122
Young, Neil, 156
Young at Heart/Wise In Time, 35
Young Lions, 4, 7-12, 206
You're Under Arrest, 78
You've Got to Pay the Band, 10

Z., Rachel, 7
Zabar, Kahil El, 45
Zanzibar (club), 3
Zanzibar Blue (club), 203
Zappa, Frank, 78
Zawinul, Joe, 6, 95, 116
Zinno's (club), 3
Zoa festival, 51
Zoar Records, 167, 168
Zorn, John, 62, 63, 109, 148, 158,
    169-76, 185, 187, 188, 189
"Zumman Zummo," 44